I was pleasantly surprised by its content. It t
of team building and leadership in a novel
even say head on, and I rather enjoyed learning about it
through quotations. I didn't expect to find Terry Pratchett in it
but there he was right at the end.
David Thomas ~ Retired Teacher, Cardiff, Wales

Wow, I really love this new book of gathered inspiration,
Roger. I truly could not add another thing to be honest as I
usually look to Mr Google for inspiration and motivation. I
found several quotes that are so motivating to me personally
and I thank you for sharing your book.
Dawn Thompson ~ Competitive Swimmer

Insightful quotes to help the average person deal with
leadership in the workplace and daily life. A good read, with
lots of surprises from well-known people.
Tracy Hobson ~ Small Business Owner

This book has so many quotes and so much history behind
them. This is the first one of this kind I have ever read and I
truly enjoyed the though provoking, helpful and fascinating
quotations on such a wide variety of subjects.
Corina McElduff ~ Children's Activity Consultant

A comprehensive compendium of quotes, phrases and words
of wisdom providing an invaluable resource for those seeking
to be confident, well informed leaders who aim to build strong
teams based on the experience and learnings of those would
have already walked the paths of life they now follow.
Michelle Cutting ~ Police Forensic Scientist

Roger's produced an interesting concept on teaching team
building for those people who become easily bored with the
run-of-the-mill books. Contains everything you would need to
know and some. The opening of the book is hard-hitting but

true, something which most leadership books don't cover. If I had to give it a score, it would be 7 out of 10.

David Layton ~ Retired Construction Executive, Toronto, Canada

Having been forced to sit down and listen to Human Resource Management ramble on about teamwork and teambuilding in a monotonous tone simular to a drunken giant bumblebee for a whole day, I found this book refreshing primarily because whenever I got bored with it I could put it down and come back to it.

Shaun Morsby ~ Electrical Engineer, Sydney, NSW, Australia

I was expecting a load of 'do this - do that' gibberish when I received the manuscript, especially as it had been written by an ex-military man. I was pleasantly surprised. I never realised how quickly people can size you up. There are ample quotes on everything, and the majority of them are interesting. When it comes out I will certainly buy a copy for my daughter as she is leaving school this year and this will help her understand the workplace.

Diana Hooper ~ Housewife, Maitland, NSW, Australia

I'm a practical person and not very good at putting things into words. You can learn a lot from quotes and what I have read in this book has a lot of meaning and sense. I found it an interesting read, especially the wide variety of people who made these quotes throughout their life's journey. I wish my team leader and manager would read this book and put half of it into practice.

John Rich ~ Computer Technician, Bridgend, South Wales

At 92 years of age the last thing I expected was to be asked to review a leadership book. But after serving in the British Airborne Forces during the 2nd World War and surviving it, I suppose a little light reading isn't going to kill me. I never had

all this airy fairy stuff in those days, they couldn't afford to be nice to you as you might want to go home to mother in the middle of a battle. My grandson he tells me that his supervisor should read it and then practice it. Leadership is important, well it was in my day to, but it was a different kind of leadership. But I read it and it makes common sense.
Bill Alcock OAM ~ Retired, Canberra, NSW

I thought I would be bored out of my mind reading this book as quotes aren't really my thing, but I was pleasantly surprised by the variety. I can see where someone who knows nothing about leadership might pick up a few tips.
Ronald B ~ Aircraft Mechanic, Melbourne, Australia

The Leadership Bucket List is an interesting concept as a learning aid. There are plenty of quotes that show you what you need if you're not sure what to do. It has a fascinating introduction, and an interesting acknowledgement about the author's teamwork experiences, and at the very end light-hearted funny favourite quotes to round off your reading.
Katherine W ~ Retired Teacher, Baton Rouge, Luisianna

Success is no accident. It is hard work, perseverance, learning, studying, sacrifice, honesty, and most of all, love of what you are doing or learning to do.

~ Pele

The Team Leadership Bucket List

How to Develop
Team Building
and
Leadership Skills Using
Quotable Quotes

Roger Payne OAM

This edition published in Australia by Aurora House
www.aurorahouse.com.au

Typesetting: Linda Lycett
Cover Design: Linda Lycett

Roger Payne OAM
The Team Building Bucket List
ISBN: 978-1-922403-27-8

Dedication

To my grandchildren Sarah, Georgia, Darcy Mae, Thomas, and Isabelle: Be like your Grandmother Ann and read ~ 'The more that you read, the more things you will know. The more you learn, the more places you'll go!' From Dr Seuss 'I Can Read with My Eyes Shut'

Thanks

To my beautiful wife, Ann, she is the one thing in my life I really cherish, along with my children Tracy, Julie and Gareth, all of who think I'm totally insane. Well I have a certificate from my Psychiatrist that says I'm not completely insane these days, just mildly so.

Special Thanks

To Linda Lycett of Aurora House Publishing who believed in me and held out a hand and gave me the confidence to take the next step and publish this book.

Acknowledgment

To the hundreds of men and women in both the British and Australian military who I had the privilege to soldier alongside, sometimes in the most dangerous of circumstances, yet never once did I ever feel that anyone would not fulfil their role, and if necessary make the ultimate sacrifice to help the team achieve its goals. It was teamwork at its finest.

I learned more about leadership and team building in the rough and tumble of the 'University of Military Life' than I ever did in the years that followed. Life since those days has never been the same. It is now mundane and tame compared to what we used to do...

Thank you for the spin with the anthropomorphic personification, Death, with his long black hooded cloak, scythe, piercing green eyes, deep voice and his magnificent pure white stallion named 'Binky', his granddaughter Susan Sto Helit, and his personal assistant Albert who looks after the billions of life clocks, one of which is mine and another is yours.

You have brains in your head. You have feet in your shoes. So you can steer yourself in any direction you choose.
~ Dr Seuss ~

Contents

Foreword

Leadership is topic that is on many people's minds, and who would be surprised by that?

In the current climate of uncertainty with an uncertain and volatile social and political landscape, the question and role of leadership is often spoken about as one of the things we seem to be lacking.

All of which leads to some important questions – what is leadership? What makes a leader? Can you learn to be a leader or is it a gift that some possess and others don't? Is leadership about strength and single mindedness or is it about collaboration, mentoring and developing others?

Many would say the times demand strong leadership, whether it be in politics, in business or in social institutions. Others, and I include myself in this category, may worry the talk about strong leadership can lead to a slide towards authoritarianism, and prefer to tread warily down that path. How do we balance these perspectives?

Roger Payne is well qualified to talk about leadership and its qualities.

Born in South Wales, at age fifteen he began a working life that led to a distinguished career in the military, eventually rising to the position of Chief Instructor of fitness training to the Corps of Infantry. He also received the highest award a serving member of the Defence Forces could receive. The Chief of Defence Force Commendation, then one year later an unprecedented Order of Australia, one of the highest awards an Australian citizen can achieve. He is still the only Australian serviceman to receive both.

With this background it is fitting that he has decided to share his insights and knowledge on the question of leadership

The Team Building Bucket List does not set out to be a standard textbook providing to answer these questions directly but instead takes an innovative approach that will encourage the reader to devise their own ideas and develop their own framework for applying the lessons and ideas to their own life.

That is *The Team Building Bucket List* is not a conventional narrative in structure but consists of quotes from a wide range of people from all walks of life and all periods of history, who have had something to say or observe about what leadership is, what it means and where it is important.

It is great to see the range of quotes presented, and although the arrangement may not always indicate context, the depth and breadth of the range of topics and contributors is tremendous. That such names as Dr Seuss, Ella Fitzgerald and Tupac Shakur appear alongside such recognizable and influential names as Winston Churchill, Nelson Mandela and Steve Jobs I think is a great testament to Roger Payne's own ability to think and read broadly and imaginatively about his topic.

Of course readers will have to understand quotes from earlier centuries or previous generations will reflect a degree of gender bias that will have to be absorbed by each reader, but it is a truthful reflection of the times.

It is probably a staple for anyone delivering a speech or address before an audience to want to use a telling quote to introduce or enliven their presentation, and anyone who approaches *The Team Building Bucket List* from that perspective will certainly not be disappointed.

However, if that as the only reason to dip into the pages they will miss the point of what the author is trying to achieve. The impact of reading a succinct and insightful quote is that the best of them have a distilled and concise wisdom that can help us see things much more clearly and rationally. We instinctively know when we hear an essential truth expressed in a few words, something which is based on life experience and the ability to think clearly about the lessons, tinged with a degree of self-awareness.

As Roger Payne writes in his introduction, *'Quotes are simple words of wisdom that make sense.'*

Perhaps what is also important in approaching this book, is remembering that whilst not everyone will think of themselves as a leader or feel driven to aspire to a leadership role, life has a way of changing or providing moments where we are forced into a role we are not immediately comfortable with. These moments may occur in families, or with friends or with work colleagues, and that is where having a strong moral grounding in the qualities of leadership will become apparent

What is also apparent is that a quote or piece of wisdom that perhaps does not speak clearly to you one day may, in another time and with another set of circumstances, be the precise thing we need. It's not possible to agree with every quote by every contributor, but with time and space we learn and see things differently

The book is divided into many chapters, each on a specific

theme, and I'm glad that in addressing the question of how leadership can easily be turned into authoritarianism I think it is important to consider the importance of the chapters on Integrity and Ethical Behaviour.

Readers will also appreciate the author's final chapter "My Favourite Quotes"

What speaks to me?

So much really, but I'd like to point to one simple piece of wisdom from Anthea Turner, and it's so truthful in its bluntness and simplicity, *the first rule of management is delegation. Don't try and do everything yourself because you can't.*

That's right, it seems so obvious doesn't it? But for me, when I finally realised that I couldn't do everything on my own and delegating was not a sign of weakness, it was the most liberating thing imaginable. I got my sense of purpose back and found my staff developing and growing as a result.

The Team Building Bucket List was an unconventional reading experience for me, but one that I felt rewarded by as I continued to delve more deeply into the contents.

Peter Woodley
Information Systems Coordinator
Planning Environment & Lifestyle | Maitland City Council

Why Quotations?

There is an argument that says quotes are of no value in teaching you anything. I can dispute this because when I served in the military quotes were constantly used to remind us of a multitude of things, and at the end of the day, to motivate us.

One in particular I can vividly remember; *'The Strong Shall Live and The Weak Shall Die.'* This was the motto of the elite British Parachute Regiment. It was used to inform us of the mental and physical pain we'd have to go through before we could enter the regiment. Another was 'KISS', *Keep It Simple Stupid,* meaning keep everything simple so that everyone could digest it quickly. Then there was the famous *Know Your Stuff Never Bluff* and *Practice What You Preach.* Simply put it means, know your subject matter thoroughly, don't try to fool anyone, and be a product of what you teach. The right quotes survive the test of time, and they all have a unique characteristic. They give you a way forward, and are an actionable intelligence that provides clarity and direction. They also help you connect with the vital spark that lights the fire inside your belly.

Quotes are simple words of wisdom that make sense. They come from life experiences. The people who think of them have struggled through the same problems you are struggling through, and have won the battle. Quotes have impact and they create the desire to take that first step. Sometimes all you need to do is read them once and you can repeat them time and again because they have touched a chord within you. It is also helpful to read various quotes about the same subject, and to understand how different people arrived at the same answer. By doing so you add the final piece to the mental jigsaw puzzle you have been trying to solve.

Quotes invariably help us by changing our focus from the problem to the solution, from the question to the answer. They provide resolution to the questions we have been looking for. Sometimes problems seem overwhelming and answers don't appear to exist, but the fact of the matter is that there are no new problems, yet there are plenty of new ideas. Remember - others have faced the problems you are now facing and have overcome them. Their quotes can provide you with clearly defined solutions that can light the way down the darkest of tunnels on the longest of days. I hope the quotes in this book do just that.

Leadership is not about a title or a designation. It's about impact, influence, inspiration. Impact involves getting results, influence is about spreading the passion you have for your work, and inspiration is all about motivating your team.
*~ **Robin S. Sharma** ~*

The Team Leader's Conundrum

When your new team finds out who is going to be their next team leader you can bet they are going to reach out and use their contacts to check up on you before you arrive.

Their background check will be as thorough as any government intelligence community could ever do, so when you walk into the team area that first time they'll have a fair idea who they are dealing with. Don't believe for one moment they care how well qualified you are. Your Master's Degree in Core Leadership or Quantum Mechanics means absolutely nothing to them. What they want to know is how good you are at practical team leading, the genuine deal, not the university graduate nonsense. You can give the greatest introduction speech of your life, it still won't guarantee they will accept you.

Your team are looking for three things in their new leader – Will you respect them? Do you have integrity? Are you a person who will be loyal to them when the cards are down? Sounds too simple doesn't it?

Now think about this. While you are telling them how good you are and what you are going to do for them they've taken a mere 1/10th of a second to read your face and seven to ten seconds to unconsciously decide what kind of a person you really are. How? By simply reading your body language.

Still unconvinced?

Then ponder on this. Should you be found wanting in those few short seconds then it is unlikely you will ever be able to motivate them to a level where you will be recognised as a good team leader; the odds are against you simply because you appear to be lacking in one or more of those three key areas. Now if you are really lucky and you've won them over, then you have the potential to become a great team leader. But don't get too cocky; team leading isn't easy, you have to constantly work at it, but at least you have a good team behind you who'll tolerate your many mistakes, and you will make lots of mistakes. Not to worry the world is now your oyster, go open it up...

RESPECT: A feeling of deep admiration for someone or something brought about by their above average abilities, qualities, or achievements.
INTEGRITY: The quality of being honest and having strong moral principles.
RESPECT + INTEGRITY = the first step in the leadership ladder.
The next step is: LOYALTY: a strong feeling of commitment to the team.

RESPECT + INTEGRITY + LOYALTY = LEADERSHIP POTENTIAL AND GROWTH
~ Roger Payne ~

Today you are You, that is truer than true. There is no one alive who is 'better' than you.
~ Dr Seuss ~

I have been impressed with the urgency of doing. Knowing is not enough; we must apply. Being willing is not enough; we must do.
~ Leonardo da Vinci 1452-1519 ~

If you look at what you have in life, you'll always have more. If you look at what you don't have in life, you'll never have enough.
~ Oprah Winfrey ~

You will never reach your destiny if you stop and throw stones at every dog that barks at you along the way.
~ Winston Churchill 1874-1965 ~

If you think you are leading and turn around to see no one following, then you are just taking a walk.
~ Benjamin Hooks ~

Nearly all men can stand adversity, but if you want to test a man's character, give him power.
~ Abraham Lincoln ~

The task of leadership is not to put greatness into humanity, but to elicit it, for the greatness is already there.
~ John Buchan ~

What you do has far greater impact than what you say.
~ Stephen Covey ~

Poor leaders lose the faith and trust of the people they lead, while great leaders seem to lead without effort.
~ Anonymous ~

Great leaders are almost always great simplifiers who can cut through argument, debate and doubt to offer a solution everybody can understand.
~ Collin Powell ~

The same people HEAR your words, but FEEL your attitude.
~ John Maxwell ~

Leaders who don't listen will eventually be surrounded by people who have nothing to say.
~ Andy Stanley ~

Being a leader is not simply about you. It's about the people on your team and how you can make every one of them successful.
~ Susan Vobejda ~

If you're not helping to make it right, then stop complaining that it's wrong.
~ Anonymous ~

Only three things happen naturally in organizations: friction, confusion, and underperformance. Everything else requires leadership.
~ Peter F. Drucker ~

I fear the day when technology will surpass our ability to simply talk to one another. When that day happens we are on the way to having a world full of idiots.
~ Albert Einstein 1879-1955 ~

The key to a good life is this: If you're not going to talk about something during the last hour of your life, then don't make it a top priority during your lifetime.
~ Richard Carlson ~

In this book the term 'ANONYMOUS' simply means that I cannot find an attributed author of a quote. I have also added the date of birth and death of attributed authors prior to the year 1900 to show how old many of the quotes are, yet they are still relevant today simply because leadership hasn't changed.

Step with care,
step with tact,
just remember that life's a great balancing act.
~ *Dr Seuss* ~

1

THE TEAM LEADER

Whether they lead a small team, a department, a large company, or a country, the best team leaders understand the importance of providing the motivation and direction to achieve important goals. Poor leaders soon lose the faith and trust of the people they are supposed to lead, while good leaders seem to lead without any effort. The character, actions and thoughts of a leader, good or bad, soon permeate a team however large. Your goal should be to demonstrate the best qualities of a leader while encouraging the same for those who follow you.

~ *Nicole Fallon Taylor* ~

1. *Leadership experience isn't just about what you bring to the table. It's about what you learn when you get there.* ~ **Peter DeWitt**

2. *Being a leader is more than just wanting to lead. Leaders have empathy for others and an ability to find the best in people, not the worst, by truly caring for them and their needs.* ~ **Henry Crutand**

3. *The illogical thing about workplace team building and leadership is that with very little formal training, or even no training, you are expected to take a group of people who are of different ages, sexes, religions, attitudes and values; and*

through your influence, require each to sufficiently modify their behaviour so that all of you can achieve a common goal with little or no interpersonal friction. ~ **Roger Payne**

4.   *Cultivate a deep understanding of yourself - not only what your strengths and weaknesses are but also how you learn, how you work with others, what your values are, and where you can make the greatest contribution. Because only when you operate from strengths can you achieve true leadership excellence.* ~ **Peter F. Drucker**

5.   *Rank does not confer privilege or give power. It imposes responsibility.* ~ **Peter F. Drucker**

6.   *As a leader your principal job is to create an operating environment where others can do great things.* ~ **Richard Teerlink**

7.   *The character, actions and thoughts of a leader, good or bad, permeate every team. Your goal should be to demonstrate the best qualities of a leader while encouraging the same from those in your team.* ~ **Nicole Fallon Taylor**

8.   *The three most charismatic leaders in this century inflicted more suffering on the human race than almost any trio in history: Hitler, Stalin, and Mao. What matters is not the leader's charisma. What matters most is the leader's mission.* ~ **Peter F. Drucker**

9.   *Leadership is about being in the service of others, not being served by others, being a mentor, not a boss.* ~ **Anonymous**

10. *A good team leader listens, then talks to his team to find the individual strengths and weaknesses of each team member, then builds on them.* ~ **Lorenzo Molina Montilla**

11. *Ultimately, leadership IS NOT about glorious crowning acts. It's about keeping your team focused on a goal and motivated to do their best to achieve it, especially when the stakes are high and the consequences really matter. It is about laying the groundwork for others' success, and then standing back and letting them shine.* ~ **Chis Hadfield**

12. *You cannot be effective if those who work for you are not. So building their effectiveness ought to be a high priority.* ~ **Richard N. Haass**

13. *The signs of outstanding leadership appear primarily among the followers. They follow because they have a good leader.* ~ **Anonymous**

14. *I never thought in terms of being a leader, I simply thought in terms of helping people.* ~ **John Hume**

15. *The challenge of leadership is to be strong, but not rude; be kind, but not weak; be bold, but not a bully; be humble, but not timid; be proud, but not arrogant; have humour, but without folly.* ~ **Jim Rohn**

16. *The X-Factor of great leadership is not personality, its humility.* ~ **Jim Collins**

17. *Leaders learn the most when they are teaching others.* ~ **Peter F. Drucker**

18. *He who cannot be a good follower will never be a good leader.* ~ **Aristotle 384-322 BC**

19. *The ultimate measure of a man is not where he stands in moments of comfort, but where he stands at times of challenge, controversy and adversity.* ~ **Martin Luther King Jr.**

20. *Before you are a leader, success is all about growing yourself. When you become a leader, success is all about growing someone else.* ~ **Jack Welch**

21. *Leadership is the art of giving a team a platform for spreading their wings and their ideas.* ~ **Seth Godin**

22. *The leader of the past was a person who knew how to tell. The leader of the future will be a person who knows how to ask and listen to what he is told.* ~ **Peter F. Drucker**

23. *Leaders aren't born they are made. And they are made just like anything else, through hard work. And that's the price we'll have to pay to achieve that goal, or any goal.* ~ **Vince Lombardi**

24. *Leadership is based upon inspiration, not domination, on co-operation, not intimidation.* ~ **William Arthur Wood**

25. *You may be the boss, but you're only as good as the people who work for you.* ~ **Rear Admiral William Leahy**

26. A good team leader takes a little more than his share of the blame and a little less share of the credit. ~ **John Maxwell**

28. When you put together a deep knowledge about a subject that intensely matters to you, charisma happens. You gain courage to share your passion, and when you do that, folks follow. ~ **Jerry Porras**

29. My job is not to be easy on people. My job is to take these great people we have and to push them and make them even better. ~ **Steve Jobs**

30. The same boiling water that softens the potato hardens the egg. It's about what you're made off, not your circumstances. ~ **Anonymous**

31. No team leader has ever suffered because his subordinates were strong and effective. ~ **Peter F Drucker**

32. A leader is best when people barely know he exists, when his work is done, his aim fulfilled, they will say: we did it ourselves. ~ **Lao Tzu 604-531 BC**

33. Become the kind of leader that people would follow voluntarily; even if you had no title or position. ~ **Brian Tracy**

34. Talk to people and compliment them. By doing so you magnify their strengths, not their weaknesses. ~ **Anonymous**

35. In the final analysis you have to ask yourself, what kind of *a leader would you follow? ~ **Roger Payne***

*36. If you want to know what a man's like, take a look at how he treats his inferiors not his equals. ~ **Sirius Black (Harry Potters God father)***

*37. A leader is like a shepherd, he stays behind the flock, letting the most nimble go out ahead, whereupon the others follow, not realizing that all along they are being directed from behind. ~ **Nelson Mandela***

*38. Everyone's leadership methods differs slightly, but to get it right you need to make your team achieve more than they thought they could. You do this not through fear, intimidation or titles, but by involving everyone at every stage and then creating a consensus of opinion around a common goal. ~ **Anonymous***

*39. Don't be trapped by dogma, which is living with the results of other people's thinking. Don't let the noise of other's opinions drown out your own inner voice; and most important, have the courage to follow your heart and intuition. Somehow they already know what you truly want to become. Everything else is secondary. ~ **Steve Jobs***

*40. True leaders always practice the three R's. Respect for self, respect for others, Responsibility for their actions. ~ **Anonymous***

*41. One of the tests of leadership is the ability to recognise a problem before it becomes an emergency. ~ **Arnold H. Glasow***

42. *The critical question is not "How can I achieve?" but "What can I contribute?"* ~ **Peter F. Drucker**

43. *Leadership is the art of serving others by equipping them with training, tools, time, energy and emotional intelligence so that they can realize their full potential, both personally and professionally.* ~ **Daphne Mallory**

44. *The secret of a leader lies in the tests he has faced over the whole course of his career and the actions he develops in meeting those tests.* ~ **Gail Sheehy**

45. *No matter how good you think you are as a leader the people around you will have all kinds of ideas for how you can get better. So for me, the most fundamental thing about leadership is to have the humility to continue to get feedback and to try to get better - because your job is to try to help everybody else get better.* ~ **Jim Yong Kim**

46. *The greatest leader is not necessarily the one who does the greatest things. He is the one that gets the people to do the greatest things.* ~ **Ronald Reagan**

47. *Good business leaders create a vision, articulate the vision, passionately own the vision, and relentlessly drive it to completion.* ~ **Jack Welch**

48. *You cannot build character and courage by taking away a man's initiative and independence.* ~ **William Henry Boetcker 1873-1962**

49. The final test of a leader is that he leaves behind him in other men the conviction and the will to carry on. The genius of a good leader is to leave behind him a situation which common sense, without the grace of genius, can deal with successfully. ~ **Walter Lippmann**

50. Effective leadership is not about making speeches or being liked; leadership is defined by results not attributes. ~ **Peter F. Drucker**

51. Successful leaders see the opportunities in every difficulty rather than the difficulty in every opportunity. ~ **Reed Markham**

52. Don't tell people how to do things, tell them what to do and let them surprise you with their results. ~ **General George S. Patton Jr.**

53. If you can't swallow your pride, you can't lead. Even the highest mountain has animals that step on it. ~ **Jack Weatherford**

54. There is a difference between being a leader and being a boss. Both are based on authority. A boss demands blind obedience; a leader earns his authority through understanding and trust. ~ **Klaus Balkenhol**

56. Real leaders are ordinary people with extraordinary determination. ~ **John Seaman Garns**

57. *The secret of leadership is simple: Do what you believe in. Paint a picture of the future. Go there. People will follow. ~* **Seth Godin**

58. *You have to look at leadership through the eyes of the followers and you have to live the message. What I have learned is that people become motivated when you guide them to the source of their own power and when you make heroes out of employees who personify what you want to see in the organization. ~* **Anita Roddick**

59. *Too many companies believe people are interchangeable. Truly gifted people never are. They have unique talents. Such people cannot be forced into roles they are not suited for, nor should they be. Effective leaders allow great people to do the work they were born to do. ~* **Warren Bennis**

60. *Great leaders don't set out to be a leader, they set out to make a difference. It's never about the role, it's always about the goal. ~* **Lisa Kaish**

61.   ***The Poem 'The Team Leader'***
IF you can keep up interest while around you others fail, and maintain your obvious keenness and avoid becoming stale.
And
IF you are truly certain that you're ideas got across, that the team has got real value, and their time was not a loss.
And
IF you can stress the things that count, not imparting all you know, to make a great impression on each team member down below.

And

IF you can paraphrase the pamphlet use 'HOLE' not 'ORIFICE' and use straightforward language in a way the team can't miss.
And
IF you're a certain master of the things you have to teach, and can keep down to the brass tacks that is well within the whole teams reach.
And
IF your diagrams and examples can be seen by everyone, and your team is motivated when everything is done.
And
*IF combined with all these things you're natural and real, then you're a pretty good Team Leader, in fact, almost ideal. ~ **A British Soldier circa 1950***

62. *Unless someone like you cares a whole awful lot, nothing is going to get better. It's not. ~ **Dr Seuss***

63. *You don't lead by pointing and telling people some place to go. You lead by going to that place and making a case. ~ **Ken Kesey***

64. *No man will make a great leader who wants to do it all himself, or to get all the credit for doing it. ~ **Andrew Carnegie***

65. *The character of a leader is how they treat others who can do nothing for them. ~ **Anonymous***

66. *What makes Superman a hero is not that he has power, but that he has the wisdom and the maturity to use the power wisely. ~ **Christopher Reeve***

67. *In matters of the right leadership method to use the answer is easy, always swim with the current. In matters of principle always stand like a rock.* ~ **Thomas Jefferson 1743-1826**

68. *Loyalty is hard to find, trust is easy to lose, and actions speak louder than words.* ~ **A.L.P.**

69. *The best leaders don't know one style of leadership. They're skilled at several and have the flexibility to switch between styles as circumstances dictate.* ~ **David Coleman**

70. *There is no one type of refereeing for all games. The referee has to develop an almost chameleon capacity to be able to adapt his own abilities to the requirement of the match. All matches are different, and therefore have to be dealt with in completely different ways. What has to prevail is a pragmatic style of refereeing, suitable for the type of match and the particular moment within the match.* ~ **Pierluigi Collina**

71. *I do not yet know of a man who became a great leader after having undergone a leadership course.* ~ **Lee Quan Yeu**

72. *Leadership is not about titles. It's not about seniority. It's not about status. It's not about management. Leadership is about power and to know when and how to use it to INFLUENCE the people around you to DO MORE and BECOME MORE.* ~ **Terina R. Allen**

73. *People don't follow you because you are nice, they follow you because they believe the place you are taking them is better*

than the place they are. ~ **Scott Hammerle**

74. *Leadership is all about caring, daring, and sharing! Caring for people, daring to act fearlessly, and sharing the success with all!* ~ **Suit Lalwani**

75. *As a leader every action has a consequence, make sure it is the one you intended.* ~ **Katherine Bryant**

76. *A GOOD LEADER leads the people from above them. A GREAT LEADER leads the people from within.* ~ **M.D. Arnold**

77. *If you delegate tasks you create followers. If you delegate authority you create leaders.* ~ **Craig Groeschel**

78. *A person that feels appreciated will always do more than expected.* ~ **Anonymous**

79. *No matter how effective your strategy, your vision, or your communication, you will fail to achieve the desired results for your team if you cannot inspire trust.* ~ **Bill George**

80. *Leadership is not magnetic personality that can just as well be a glib tongue. It is not 'making friends and influencing people', that is flattery. Leadership is lifting a person's vision to higher sights, the raising of a person's performance to a higher standard, the building of a personality beyond its normal limitations.* ~ **Peter F. Drucker**

2

TEAMWORK

Most of us have been a part of that group project run by Human Resources. You know, the project where one person takes the lead, leading some members to conclude their ideas are unwelcome, while a select few ride the others coattails. Thanks to experiences like this, it's no surprise why so many people have been scarred by the nightmares of past group projects. And yet, something incredible happens when teamwork happens the way it's supposed to happen. Things change when everyone on the team is equally invested in the overall purpose and goal. You find yourself working faster, finding mistakes more easily, and innovating better. Ultimately, you reach a point where you're certain each person on your team has your back and both your job satisfaction and performance skyrocket.

*~ **Megan Conley** ~*

1. *I'm part of a team, and I'm no better or no worse than any single player on the team. That's the approach I've always taken and will continue to take. It's not about me. It has never been all about me. If it had, this would have been a long and lonely journey. ~* **Mia Hamm**

2. *When a team outgrows individual performance and learns all about team confidence then excellence becomes a reality. ~* **Joe Paterno**

3.   *There is absolutely nothing like being part of a team that will go the distance.* ~ **Chuck Daly**

4.   *NOTE TO SELF: I am going to be the type of team leader that contributes positively every day, being negative is not going to cross my mind. If we cannot work together as a team then we cannot possibly achieve our goals.* ~ **Anonymous**

5.   *You can't always have the best team, there is always a compromise. But that compromise can still make it a very good team.* ~ **Alain Prost**

6.   *Your team is your second family. You may fight each other on occasions; you may even threaten to throttle each other and throw each other out of the window, but that happens in the best of families. In the end they are still your family, so you make up and get on with doing what you all do best work as a team.* ~ **Anonymous**

7.   *You are not a team because you work together. You are a team because you respect, trust and care for each other.* ~ **Vala Afshare**

8.   *I'm going to tell you the story about the geese that fly 5,000 miles from Canada to France every year. They fly in a 'V' formation as it conserves their energy. Each bird flies slightly above the bird in front of him, resulting in a reduction of wind resistance. The birds take turns being in the front, falling back to the rear when they get tired. In this way, the geese can fly for a long time before they must stop for rest. Now this is what real*

*teamwork is all about. ~ **Alex Ferguson***

9. *Alone we can do so little. Together we can do so much. ~* ***Helen Keller 1889-1968***

10. *Talent wins games, but teamwork and intelligence wins championships. ~ **Michael Jordan***

11. *In any team the team leader's job isn't to have all the ideas. It's to make sure ALL the ideas are heard and then the best one wins and is put into practice. ~ **Chris Hawker***

12. *A team is more than a collection of people. It is a process of give and take. ~ **Barbara Glacel***

13. *Sometimes the most ordinary things can be made extraordinary simply by doing them with the right people. ~ **Nicholas Sparks***

14. *I CAN'T, but we all CAN. ~ **Anonymous***

15. *We trained hard, but it seemed every time we were beginning to form up into teams, we would be reorganized. I was to learn later in life that we tend to meet any new situation by reorganizing and a wonderful method it can be for creating the illusion of progress while producing confusion, inefficiency and demoralization. ~ **Petronii Arbitri Satyricon AD 66***

16. *One man can be a crucial ingredient on a team, but one man cannot make a team. ~ **Kareem Abdul Jabbar***

17. *I am a member of a team and I rely on the team. I defer to it and I sacrifice for it, because the team, and not the individual is the ultimate winner.* ~ **Mia Hamm**

18. *The greatest danger a team faces isn't that it won't become successful, but that it will, and then it ceases to improve.* ~ **Mark Sanborn**

19. *No matter what accomplishments you make, somebody helped you.* ~ **Althea Gibson**

20. *Team player: One who unites others toward a shared destiny by providing information and ideas, empowering others to grow and by doing so developing trust.* ~ **Dennis Kinlaw**

21. *As a team If we don't communicate, we certainly can't get much done, and if we don't communicate authentically, what we get done is less effective.* ~ **Michele Jennae**

22. *There is no such thing as a 'one man show' in a winning team.* ~ **Jose B. Cabajar**

23. *When was ever honey made with only one bee in a hive?* ~ **Thomas Hood**

24. *To play a good game you need a few good players.* ~ **Anonymous**

25. *After a snowstorm no individual snowflake in an avalanche ever feels responsible.* ~ **Stanisław Jerzy Lec**

26. *Finding each other is the beginning, staying together is the process, working together is the success. ~* **Maegan Gunderson**

27. *The ratio of We's to I's is the best indicator of the development of a team. ~* **Lewis B. Ergen**

28. *No one can whistle a symphony. It takes a whole orchestra to play it. ~* **H.E. Luccock 1865-1961**

29. *The best teamwork comes from men who are working independently toward one goal in unison. ~* **James Cash Penney 1875-1971**

30. *You can't stay in your corner of the forest waiting for others to come to you. You have to go and find them. ~* **A. A. Milne**

31. *It is amazing what you can accomplish if you do not care who gets the credit. ~* **Harry S. Truman 1884-1972**

32. *For a team to succeed everyone must pull as one in the right direction. ~* **Anonymous**

33. *There is no 'I' in team but there is in 'WIN'. ~* **Michael Jordan**

34. *Ultimately, leadership is not about glorious crowning acts. It's about keeping your team focused on a goal and motivated to do their best to achieve it, especially when the stakes are high and the consequences really matter. It is all about laying the groundwork for others to succeed and then standing back and*

letting them shine. ~ **Chris Hadfield**

35. *Don't get upset with the results you didn't get because of the work you didn't do.* ~ **Anonymous**

36. *Teamwork means never saying never because limits, like fears, are often just an illusion.* ~ **Michael Jordan**

37. *No matter how brilliant your mind or strategy, if you're playing a solo game, you'll always lose out to a team.* ~ **Reid Hoffman**

38. *The achievements of an organization are the results of the combined effort of each individual.* ~ **Vincent Lombardi**

39. *Leaders who never listen end up with people who never have anything to say.* ~ **Andy Stanley**

40. *How could you have a soccer team if everyone were goalkeepers? What would happen if an orchestra were all French horn players?* ~ **Desmond Mpilo Tutu**

41. *The strength of the team is each individual member. The strength of each member is the team.* ~ **Philip Jackson**

42. *Individually we are one drop. Together we are an ocean.* ~ **Ryunosuke Satoro**

43. *Conflict is inevitable in a team.....in fact, to achieve synergistic solutions, a variety of ideas and approaches are needed. These are the ingredients for conflict.* ~ **Susan K. Gerk**

44. *If you want to be incrementally better: Be competitive. If you want to be exponentially better: Be cooperative.* ~ **Mitchell Anthony**

45. *If everyone helps to hold up the sky then not one person becomes tired.* ~ **Askhari Johnson Hodaric**

46. *My model for business is 'The Beatles'. They were four guys who kept each other's kind of negative tentacles in check. They balanced each other and the total was greater than the sum of the parts. That's how I see business: great things in business are never done by one person, they're done by a team of people.* ~ **Steve Jobs**

47. *People have been known to achieve more as a result of working with others than against them.* ~ **Dr. Allan Fromme**

48. *A leader must INSPIRE his team or his team will EXPIRE.* ~ **Orrin Woodward**

49. *When you score a goal, hit a three, or get a touchdown, you don't do it for yourself, you do it for the team 'cause the name on the front of the shirt is more important than the name on the back.* ~ **Anonymous**

50. *A group becomes a team when an individual is sure enough of himself to praise the work of the others.* ~ **Norman Shidle**

51. *The workings of a successful team is like the beating of a heart, everyone is beating in sync.* ~ **Anonymous**

52. *Only by binding together as a single force will we remain strong and unconquerable. ~* **Chris Bradford**

53. *ALONE we can do so little; TOGETHER we can do so much.* *~* **Helen Keller 1889-1968**

54. *My opinion, my conviction, gains immensely in strength and sureness the minute a second mind has adopted it. ~* **Novalis 1772-1801**

55. *Find a group of people who challenge and inspire you, spend a lot of time with them, and it will change your life. ~* **Amy Poehler**

56. *We are a team. One person struggles, we all struggle. One person triumphs we all triumph. ~* **Paul Bowers**

57. *The teamwork recipe for success: Heat up an idea, take action, mix it up with passion and belief, then add a big dash of persistence. ~* **Anonymous**

58. *Uniqueness IS NOT going away from the team and working, it's like being in the team and still doing things differently!!! ~* **Manivasagam Karunakaran**

59. *One piece of log creates a small fire, adequate to warm you up, add just a few more pieces to blast an immense bonfire, large enough to warm up your entire circle of friends; needless to say that individuality counts but team work dynamites. ~* **Jin Kwo**

60. *Respect your fellow human being, treat them fairly, disagree with them honestly, enjoy their friendship, explore your thoughts about one another candidly, work together for a common goal and help one another achieve It.* ~ **Bill Bradley**

61. *When you win as a team. It doesn't matter if one person had more hits or another person barely touched the ball. You won as a team.* ~ **Anonymous**

62. *What we need to do is learn to work in the system, by which I mean that everybody, every team, every platform, every division, every component, is there not for individual competitive profit or recognition, but for contribution to the system as a whole on a win win basis.* ~ **W. Edward Deming**

63. *Unity is strength. Where there is collaboration wonderful things can be achieved.* ~ **Mattie J.T. Stepanek**

64. *Trust is knowing that when a team member does push you, they're doing it because they care about the team.* ~ **Patrick Lencioni**

65. *Many of us are more capable than some of us, but none of us is as capable as all of us.* ~ **Tom Wilson**

66. *Many corporate leaders and employees have all the right intentions, but it can be overwhelming when you consider how everything is about leadership styles, organizational structures, employee engagement, and customer service in a particular marketplace. It's all about fancy words and fandangled ideas*

just to keep Human Resources happy. ~ **Simon Mainwaring**

67. *A good objective of leadership is to help those who are doing poorly to do well and to help those who are doing well to do even better.* ~ **Jim Rohn**

68. *In teamwork, silence isn't golden. It's deadly.* ~ **Mark Sanborn**

69. *People are definitely a company's greatest asset. It doesn't make any difference whether the product is cars or cosmetics.* ~ **Mary Kay Ash**

70. *I love teamwork. I love the idea of everyone rallying together to help me win.* ~ **Jarod Kintz**

71. *Mistakes are part of the game. It's how well the team recovers from them that's the mark of a great team.* ~ **Alice Cooper**

72. *'A just the job employee' does just enough to keep their job while complaining about what's not fair or right at work. 'A team player' works positively together with everyone to get the job done the best way possible. SEE THE DIFFERENCE?* ~ **Ty Howard**

73. *We are not a team because we work together. We are a team because we respect each other and care for each other.* ~ **Vala Afshar**

74. *The thing you can do to make your team a more interesting*

place to work is to enable those under you to feel they control their own areas of work. In this way they acquire a sense of ownership in what gets done and how they do it. ~ **Kenneth Ashworth**

75. *Most people don't want to be a part of the process, they only want to be a part of the outcome. But the process is the part where you figure out who is worth being a part of the outcome.* ~ **Carey Lohrenz**

76. *Successful teams struggle, fight and often bicker. The difference between a successful team and a failing team is when these challenges happen, successful teams acknowledge and resolve them quickly because the vision, harmony, constant production and success of the team, is more important than the 'he said or she said' drama or counterproductive foolishness of an individual.* ~ **Ty Howard**

77. *The kinds of nets we know how to weave determine the kind of nets we caste. These nets, in turn, determine the kind of fish we catch.* ~ **Elliot W. Eisner**

78. *Teamwork begins by building trust. And the only way to do that is to overcome our need for invulnerability.* ~ **Patrick Lencioni**

79. *You put together the best team that you can with the players you've got, and replace those who aren't good enough.* ~ **Robert Crandal**

80. *Every high performance team believe it exists for a compelling reason and that the world will be better for what it does. Its purpose is not the task or the work it does but the benefit it delivers. So surround yourself with a great team and build that team slowly. Your team is going to be one of your most important investments, so if you are careful about hiring only the best people, it will pay dividends. ~* ***Kinda Hil and Sheala Johnstone***

3
MANAGING PEOPLE

A leader is the one who can outline the broad vision and the direction, and says this is where we are going, here's why we need to go there, and here's how we are going to get there. A manager is the one who actually gets up under the hood and tunes the carburettor so you can get there at top speed.

~ Mike Huckabee ~

1.   *Effective leadership is putting first things first. Effective management is about the discipline, to carry it out. ~ **Stephen Covey***

2.   *Managing and leading people means caring for them, respecting them, rewarding them, winning them over, focusing on intangibles, teaching them constantly, delegating tasks to them, communication clearly to them, creating leadership opportunities, relishing diversity, promoting differences and constantly being enthusiastic however bad you feel inside. On the other side of the coin it also means talking tough at times and disciplining them when required. ~ **Tom Peters***

3.   *As a manager one of the important things you need to instil into your team is that they all need to learn that their words and actions DO affect other people. So they should be CAREFUL when doing something or saying something, as it's not always*

about them, it's about everyone around them. ~ **Anonymous**

4.   *A man is sitting under a giant oak tree in a park in the middle of a city today because someone in authority made the decision to plant a tiny seed all those years ago. Management is seeing into the future while planning for today.* ~ **Anonymous**

5.   *As a leader, whether you're the team leader or the manager, it's incumbent upon you to practice the behaviour you want your team to follow.* ~ **Hiamnshu Bhatia**

6.   *Management is about arranging and telling. Leadership is about nurturing and enhancing.* ~ **Tom Peters**

7.   *Management is nothing more than learning to constantly motivate other people.* ~ **Lee Cacocca**

8.   *Reading a book about management isn't going to make you a good manager any more than a book about guitars will make you a good guitarist, but it can get you thinking about the most important concepts.* ~ **Drew Houston**

9.   *The first rule of management is delegation. Don't try and do everything yourself because you can't.* ~ **Anthea Turner**

10.   *Our greatest assets walk out the door each evening. Our job as a manager is to make their work so interesting that they walk back in the next morning.* ~ **N.R. Narayana Murthey**

11.   *The productivity of work is not the responsibility of the worker but of the team manager.* ~ **Peter F Drucker**

12. *Never give an order that can't be obeyed. ~* **General Douglas MacArthur**

13. *If everyone is moving forward together, then success will take care of itself. ~* **Henry Ford 1863-1947**

14. *Hire people who are better than you are, then leave them to get on with it. Look for people who will aim for the remarkable, who will not settle for the routine. ~* **David Ogilvy**

15. *The conventional definition of management is getting work done through people, but real management is developing people through work. ~* **Agha Hasan Abedi**

16. *Effective leadership is putting first things first. Effective management is discipline, carrying it out. ~* **Stephen R. Covey**

17. *Management is efficiency in climbing the ladder of success; leadership determines whether the ladder is leaning against the right wall. ~* **Stephen R. Covey**

18. *When you manage people you must first convince them they need managing. So you create the problems and let the people cry for solutions. ~* **Barbara Marcainiak**

19. *Coming together is a beginning. Keeping together is progress. Working together is success. ~* **Henry Ford 1863-1947**

20. *Management is about human beings. Its task is to make people capable of joint performance, to make their strengths*

effective and their weaknesses irrelevant. ~ **Peter F. Drucker**

21.   *To be honest, the fact that people trust you gives you a lot of power over people. Having another person's trust is more powerful than all other management techniques put together.* ~ **Linus Torvalds**

22.   *Good Management is the art of making problems so interesting, so constructive, that everyone wants to come to work and deal with them.* ~ **Paul Hawking**

23.   *The three rules of management: Out of clutter find SIMPLICITY. From discord find HARMONY. In the middle of difficulty lies OPPORTUNITY.* ~ **Albert Einstein 1879-1955**

24.   *Most of management is nothing more than motivating other people.* ~ **Lee Iacocca**

25.   *A good manager is a man who isn't worried about his own career but rather the careers of those who work for him.* ~ **H.S.M. Burns**

26.   *The secret of successful managing is to keep the five guys who hate you away from the four guys who haven't made up their minds.* ~ **Casey Stengel**

27.   *Facebook and Twitter aren't the real problems in the office. The real problems are what I like to call the M&Ms, the Managers and the Meetings.* ~ **Jason Fried**

28.   *Organisation doesn't really accomplish anything. Plans*

don't accomplish anything, either. Theories of management don't much matter. Endeavours succeed or fail because of the people involved. Only by attracting the best people will you accomplish great deeds. ~ **General Colin Powell**

29. Fit no stereotypes. Don't chase the latest management fads. The situation dictates which approach best accomplishes the team's mission. ~ **General Colin Powell**

30. Good managers always recognise that human individuals are ends, and do not use them as a means to your end. ~ **Immanuel Kant 1724-1804**

31. Reduce the layers of management. They put unnecessary distance between the top of an organization and the customers. ~ **Donald Rumsfeld**

32. Management manages by making decisions and by seeing that those decisions are implemented. ~ **Harold S. Geneen**

33. Good management consists in showing average people how to do the work of superior people. ~ **John D. Rockefeller 1839-1937**

34. Some people are better at managing situations. A lot of times it is the inability to deal with those life events that can be a trigger for anger. ~ **Sherri Miller**

35. Management is about arranging and telling. Leadership is about nurturing and enhancing. ~ **Tom Peters**

36. *A key to achieving success is to assemble a strong and stable management team.* ~ **Vivek Wadhawa**

37. *When there is an acute talent shortage someone has to be the manager. Why not you?* ~ **Anonymous**

38. *You manage things; you lead people.* ~ **Rear Admiral Grace Murray Hopper**

39. *So much of what we call management consists in making it difficult for people to work.* ~ **Peter F Drucker**

40. *A good manager is best when people barely know that he exists. It's not so good when people obey and acclaim him, it's at its worst when they despise him.* ~ **Lao Tzu 604-531 BC**

41. *The desk in your office is a dangerous place to view the world from.* ~ **John Le Caré**

42. *Lead and inspire people. Don't try to manage and manipulate people. Inventories can be managed but people must be lead.* ~ **Ross Perot**

43. *If you have a workforce that enjoys each other, they trust each other, they trust management, they're proud of where they work, then they're going to deliver a good product.* ~ **Jeff Smisek**

44. *The art of effective listening is essential to clear communication, and clear communication is necessary to management success.* ~ **James Cash Penney**

45. *People are definitely a company's greatest asset. It doesn't make any difference whether the product is cars or cosmetics. A company is only as good as the people it keeps.* ~ **Mary Kay Ash**

46. *When we own portions of outstanding businesses with outstanding management, our favourite holding period is forever.* ~ **Warren Buffet**

47. *Anyone can hold the helm when the sea is calm.* ~ **Publilius Syrus**

48. *When people cut you down or talk behind your back, remember that they took time out of their pathetic little lives to think about you. So you must mean something to them.* ~ **Anonymous**

49. *It takes years for anyone in a management position to build a solid reputation and only 5 minutes to ruin it. If you think about that you'll often do things differently.* ~ **Warren Buffett**

50. *Checking the results of a decision against its expectations shows managers what their strengths are, where they need to improve, and where they lack knowledge or information.* ~ **Peter F. Drucker**

51. *Managers start with good people, lay out the rules, communicate with your team, then motivate them and reward them. If you do all these things then you cannot miss.* ~ **Lee Iacocca**

52. *Good management is the art of making problems so interesting and their solutions so constructive that everyone wants to get to work and deal with them.* ~ **Paul Hawken**

53. *Today, a skilled manager makes more than the owner. And owners fight each other to get the skilled managers.* ~ **Mikhail Khodorkovsky**

54. *We don't have as many managers as we should, but we would rather have too few than too many.* ~ **Larry Page**

55. *Our mission statement about treating people with respect and dignity is not just words but a creed we live by every day. You can't expect your employees to exceed the expectations of your customers if you don't exceed the employees' expectations of management.* ~ **Howard Schultz**

56. *Managing to have a sense of humour makes it a lot easier to manage people.* ~ **Steve Wilson**

57. *If you want to build a ship, don't drum up people to collect wood and then assign them tasks and work, but rather teach them to long for the endless immensity of the sea.* ~ **Antoine de Saint Exuper**

58. *Hiring people is an art, not a science, and resumes can't tell you whether someone will fit into a company's culture. When you realize you've made a mistake, you need to cut your losses and move on.* ~ **Howard Schultz**

59. *Employees who believe that management is concerned about them as a whole person, not just as an employee, are more productive, more satisfied, more fulfilled. Satisfied employees mean satisfied customers, which leads to greater profitability.* ~ **Anne M. Mulcaghy**

60. *If you want to be a good manager don't swear, and don't ever raise your voice, simply make a damn good argument, then tell them to do it.* ~ **Anonymous**

61. *A good manager is a man who isn't worried about his own career but rather the careers of those who work for him. My advice: Don't worry about yourself. Take care of those who work for you and you'll float to greatness on their achievements.* ~ **H.S.M. Burns**

62. *We're not a team simply because we work together. We're a team because we respect, trust and care for each other.* ~ **Vala Alfshar**

63. *Management isn't simply about organisation or perfection. It's about efficiency, reducing stress and clutter, saving time and money and improving your teams overall quality of life.* ~ **Christina Scalise**

64. *Manager quote 21: Everyone who comes here makes us happy. Some when they arrive, some when they stay, some when they leave.* ~ **Anonymous**

65. *If you have a workforce that enjoys each other, they trust each other, they trust management, they're proud of where they*

work - then they're going to deliver a good product. ~ **Jeff Misek**

66. *The Stage Managers Prayer: Lord grant me the serenity to accept the things I cannot change, the courage to change the things I can, and the wisdom to hide the bodies of the actors I had to kill because they really pissed me off!* ~ **Anonymous**

67. *Research indicates that workers have three prime needs: Interesting work, recognition for doing a good job, and being let in on things that are going on in the company.* ~ **Zig Ziglar**

68. *I consider my ability to arouse enthusiasm among men the greatest asset I possess. The way to develop the best that is in a man is by appreciation and encouragement.* ~ **Charles Schwab**

69. *Given the right circumstances, from no more than dreams, determination, and the liberty to try, quite ordinary people consistently do extraordinary things.* ~ **Dee Hock**

70. *Rule number one for managers: it is better to offer no excuse for failure than a bad one.* ~ **Peter Brennan**

71. *If you, as a manager, are building a culture where honest expectations are communicated and peer accountability is the norm, then the group will address poor performance and attitudes.* ~ **Henry Cloud**

72. *One of the most important task of a manager is to eliminate his people's excuses for failure.* ~ **Robert Townsend**

73. *All of the great leaders have had one characteristic in*

common: it was the willingness to confront unequivocally the major anxiety of their people in their time. This, and not much else, is the essence of leadership. ~ **John Kenneth Galbraith**

74. We cling to hierarchies because our place in a hierarchy is, rightly or wrongly, a major indicator of our social worth. ~ **Harold J. Leavitt**

75. The Four Keys to finding Great Managers: When selecting someone, select for talent ... not simply experience, intelligence or determination. When setting expectations, define the right outcomes ... not the right steps. When motivating someone, focus on strengths ... not on weaknesses. When developing someone, help him find the right fit ... not simply the next rung on the ladder. ~ **Marcus Buckingham**

76. People want guidance, not rhetoric. They need to know what the plan of action is and how it will be implemented. They want to be given responsibility to help solve the problem and the authority to act on it. ~ **Howard Schultz**

77. Focus on a few key objectives ... I only have three things to do. I have to choose the right people, allocate the right number of dollars, and transmit ideas from one division to another with the speed of light. So I'm really in the business of being the gatekeeper and the transmitter of ideas. ~ **Jack Welch**

78. If you focus on results you will never get change. If you focus on change you will get results. ~ **Jack Dixon**

79. The job of management is not to select the best ideas; it is

to create a system that allows the best ideas to emerge. ~
Anonymous

80. I describe management as arts, crafts and science
orientated. It is a practice that draws on arts, crafts and science,
and there is a lot of art, meaning experience involved. There is
a certain amount craft, meaning insight, creativity and vision,
and there is also the use of science for technique and analysis.
Remember that people are not clones, every single one of them
is different and you have to fit those differences together like a
jigsaw puzzle so that they can do their arts, crafts and science.
~ **Henry Mintzberg**

The first rule of management is delegation. Don't try and
do everything yourself because you can't.

~ **Anthea Turner** ~

4
DELEGATION

When you delegate always start by specifying the outcome you desire to the people you trust to deliver it. Establish controls, identify limits to the work and provide sufficient support, but resist upward delegation. Keep up to date with progress, and focus on results rather than procedures. Finally, when the work is completed, give recognition where it's deserved.
~ Alex Raths ~

1. *The secret to sustainable growth is to spend your time on what adds most value to your business and delegate the rest. ~* **Even Carmichael**

2. *A key aspect of leadership is delegation. If you don't delegate tasks to your subordinates your team will become demoralized and inefficient. ~* **Anonymous**

3. *If you really want to grow as an entrepreneur then you have to delegate. ~* **Richard Branson**

4. *Few things help a person more that to place responsibility upon him, and to let him know that you trust him. ~* **Booker T. Washington 1856-1915**

5. *I'm going from doing all of the work to having to delegate the work – which is harder for me than doing the work myself.*

*I'm a lousy delegator, but I'm learning. ~ **Alton Brown***

6. *A king, realizing his incompetence, can either delegate or abdicate his duties. A father can do neither. If only sons could see the paradox, they would understand the dilemma. ~* **Marlene Dietrich**

7. *When you delegate work to a member of the team, your job is to clearly frame success and describe the objectives. ~ **Steven Sinofsky***

8. *If you want to do a few small things right, do them yourself. If you want to do great things and make a big impact, learn to delegate. ~ **John C. Maxwell***

9. *The best executive is the one who has sense enough to pick good men to do what he wants done, and self-restraint to keep from meddling while they do it. ~ **Theodore Roosevelt 1858-1919***

10. *If you don't know what to do with many of the papers piled on your desk, stick a dozen colleagues' initials on them and pass them along. When in doubt, reroute. ~ **Malcolm S. Forbes***

11. *Delegation is giving others the opportunity to participate in the story. If you have a good story, people will line up to get involved – to play a part in the story. ~ **Eric Phillips***

12. *Identify your best skill and devote your time to performing it. Delegate all other skills. ~ **Ronald Brown***

13.   *No person will make a great business who wants to do it all himself, or get all the credit.* ~ **Andrew Carnegie**

14.   *Hire people who are better than you are, then leave them to get on with it . . . Look for people who will aim for the remarkable, who will not settle for the routine.* ~ **David Ogilvy**

15.   *If you pick the right people and give them the opportunity to spread their wings and put compensation as a carrier behind it, you almost don't have to manage them.* ~ **Jack Welch**

16.   *You cannot talk about leadership without talking about responsibility and accountability. You can't separate them. When you delegate make sure whoever you delegate to know they are responsible for every aspect of the work they are doing.* ~ **James Hargrave**

17.   *Delegating means letting others become the experts and hence the best.* ~ **Timothy Firnstahl**

18.   *Are we limiting our success by not mastering the art of delegation? ...it's simply a matter of preparation meeting opportunity.* ~ **Oprah Winfrey**

19.   *DELEGATE: Busy is not a good word. It's not a good excuse. Get it done. Delegate it!* ~ **Paul Orfalea**

20.   *As we look ahead into the next century, leaders will be those who empower others.* ~ **Bill Gates**

21.   *As long as you have the right people in place and you've*

organized your leadership team so they're aligned with the company's goals, you should get out of the way and let them do their jobs. ~ **Steve Tobak**

22. *The inability to delegate is one of the biggest problems I see with managers at all levels.* ~ **Eli Broad**

23. *Delegation doesn't lose you any power it simply distributes your power more effectively.* ~ **Anonymous**

24. *The fact you delegate a task to someone shows them you trust them so they are extremely unlikely to let you down. In fact they will most likely go out of their way to do the best job possible so that you will delegate to them again.* ~ **Roger Payne**

25. *Delegation requires the willingness to pay for short term failures in order to gain long term competencies.* ~ **Dave Ramsey**

26. *Delegation is not a binary thing. There are shades of grey between a dictatorship and an anarchy.* ~ **Jurgen Appelo**

27. *Don't wait to delegate. You need to start getting people to do stuff for you even before you feel you are ready.* ~ **Kevin Kruse**

28. *If there is any one axiom that I have tried to live up to in trying to become successful in business, it is the fact that I have tried to surround myself with associates that know more about business than I do. It's delegation by natural selection. This policy has always been very successful and is still working for*

me. ~ **Monte L. Bean**

30. *If you delegate a job to someone and he accepts it he should be under no illusions that every aspect of the job is HIS responsibility. There can be NO EXCUSES for not completing the job to the standard you require and within the time frame laid down.* ~ **Roger Payne**

31. *If you want it done right you don't have to do it yourself.* ~ **Donna M. Genell.**

32. *To truly understand any team you first have to wear all the hats before you can take some off and give them to someone else.* ~ **Jim McNelis**

33. *The 5 stages of delegation: I do – I do, you watch – we do – you do, I watch – I watch.* ~ **Anonymous**

34. *Team Leading is about striving to become better than we are, and helping everything and everyone around us to become better too. Delegation is a tool that helps team members get better at what they do.* ~ **Lolly Daskal**

35. *The role of leaders is not to just get other people to follow them but to empower others to lead and within that falls the role of delegation.* ~ **Bill George**

36. *An empowered organization is one in which individuals have the knowledge, skill, desire, and opportunity to personally succeed in a way that leads to collective organizational success.* ~ **Stephen Covey**

37. *Surround yourself with the best people you can find, delegate authority, and don't interfere as long as the policy you've decided upon is being carried out. ~ **Ronald Reagan***

38. *From a young age, I learned to focus on the things I was good at and delegate to others what I was not good at. That's how Virgin is run. Fantastic people throughout the Virgin Group run our businesses, allowing me to think creatively and strategically. ~ **Richard Branson***

39. *I don't have a problem with delegation. I love to delegate. I'm either a lazy person, which I'm not, or I'm too busy, which I am. I trust those I delegate too, which I do. The notion that leaving the task in someone else's lap is foolish never occurs to me. The whole concept is very attractive to both parties. ~ **John Ortberg***

40. *Remember – Delegation does not mean passing off work you don't enjoy, that's being lazy. Delegation means giving others work that stretches their imagination, skills and judgement. ~ **Harvey Mackay***

41. *Delegation means handing some of your powers downwards to a subordinate, a trusted team member. It's about assigning responsibility to others. Over time involve as many team members in the process as possible. The more responsible ones have greater responsibility. The more you do it the greater the confidence each individual becomes and you not only teach them how to take control of certain aspects of the team's work you're showing them that you trust them, which is equally as*

important. ~ **Bobby Mayne**

42. *The only reason I have been able to run the business is because I've been able to delegate successfully, and those I've delegated too have also delegated.* ~ **Larry Wall**

43. *If there is any one axiom that I have tried to live up to in trying to become successful in business, it is the fact that I have tried to surround myself with associates that know more about business than I do. This policy has always been very successful and is still working for me.* ~ **Monte L. Bean**

44. *Delegate to train people well enough so they can leave. Delegate to train people well enough so they don't want to leave.* ~ **Richard Branson**

45. *You don't build a team, you build people in that team. Then you delegate and let the people build continue to build the team.* ~ **Richard Branson**

46. *Not many of us will be leaders; and even those who are leaders must also be followers much of the time. This is the crucial role. Followers judge leaders. Only if the leaders pass that test do they have any impact. The potential followers, if their judgment is poor, have judged themselves. If the leader takes his or her followers to the goal, to great achievements, it is because the followers were capable of that kind of response.* ~ **Garry Wills**

47. *Because our organisation has grown so much and in so many ways the delegation process places responsibility and*

authority on the shoulders of people you can watch grow and watch the way they treat others. ~ **Vince McMahon**

48. *Delegation is giving others the chance to participate in your story. If you have a really good story, people will line up to get involved, to play their part in the story.* ~ **Eric Phillips**

49. *People want guidance, not rhetoric. They need to know what the plan of action is and how it will be implemented. They want to be given responsibility to help solve the problem and the authority to act on it.* ~ **Howard Schultz**

50. *What happens when you pass a project to one of your lieutenants? He or she might take the ball and run a different route than you would. One that might not work. Scary? Yes, but at some point, you've got to trust your people.* ~ **Lisa Mckale**

51. *You walk into the class in second grade. You can't read. What are you going to do if you're going to make it? You identify the smart kid. You make friends with him. You sit next to him. You grow a team around you. You delegate your work to others. You learn how to talk your way out of a tight spot.* ~ **Malcolm Gladwell**

52. *If you have discipline, drive, determination, and the confidence to delegate, then nothing is impossible.* ~ **Dana Lyn Bail**

53. *Followers who tell the truth when something didn't go right, and leaders who listen to it, are an unbeatable combination.* ~ **Warren Bennis**

54. Our organization has grown so much and in so many different ways, the delegation process places responsibility and authority on the shoulders of people you can watch grow and watch the way they treat others which is equally as important. ~ **Vince McMahon**

55. Never try to teach a pig to sing; it wastes your time and it annoys the pig. ~ **Paul Dickson**

56. Make sure you thoroughly brief anyone you delegate a task to. Make sure they know that if they are having problems with the task they come and see you before it gets out of hand. Show them how to solve the problem then let them finish it. Remember, everyone makes mistake, even you. ~ **Roger Payne**

57. Delegating work works, providing whoever is delegating works too. ~ **Robert Half**

58. Not many of us will be leaders; and even those who are leaders must also be followers much of the time, that's called delegation. This is the crucial role. Followers judge leaders. Only if the leaders pass that test do they have any impact. The potential followers, if their judgment is poor, have judged themselves. If the leader takes his or her followers to the goal, to great achievements, it is because the followers were capable of that kind of response. ~ **Garry Wills**

59. The role of leaders is not to get other people to follow them but to empower others to lead. ~ **Bill George**

60. *Delegating means letting others become the experts and hence the best.* ~ **Timothy Firnstahl**

61. *As all entrepreneurs know, you live and die by your ability to prioritize. You must focus on the most important, mission-critical tasks each day and night, and then share, delegate, delay or skip the rest.* ~ **Jessica Jackley**

62. *There are two ways of spreading light: to be the candle or the mirror that reflects it.* ~ **Edith Wharton**

63. *When in doubt, mumble; when in trouble, delegate; when in charge, ponder.* ~ **James Boren**

64. *As we look ahead into the next century, leaders will be those who empower others.* ~ **Bill Gates**

65. *Nobody is going to delegate a lot of power to a secretary that only controls her desk.* ~ **Michael Bloomberg**

66. *Delegation is an issue of respect and how much we respect those that are under us on our team.* ~ **Dr. Hans Finzel**

67. *The best advice in two line that you can get: 'Silence is the best answer for all questions', 'and a Smile is the best reaction in all situations.'* ~ **Anonymous**

68. *The world is full of willing people, some willing to work, the rest willing to let them.* ~ **Robert Frost**

69. *In order that people may be happy in their work, these three*

things are needed: They must be fit for it. They must not do too much of it. And they must have a sense of success in it. ~ **John Ruskin 1819-1900**

70. When you have had work delegated to you the quality of your work, in the long run, is the deciding factor on how much your services are valued in the future. ~ **Orison Swett Marden 1848-1924**

71. The secret of joy in work, delegated or not, is contained in one word - excellence. To know how to do something well is to enjoy it. ~ **Pearl Buck**

72. Success in business requires training, discipline and hard work. If you're not frightened by these things, the opportunities are just as great today as they ever were. ~ **David Rockefeller**

73. People and organizations don't grow much without delegation and teamwork because they both reflect personal strengths and team weaknesses. ~ **Stephen Covey**

74. You run a major risk when you assume that you alone have all the answers: You don't, and that's okay. You don't have to be afraid to admit there are certain things you either don't like to do or aren't any good at. You reach a goal by covering all your bases, and you cover all your bases by hiring good people. ~ **Georgette Mosbacher**

75. I don't keep a dog and bark myself. ~ **Elizabeth I 1533-1603**

76. I find that many entrepreneurs are trying to do everything

*when it would be cheaper and more time-efficient to delegate, even if there are monetary costs associated with that. ~ **James Altucher***

77. *When I put out to sea, I do not offer advice to the skipper about the management of the ship.*
*~ **Elsa Barker***

78. *As much as you need a strong personality to build a business from scratch, you also must understand the art of delegation. I have to be good at helping people run the individual businesses, and I have to be willing to step back. The company must be set up so it can continue without me. ~ **Richard Branson***

79. *I have received delegations of working men who come, apparently speaking of the utmost sincerity, have declared that they would regard it as a genuine hardship to be deprived of their beer. ~ **Woodrow Wilson 1856-1924***

80. *If you delegate tasks you create followers. If you delegate power you create leaders ~ **Craig Gallagher***

.

5
DECISION MAKING

Decision making is the thought process of selecting a logical choice from all the available options. When trying to make the right decision you must weigh the positives and negatives of each possible action, and consider every alternative. For effective decision making you must not only select the best choice you must be able to forecast the outcome of each option as well, and based on all these choices, determine which is the best for that particular situation.

~ *Roger Payne* ~

1.   *Sometimes in life you have to make hard decisions that are BEST for YOU, but NOBODY ELSE.* ~ **Peter F. Drucker**

2.   *Don't make decisions based upon the advice of people that don't have to live with the outcome of that decision.* ~ **Andy Lehey**

3.   *You have a choice, a single choice whatever ever it might be; you have to live with the consequences of that choice, and only that single choice, every time you make a choice. That's all, a SIMPLE CHOICE.* ~ **Anonymous**

4.   *When you need to make a hard decision flip a coin. WHY? Because when that coin is in the air you suddenly know the*

answer you're looking for. ~ **Anonymous**

5.   *Wherever you see a successful business, someone once made a courageous decision.* ~ **Peter F Drucker**

6.   *You have a choice when making a decision. So think carefully, plan and prepare it, and once your preparations are finished, don't hesitate, go with it. The worst that can happen is you were wrong for all the right reasons. Better that than you were wrong for all the wrong reasons.* ~ **William Giles 1791-1862**

7.   *Whatever you decide upon, there is always someone to tell you that you are wrong. There are always difficulties arising that tempt you to believe that your critics are right. To map out a course of action and follow it to an end requires courage.* ~ **Ralph Waldo Emerson 1803-1882**

8.   *It is hard to imagine a more stupid or more dangerous way of making decisions than by putting those decisions in the hands of people who pay no price for being wrong.* ~ **Thomas Sowell**

9.   *On an important decision one rarely has 100% of the information needed for a good decision no matter how much one spends thinking about it, or how long one delays. And, if one waits too long, you have a different problem and have to start all over. This is the terrible dilemma of the hesitant decision maker.* ~ **Robert K. Greenleaf**

10.   *Sometimes the hardest decision and the right decision are*

*one and the same. ~ **Anonymous***

11.   *One of the hardest decisions you'll ever make is deciding to walk away or keep on fighting. ~ **Anonymous***

12.   *The worst business decision you can make is no decision. The needs are not going to go away. Waiting is what's gotten you in the situation you're in now. ~ **John Peace***

13.   *Forget about all the reason why something might not work. You only need to find one reason why it might work. ~ **Curiano.com***

14.   *The only people who never tumble are those who never mount the high wire. This is your moment. Mount it then own it. ~ **Oprah Winfrey***

15.   *Decisions are the hardest thing to make especially when it is a choice between where you are and where you want to be. ~ **Martin Eynon***

16.   *We are the creative force of our life, and through our own decisions rather than our conditions, if we carefully learn to do certain things, we can accomplish those goals. ~ **Stephen Covey***

17.   *Decision is the spark that ignites action. Until a decision is made, nothing happens. A Decision is the courageous facing of issues, knowing that if they are not faced, problems will remain forever unanswered. ~ **Wilfred A. Peterson***

18. *It doesn't matter which side of the fence you get off on sometimes. What matters most is getting off. You cannot make progress without making decisions.* ~ **Jim Rohn**

19. *When defeat comes, accept it as a signal that your plans are not sound, rebuild those plans, and set sail once more toward your coveted goal. If you give up before your goal has been reached, you are a 'quitter'. A quitter never wins, and a winner never quits.* ~ **Napoleon Hill 1883-1970**

20. *What's called a difficult decision is a difficult decision because either way you go there are penalties.* ~ **Elia Kazan**

21. *In the final analysis there is no other solution to man's progress but the day's honest work, the day's honest decision, the day's generous utterances, and the day's good deed.* ~ **Clare Boothe Luce**

22. *The brick walls are there for a reason. The brick walls are not there to keep us out. The brick walls are there to give us a chance to show how badly we want something, because the brick walls are there to stop the people who don't want it badly enough. They're there to stop the other people.* ~ **Randy Pausch**

23. *Everything in your life is a reflexion of the choices you made. If you want a different result then make a different choice.* ~ **Anonymous**

24. *Just really, really believe in what you're trying to do. Don't let people alter that. Let people advise you and lead you down*

*paths to make smart business decisions. But in the end trust your instinct and that overwhelming drive that made you put all your dreams and everything on the line. ~ **Luke Bryan***

25. *Everything in your life is a reflexion of the choices you made. If you want a different result then make a different choice. ~ **Anonymous***

26. *You have a choice, a single choice, whatever that choice might be YOU have to live with the consequences that it might bring. That's all. A CHOICE. ~ **G. Gutierrez***

27. *Don't make any decisions based upon a temporary emotion, think before you leap. ~ **Anonymous***

28. *A peacefulness follows any decision, even the wrong one. ~ **Rita Mae Brown 1842-1910***

29. *Sometimes you can head off a decision you'll regret by looking into your heart and finding regret already there. ~ **Robert Brault***

30. *For all its accolades and celebrated recognition as sound guidance, I have personally noticed that sometimes 'Follow your heart,' is really bad advice. ~ **Steve Maraboli***

31. *Some people are very decisive when it comes to avoiding decisions. ~ **Brendan Francis***

32. *Life is the sum of all your choices. ~ **Albert Camus***

33. *What is the secret of success? 'Make The Right Decisions.'* *And how do you make the right decisions? 'Experience.' And how do you gain experience? 'By Making Mistakes.'* ~ **Abdul Kalam**

34. *Although every man believes that his decisions and resolutions involve the most multifarious factors, in reality they are mere oscillation between flight and longing.* ~ **Herman Broch**

35. *When you have to make a choice and don't make it, that is in itself a choice.* ~ **William James 1842-1910**

36. *Even though you've deliberated long and hard. When you make that final choice from all the ones laid out in front of you, what you're really doing is diving into a strong swirling, turbulent current in the hope that you are strong enough to swim to the opposite shore before being carried into places you never dreamed of going when you made the decision. Curiously, nine times out of ten you can.* ~ **Paul Coelho**

37. *To finally decide is to walk facing forward with nary a crick in your neck from looking back at the crossroads.* ~ **Betsy Cañas Garmon**

38. *In a minute there is time for decisions and revisions which a minute will reverse.* ~ **T.S. Eliot 1888-1965**

39. *Every morning you are faced with two choices: You can aimlessly stumble through the day not knowing what's going to happen and worry about it; or you can go through the day*

directing your own life and making your own decisions and destiny. ~ **Brittney Josephina**

40. *It was that moment all men anticipate, some with eagerness and some with dread, when you finally confront your dream and you must decide, once and for all, if you want it. To the young and still dreaming, it seems an obvious choice. But to the middle aged and responsible, it marks life's turning point.* ~ **Joe Kita**

41. *Decision making is regarded as a process resulting in the selection of a course of actions from amongst many alternatives. Every decision produces a single choice that either prompts action or not. Providing you have weighed up every possibility this is decision making at its best.* ~ **Anonymous**

42. *I am always wary of decisions made hastily. I am always wary of the first decision, that is, the first thing that comes to my mind if I have to make a decision. This is usually the wrong thing. I have to wait and assess, looking deep into myself, taking the necessary time.* ~ **Pope Francis**

43. *The inability to make a decision has often been passed off as patience.* ~ **Anonymous**

44. *If you insist on making teenage decision in your adult life then you can only expect teenage results.* ~ **Melanie Joy**

45. *The hardest thing to learn in life is which bridge to cross and which to burn.* ~ **David Russell**

46. *Sometimes you make the right decision; sometimes you make the decision right.* ~ **Phil McGraw**

47. *One of the hardest decisions in your life is choosing whether to walk away or keep on trying.* ~ **Anonymous**

48. *It is in your moments of decision that your destiny is shaped. Never cut a tree down in the wintertime. Never make a negative decision in the low time.* ~ **Ralph Waldo Emerson 1803-1882**

49. *I found every single successful person I've ever spoken to had a turning point. The turning point was when they made a clear, specific unequivocal decision that they were going to achieve success. Some people make that decision at fifteen and some people make it at fifty, and most people never make it at all.* ~ **Brian Tracy**

50. *An important decision I made was to resist playing the Blame Game. The day I realized that I am in charge of how I will approach problems in my life, that things will turn out better or worse because of me and nobody else, that was the day I knew I would be a happier and healthier person. And that was the day I knew I could truly build a life that matters.* ~ **Steve Goodier**

51. *There are people who can come to no decision on any matter without first having slept over it. This is all very well; but cases may occur where on this plan you risk being captured, bed and all.* ~ **Georg Christoph Lichtenberg 1742–1799**

52. *If being and remaining whole and healthy is a priority for you then you have to make some tough decisions on who and what you'll allow into your life. Love yourself enough to make the right decisions for your well-being and have no regrets or apologies. ~ **Abena***

53. *Your life changes the moment you make a new and committed decision. ~ **Anthony Robbins***

54. *Too often, the opportunity knocks, but by the time you push back the chain, push back the bolt, unhook the two locks and shut off the burglar alarm, it's too late. ~ **Rita Coolidge***

55. *Unnecessary fear of a bad decisions is a stumbling block for good decisions. ~ **Jim Camp***

56. *Decision is a sharp knife that cuts clean and straight; indecision, a dull one that hacks and tears and leaves ragged edges behind it. ~ **Gordon Graham***

57. *There is no more miserable human being than one in whom nothing is habitual but indecision. ~ **The Principles of Psychology 1890***

58. *One of the saddest lines in the world is, 'Oh come now be realistic.' The best parts of this world were not fashioned by those who were realistic. They were fashioned by those who dared to look hard at their wishes and gave them horses to ride. ~ **Richard Nelson Bolles***

59. *If you're not making mistakes, you're not taking risks, and*

that means you're not going anywhere. The key is to make mistakes faster than the competition, so you have more changes to learn and win. ~ **John W. Holt Jr**

60. *The percentage of mistakes in quick decisions is no greater than in long drawn out vacillation, and the effect of decisiveness itself 'makes things go' and creates confidence.* ~ **Anne O'Hare McCormick**

61. *Decisions. We can think about things, turn them over a million times in our head, play out the possible scenarios, but really when it comes down to it, you have to go with your heart and move forward. Maybe things will go well. Maybe they'll turn out poorly. Every decision brings with it some good, some bad, some lessons, some luck. The only thing that's for sure is that indecision steals years from many people who wind up wishing they'd just had the courage to leap.* ~ **Doe Zantamata**

62. *The right decisions are always the hardest to make it. But they must be made in order to live the life you deserve.* ~ **Trent Sheldon**

63. *People too often forget that it is your own choice how you want to spend the rest of your life.* ~ **Anonymous**

64. *A major life decision is never a choice but rather a realization that the decision has already been made.* ~ **Doug Cooper**

65. *You are not a product of your circumstances, you are a product of your decisions.* ~ **Stephen R. Covey**

66. *Viktor Frankl wisely said, 'Between stimulus and response there is a space. In that space lies our freedom and power to choose our response ('ResponseAbility'). In our response lies our growth and our happiness. This idea is so compelling and incredible, that if we allow it to take hold of us it can profoundly influence our lives! It's not circumstances (or mere feelings), but choices that steer our direction and determine our outcomes in life. Decisions determine destiny'.* ~ **Thomas Stephens**

67. *The more alternatives, the more difficult the choice.* ~ **Abbe D'Allanival**

68. *Unsuccessful people make decisions based on their current situation. Successful people make decisions based upon where they want to be.* ~ **Anonymous**

69. *Far better it is to dare mighty things, to win glorious triumphs, even though chequered by failure, than to take rank with those poor spirits who neither enjoy nor suffer much, because they live in the grey twilight that knows neither victory nor defeat.* ~ **Theodore Roosevelt**

70. *A man who has to be convinced to act before he acts is not a man of action. You must act as you breathe.* ~ **Georges Clemmanceau 1841-1929**

71. *There comes a moment when you have to stop revving up the car and shove it into gear.* ~ **David Mahoney**

72. *If there is a trait which does characterize leaders it is opportunism. Successful people are very often those who steadfastly refuse to be daunted by disadvantage and have the ability to turn disadvantage to good effect. They are decision makers who seize opportunity and take risks. Leadership then seems to be a matter of personality and character.* ~ **John Viney**

73. *You have to enable and empower people to make decisions independent of you. As I've learned, each person on a team is an extension of your leadership; if they feel empowered by you they will magnify your power to lead. Trust is a great force multiplier.* ~ **Tom Ridge**

74. *What we think or what we know or what we believe is, in the end, of little consequence, the only consequence is what we do.* ~ **John Ruskin1819-1900**

75. *When one bases his life on principle, 99 percent of ones decisions are already made.* ~ **Anonymous**

76. *The greatest mistake you can make in life is to be continually fearing that you will make one.* ~ **Elbert Hubbard 1856-1915**

77. *Consider what you think justice requires, and decide accordingly. But never give your reasons; for your judgment will probably be right, but your reasons will certainly be wrong.* ~ **Lord Mansfield 1705-1793**

78. *To decide is to make peace within and let the chips fall where they may.* ~ **Lisa Tabak**

79. *When one bases his life on principle, 99 percent of his decisions are already made.* ~ **Anonymous**

80. *Your life is the sum result of all the choices you make, both consciously and unconsciously. If you can control the process of choosing, you can take control of all aspects of your life. You can find the freedom that comes from being in charge of yourself.* ~ **Robert Bennett**

6
MOTIVATION

Before you act, LISTEN. Before you react, THINK. Before you spend, EARN. Before you criticize, WAIT. Before you pray, FORGIVE. Before you quit, TRY. Each in its own way is a form of motivation.

~ *Anonymous* ~

1.   *The 'PRISMATIC PRINCIPLE': So called because just like a prism that separates white light into several colours you have to understand that different people in your team will react positively or negatively to different methods of motivation. What motivates one team member WILL NOT motivate another. We assume that money is the great inducement and initially it will attract someone to your team, but it is not what keeps them there. The top three factors that retain the majority of people are a Sense of Purpose: (Having something in your life that is so meaningful you don't want to give it up). The Ability to Master the skill you're employed to do: (Become an expert at it), and Autonomy when doing it: (As much Freedom as possible on how you achieve it).* ~ **Roger Payne**

2.   *Sometimes your strategy wins, sometimes it loses. Every time you should learn.* ~ ***Anonymous***

3. *Failure will never over take me if my determination to succeed is strong enough.* ~ **Og Mandino**

4. *The SUCCESS of Teamwork is COMING together at the BEGINNING. KEEPING together is PROGRESS. CONTIN-UALLY working together is SUCCESS.* ~ **Henry Ford**

5. *Whatever the mind of man can conceive and believe, it can achieve.* ~ **Napoleon Hill 1883-1970**

6. *Wake up with determination and go to bed with satisfaction.* ~ **George Lorimer**

7. *Push yourself, because no one else is going to do it for you.* ~ **Anonymous**

8. *You miss 100% of the shots you don't take.* ~ **Wayne Gretzky**

9. *Everyone you will ever meet knows something you don't.* ~ **Bill Nye**

10. *The most difficult thing is the decision to act, the rest is merely tenacity.* ~ **Amelia Earhart 1897-1937**

11. *I've learned that people will forget what you said, people will forget what you did, but people will never forget how you made them feel.* ~ **Maya Angelou**

12. *Stop doubting yourself. Work hard, and make it happen.* ~ **Anonymous**

13. *Life isn't about getting and having, it's about giving and being.* ~ **Kevin Kruse**

14. *Life is what happens to you while you're busy making other plans.* ~ **John Lennon**

15. *Life is 10% what happens to me and 90% of how I react to it!* ~ **Charles Swindoll**

16. *The mind is everything. What you think you become.* ~ **Buddha 463-483 BC**

17. *Difficult roads often lead to beautiful destinies.* ~ **Anonymous**

18. *Every professional was once an amateur. Every expert was once a beginner. So dream big and start NOW!* ~ **Anonymous**

19. *Success is not built on success. It's built on failure. It's built on frustration and sometimes it's built of catastrophe.* ~ **Sumner Redstone**

20. *The strength of the team is each individual member. The strength of each member is the team.* ~ **Phil Jackson**

21. *Winning isn't everything, but wanting to win is.* ~ **Vince Lombardi**

22. *I am not a product of my circumstances. I am a product of my decisions.* ~ **Stephen Covey**

23. *Don't stop when you're dead tired, stop when you are done.* *~ **Marilyn Monroe***

24. *The hardest thing about getting motivated to do anything is not beginning, or the middle, but sticking with it to the end.* *~ **Steve Langdon***

25. *Every child is an artist. The problem is how to get them to remain an artist once they grow up. ~ **Pablo Picasso 1871-1973***

26. *You can never cross the ocean until you have the courage to lose sight of the shore. ~ **Christopher Columbus 1451-1596***

27. *If you want to know what a man's like, take a good look at how he treats his so called inferiors, not his equals. ~ **J.K. Rowling***

28. *The reason you talk to yourself is because you're the only one that answers 'I accept!' ~ **George Carlin***

29. *Whatever you can do, or dream you can, so begin it. Boldness has genius, power and magic in it! ~ **Johann Wolfgang von Goethe 1749-1832***

30. *If you don't go after the thing you want you'll never have it. If you don't ask, the answer will always be no. If you don't step forward you're always in the same place. ~ **Nora Roberts***

31. *People often say that motivation doesn't last. Well, neither does bathing. That's why we recommend it daily. ~ **Zig Ziglar***

33. *If it's truly important to you you'll find a way to achieve it.* ~ **Anonymous**

34. *Life shrinks or expands in proportion to one's courage.* ~ **Anais Nin**

35. *One very important aspect of motivation is the willingness to stop and look at things that no one else had bothered to look at. This simple process of focusing on things that are normally taken for granted is a powerful source of creativity and impetus.* ~ **Edward De Bono**

36. *Everything you've ever wanted is on the other side of fear.* ~ **George Addair**

37. *Dreams don't work unless you do too!* ~ **Anonymous**

38. *The only person you are destined to become is the person you decide to be.* ~ **Ralph Waldo Emerson 1803-1882**

39. *If you don't see yourself as a winner, how can you expect to perform as one?* ~ **Anonymous**

40. *A positive thinker sees the invisible, feels the intangible and achieves the impossible.* ~ **Anonymous**

41. *Few things can help an individual more than to place responsibility on him, and to let him know that you trust him.* ~ **Booker T. Washington 1856-1915**

42. *The real opportunity for success lies within the individual, not the job.* ~ **Zig Ziglar**

43. *If you cannot motivate yourself how do you expect to motivate your team.* ~ **Kenneth Lynch**

44. *You can't fall if you don't climb. But there's no joy in living your whole life on the ground looking up.* ~ **Anonymous**

45. *Challenges are what make life interesting and overcoming them is what makes life meaningful.* ~ **Joshua J. Marine**

46. *Good teams incorporate teamwork into their culture, creating the building blocks for success.* ~ **Ted Sundquist**

47. *I have been impressed with the urgency of doing. Knowing is not enough; we must apply. Being willing is not enough; we must do.* ~ **Leonardo da Vinci 1452-1519**

48. *There is only one corner of the universe you can be certain of improving, and that's your corner.* ~ **Aldous Huxley 1894-1963**

49. *A river cuts through rock not because it is powerful, but because it is persistent.* ~ **Anonymous**

50. *I believe anything is possible. I see opportunity where others see impossibility. I take risks. I'm focused. I hustle. I know that nothing is unrealistic. I feel an overwhelming love for my family. I embrace my childlike wonder and curiosity. I take flying leaps into the unknown. I contribute to things bigger*

*than myself. I create. I learn. I do. I believe it's never too late to start living a dream. I am a risk taker. ~ **Anonymous***

51. *A successful team is a group of many hands and one mind. ~ **Bill Bethel***

52. *The person who says it cannot be done should not interrupt the person who is doing it! ~ **Chinese Proverb***

53. *It does not matter how slowly you go as long as you do not stop. ~ **Confucius 551-479 BC***

54. *Every failure is a LESSON. If you're not ready to fail ten times you're not ready to SUCCEED ~ **Gymholic***

55. *The speed of the boss is the speed of the team. ~ **Lee Iacocca***

56. *Stop WISHING and Start DOING! ~ **Anonymous***

57. *Stop being afraid of what could go wrong and begin thinking of all the things that could go right. ~ **Anonymous***

58. *Do not tell people your dreams, show them. ~ **William Boyce***

59. *Do something today that your future self with thank you for. ~ **Jeremy Hinds***

60. *You DID NOT wake up today to be mediocre. ~ **Anonymous***

61. *The past should be the past. It can destroy the future if you let it. Live life with what tomorrow has to offer not for what yesterday has taken away.* ~ **Anonymous**

62. *A single arrow is easily broken, but not ten in a bundle.* ~ **Japanese Proverb**

63. *If a team is to reach its potential, each player must be willing to subordinate his personal goals to the good of the team.* ~ **Bud Wilkinson**

64. *When he took time to help the man up the mountain, lo, he scaled it himself.* ~ **Tibetan Proverb**

65. *The nice thing about teamwork is that you always have others on your side.* ~ **Margaret Carty**

66. *Everyone is needed, but no one is necessary.* ~ **Bruce Coslet**

67 *In a team of 10 every team member is just as important as the other 9 members.* ~ **Anonymous**

68. *We eventually realized that none of us could be as good as all of us playing unselfishly.* ~ **Bill Bradley**

69. *People have been known to achieve more as a result of working with others than against them.* ~ **Dr. Allan Fromme**

70. *Never say never, because limits like fears are often an*

*illusion ~ **Michael Jordan***

71. *Its Monday, get a new perspective. Whatever new obstacle you're facing, it's NOT permanent. ~ **Anonymous***

72. *The one who falls and immediately gets up is so much stronger than the one who never fell. ~ **Anonymous***

73. *Until you cross the bridge of your insecurities you cannot begin to explore your pathway to possibilities. ~ **T.M. Fargo***

74. *Sometimes the worse things in our lives put us directly on the path to the best things that will ever happen to us. ~ **Rebekah Reagan***

75. *If you always put limits on everything you do, physical or anything else, it will spread into your work and into your life. There are no limits. There are only plateaus, and you must not stay there, you must go beyond them. ~ **Bruce Lee***

76. *A little motivation each day adds up to bigger results later on. ~ **Anonymous***

77. *Do it now! As some time later often becomes never. ~ **Anonymous***

78. *Life is filled with highs and lows - valleys and peaks that will test your resilience, that will push you to overcome challenges - and the lessons you'll learn on your way to the top will only make you stronger, better. ~ **Lydia Sweatt***

79. *Strength does not come from winning. Your struggles develop your strengths. When you go through hardships and decide not to surrender, that is strength. ~* **Arnold Schwarzenegger**

80. *All the adversity I've had in my life, all my troubles and obstacles, have strengthened me... You may not realize it when it happens, but a kick in the teeth may be the best thing in the world for you. ~* **Walt Disney**

7
LEARN TO BE RESILIENT

Resilience is that indescribable quality that allows some people to be overwhelmed by life yet come back stronger than ever. Rather than letting failure overcome them and drain their resolve, they somehow find a way to rise from the ashes. They tend to have a positive attitude, are optimistic, can control their emotions, and see failure as a learning curve that provides them with feedback they can utilise. Using this feedback they are able to change course, soldier on, and eventually achieve their goals.

~ Bea Stevens ~

1.   *Resilience is accepting the way things are right now, even if it's not as good as what you had before. ~ Elizabeth Edwards*

2.   *In order to succeed, people need a sense of self-efficacy, to struggle together with resilience to meet the inevitable obstacles and inequities of life. ~ Albert Bandura*

3.   *No matter how much falls on us, we keep pushing ahead. That's the only way to keep the roads clear. ~ Greg Kincaid*

4.   *I tried and failed. I tried again and again and I eventually succeeded. ~ Gail Borden*

5. *You never know how strong you are until being strong is the only choice you have. ~ **Anonymous***

6. *It may sound strange, but many champions are made champions by constant setbacks. ~ **Bob Richards***

7. *Do not judge me by my success, judge me by how many times I fell down and got back up again. ~ **Nelson Mandela***

8. *The world breaks everyone, and afterward, some are much stronger at the broken places. ~ **Ernest Hemingway***

9. *Things don't just go wrong and break your spirit so you can become bitter and give up and never try again. They break you down so you can rebuild yourself and be all you were intended to be. ~ **Charles Jones***

10. *Forget mistakes. Forget failures. Forget everything except what you are going to do right now, and do it. Today could be your lucky day – don't miss it. ~ **Will Durant***

11. *Someone was hurt before you, wronged before you, hungry before you, frightened before you, beaten before you, humiliated before you, cheated before you! Yet that someone survived. So there is NOTHING you cannot do if you choose to. ~ **Maya Angelou***

12. *Resilience is the capacity of a person to maintain their core purpose and integrity is the face of dramatically changed circumstances. ~ **Andrew Zolli***

13. *Why fit in when you were born to stand out? ~***Dr. Seuss**

14. *The thing that is really hard, and really amazing, is giving up on being perfect and beginning the work of becoming yourself. ~* **Anna Quindlen**

15. *Resilience is very different than being numb. Resilience means you experience, you feel, you fail, you hurt. You fall. But, you keep going. ~* **Yasmin Mogahed**

16. *We are not a product of what has happened to us in our past. We have the power of choice. ~* **Stephen Covey**

17. *I spent my young adult years postponing many of the small things that I knew would make me happy...I was fortunate enough to realize that I would never have the time unless I made the time. And then the rest of my life began ~* **Dr. Chris Peterson**

18. *Good judgment comes from experience. Experience comes from bad judgment. ~* **Jim Horning**

19. *It's the bounce that counts! Picking ourselves up after life's hurdle. ~* **Tessa Bielecki**

20. *Resilience is not what happens to you. It's how you react to, respond to, and recover from what happens to you. ~* **Jeffrey Gitomer**

21. *Part of resilience is deciding to make yourself miserable over something that matters, or deciding to make yourself*

miserable over something that doesn't matter. ~ **Elizabeth Edwards**

22. *Resilience is based on compassion for ourselves as well as compassion for others.* ~ **Sharon Salzberg**

23. *Resilience is being honest, faithful, reliable, sincere and true, when it would be easier to give in and be corrupted.* ~ **Anonymous**

24. *Do not let your struggle become your identity.* ~ **Rod Baker**

25. *The human capacity for burden is like bamboo - far more flexible than you'd ever believe at first glance.* ~ **Jodi Picoult**

26. *Just because your past didn't turn out to be like you wanted it to, doesn't mean that your future cannot be better than you ever imagined.* ~ **Carl Spinks**

27. *You attract people by the qualities you display, you keep them by the qualities you possess.* ~ **Frank K. Anson**

28. *The meaning of life is to find your gift. The purpose of life is to give it away.* ~ **Pablo Picasso 1881-1973**

29. *Few people are mind readers. Let them know they matter.* ~ **Dr. Chris Peterson**

30. *The truth will set you free, but first it will piss you off.* ~ **Gloria Steinem**

31.   *There's no such thing as ruining your life, it turns out to be a pretty resilient thing.* ~ **Sophie Kinsella**

32.   *Marriage is like a 5,000 piece jigsaw puzzle that's is all sky blue.* ~ **Cathy Ladman**

33.   *However long the night, the dawn will break.* ~ **African Proverb**

34.   *It's the possibility of having a dream come true that makes life interesting.* ~ **Paulo Coelho**

35.   *Resilience is accepting your new reality, even if it's less good than the one you had before. You can fight it, you can do nothing but scream about what you've lost, or you can accept that and try to put together something that's good.* ~ **Elizabeth Edwards**

36.   *I am strong because I was once weak. I am fearless because I was once afraid. I am wise because I was once foolish* ~ **Ann Barlow**

37.   *You're only given a little spark of madness. You mustn't lose it.* ~ **Robin Williams**

38.   *Be kind, for everyone you meet is fighting a hard battle.* ~ **Plato 428-348 BC**

39.   *90% of life is about remaining calm.* ~ **Dr. Chris Feudtner**

40.   *No matter what your current condition, how or where you*

grew up, or what education or training you feel you lack, you can be successful in your chosen endeavour. It is spirit, fortitude, and hardiness that matter more than where you start. ~ **Jack Ma**

41. *The most dangerous poison is the feeling of achievement. The antidote is every evening, think what can be done better tomorrow.* ~ **Ingvar Kamprad**

42. *Most people give up just when they're about to achieve success. They quit on the one yard line. They give up at the last minute of the game, one foot from a winning touchdown.* ~ **H. Ross Perot**

43. *Develop success from failures. Discouragement and failure are two of the surest steppingstones to success.* ~ **Dale Carnegie**

44. *I just love it when people say I can't do it, there's nothing that makes me feel better, because all my life, people have said that I wasn't going to make it.* ~ **Ted Turner**

45. *Failure is not the outcome - failure is not trying. Don't be afraid to fail.* ~ **Sara Blakely**

46. *Everyone experiences really tough times; it is a measure of your determination, dedication and resilience how you deal with them and how you can come through them.* ~ **Lakshmi Mittal**

47. *I'm only rich because I know when I'm wrong ... I basically*

have survived by recognizing my mistakes. ~ **George Soros**

48. *If you want to succeed, you should strike out on new paths, rather than travel the worn paths of accepted success.* ~ **John Rockefeller 1839-1937**

49. *I was set free, because my greatest fear had already been realized, and I was still alive, and I still had a daughter whom I adored, and I had an old typewriter and a big idea. And so rock bottom became the solid foundation on which I rebuilt my life.* ~ **J.K. Rowling**

50. *My inner scars remind me that I did indeed survive my deepest wounds. That in itself is an accomplishment. And they bring to mind something else, too. They remind me that the damage life has inflicted on me has, in many places, left me stronger and more resilient. What hurt me in the past has actually made me better equipped to face the present.* ~ **Steve Goodier**

51. *I knew that if I failed I wouldn't regret that, but I knew the one thing I might regret is not trying.* ~ **Jeff Bezos**

52. *If you are hardworking and determined, you will make it and that's the bottom line. I don't believe in an easy way.* ~ **Isabel dos Santos**

53. *The big secret in life is that there is no big secret. Whatever your goal, you can get there if you're willing to work.* ~ **Oprah Winfrey**

54. *Resilience is knowing that you are the only one that has the power to pick you up and carry on ~* **Mary Holloway**

55. *Resilient people immediately look at the problem and say 'What's the solution to that and what is it trying to teach me?' ~* **Mary Riddle**

56. *Its learning that some things are outside your control, so make the best of what you can control. ~* **Anonymous**

57. *Consider this when you feel broken. In Japan some broken objects are repaired in gold as the flaw is seen as an unique part of the objects history ~* **Anonymous**

58. *People may encounter objectively difficult circumstances - disaster, loss, illness, transition, heartbreak, etc., but still survive, even thrive. It seems so extraordinary, but is actually part of human adaptation, which makes it... an ordinary magic. ~* **Mel Denise**

59. *Grant me the serenity to accept the things I cannot change, the courage to change the things I can, and the wisdom to know the difference. ~* **Reinhold Niebuhr**

60. *You are indestructible in every single way. Don't let anyone get the best of you. No one has the power to break you unless you allow them. Yes, you might crumble for a moment, but you are far from destroyed. Stay strong and resilient with dignity and grace. Despite all I've been through, I'm still here and I'm still standing - stronger, better, wiser, and more determined than ever before. ~* **Haley Brown**

61. *Life doesn't get easier, or more forgiving. We simply get stronger and more resilient.* ~ **Jack Howe**

62. *Don't let people walk over you. Don't have bullies in your team. If you allow them to continue bullying you or anyone in the team, it won't be long before the team falls apart. Begin the process of dismissal which should show them you aren't going to tolerate their antics.* ~ **Roger Payne**

63. *Facing it, always facing it, that's the way to get through and defeat it.* ~ **Joseph Conrad**

64. *One small crack does not mean that you are broken. It means you were put to the test and didn't fall apart. Work out which situations you are likely to get most stressed out by. If you feel like you're getting too angry, end the conversation, take some space, and don't resume talking until you are calm and ready.* ~ **Linda Poindexter**

65. *One day all this pain will actually make sense to you.* ~ **Anonymous**

66. *Never say that you can't do something, or that something seems impossible, or that something can't be done, no matter how discouraging or harrowing it may be; human beings are limited only by what we allow ourselves to be limited by: our own minds. We are each the masters of our own reality; when we become self-aware to this: absolutely anything in the world is possible.* ~ **Mike Norton**

67. Resilience is very different to being numb. Resilience means you experience things, you feel things, you fail, you hurt, you fall, yet you never give up. ~ **Janet Holloway**

68. Man has never made anything as strong as the human spirit ~ **Bern Williams**

69. A child's talent to endure stems from the fact that they are ignorant of the alternatives ~ **Maya Angelou**

70. Hone your communication skills. If you know how to communicate a problem well, it will help prevent conflict from escalating, and could help solve the cause of things that stress you in the first place. ~ **Blake Boswell**

71. I can accept failure, everyone fails at some point in time, but I cannot accept not trying again. ~ **Michael Jordan**

72. The struggles you'll meet today are preparing you for the struggles you'll meet tomorrow and tomorrow you'll prepare to meet the struggles of the rest of your life. ~ **Anonymous**

73. Don't be afraid to turn to someone you trust. It can be a relief to share your thoughts with someone else, and it can be good to work through problems with the help of another person. ~ **John Morton**

74. Courage doesn't always ROAR. Sometimes it's a quiet voice at the end of the day that says 'I made it after all, so I will try again tomorrow.' ~ **Anonymous**

75. *What helps you persevere is your resilience and commitment.* ~ **Roy T. Bennett**

76. *Teachers everywhere generally have 3 loves: A LOVE of learning, A LOVE of learners, and a LOVE of bringing the first two together regardless of the circumstance.* ~ **Scott Hayden**

77. *Resilience is facing down rejection, ridicule and criticism and still succeeding.* ~ **Mark Macguinness**

78. *We're all a little broken, but the last time I checked broken crayons still colour the paper they are used on* ~ **Anonymous**

79. *Don't part with your illusions. When they have gone you may still exist, but you have ceased to exist.* ~ **Mark Twain 1835-1910**

80. *To me resilience simply means bouncing back higher and stronger after each setback; it becomes a strength of our character when we form the habit of bouncing back.* ~ **Paul T.P. Wong**

Life is the sum of all your choices.
~ Albert Camus

8
COMMUNICATION

Words are singularly the most powerful force available to humanity. We can choose to use this force constructively with words of encouragement, or destructively using words of despair. Words have energy and power with the ability to help, to heal, to hinder, to hurt, to harm, to humiliate and to humble.

~ Yehuda Berg ~

1.   *We all need people who will give us feedback. That's how we improve. ~* **Bill Gates**

2.   *Good communication does not mean that you have to speak in perfectly formed sentences and paragraphs. It isn't about slickness. Simple and clear go a long way. ~* **John Kotter**

3.   *The most important thing in communication is to hear what isn't being said. ~* **Peter F Drucker**

4.   *The real art of conversation is not only to say the right thing at the right place, but to leave unsaid the wrong thing at the tempting moment. ~* **Dorothy Nevill**

5.   *We have two ears and one mouth so that we can listen twice as much as we speak. ~* **Epictetus 55-135 AD**

6.   *The two words 'information' and 'communication' are often used interchangeably, but they signify quite different things. Information is giving out; communication is getting through.* ~ **Sydney J Harris**

7.   *When you ask the right questions and listen for the answers sometimes you find exactly what you were looking for before you even realised that you were looking for it. Stay open, stay positive, things can change in an instant.* ~ **Doe Zantamata**

8.   *Every criticism, judgment, diagnosis, and expression of anger is the tragic expression of an unmet need.* ~ **Marshall Rosenberg**

9.   *Speak in such a way that others love to listen to you. Listen in such a way that others love to speak to you. This encourages good communication.* ~ **Anonymous**

10. *Developing excellent communication skills is absolutely essential to effective leadership. The leader must be able to share knowledge and ideas and then transmit a sense of urgency and enthusiasm to others. If a leader can't get a message across clearly so it motivates others to act upon it, then having the information is a waste of time.* ~ **Gilbert Amelio**

11. *Any great relationship has great communication. That mean knowing how to effectively express yourself and how to listen properly.* ~ **Stephen Peak**

12.   *The biggest problem with communication is that we listen to reply not to learn and understand.* ~ **Zig Ziglar**

13.   *Strategic communication is at the core of effective leadership. Through a leader's use of verbal and written word employees are motivated or deflated, informed or confused, productive or apathetic. A leader's ability to carve off the verbal fat and get to the meat of an issue, idea or plan will find success at every turn.* ~ **Reed Markham**

14.   *Communication does not depend on syntax, or eloquence, or rhetoric, or articulation but on the emotional context in which the message is being heard. People can only hear you when they are moving toward you, and they are not likely to do that when your words are pursuing them.* ~ **Edwin H. Friedman**

15.   *I'm a great believer that any tool that enhances communication has a profound effect in terms of how people can learn from each other, and how they can achieve the kind of freedoms that they're interested in.* ~ **Bill Gates**

16.   *To effectively communicate, we must realize that we are ALL different in a way we perceive the world, and use this knowledge as a guide to our communication with others.* ~ **Anthony Robbins**

17.   *Remember, only 7% to 10% of what we say gets through. The rest is body language, how we stand, and how we gesture.* ~ **Stephen Covey**

18. *Communication is a skill that you can learn. It's like riding a bicycle. If you're willing to work at it, you can rapidly improve the quality of every part of your life, especially your leadership role. ~* **Brian Tracy**

19. *Speak when you are angry and you'll make the best speech you'll ever regret. ~* **Laurence Peters**

20. *How often could things be remedied by a single word (Sorry) and how often is it left unspoken. ~* **Norman Douglas**

21. *The most basic of all human needs is the need to understand and be understood. The best way to understand people is to listen to them. ~* **Ralph Nichols**

22. *Mother nature gave you a brain, ears, eyes and a mouth. All four of them should be in forward gear with the clutch down and brake off before you say anything. If they aren't, then shut up and wait until the clutch is down and the brake gets released. ~* **Roger Payne**

23. *There is all the difference in the world between having something to say and having to say something. ~* **John Dewey**

24. *It is greed to do all the talking but not to want to listen at all. ~* **Democritus 460-370 BC**

25. *A lot of problems in the world would be solved if we talked to each other instead of about each other. ~* **Nickey Gumbel**

26. *The most important thing in communication is to hear*

*what ISN'T being said. ~ **Peter F. Drucker***

27. *The game of life is a game of boomerangs. Our thoughts, deeds and words return to us sooner or later with astounding accuracy. ~ **Florence Scovel Shinn 1871-1940***

28. *Good healthy communication is impossible without openness, honesty, and vulnerability. ~ **Paul Kendall***

29. *Whenever you communicate with anyone use the age old KISS principle (Keep It Simple Stupid). This means use terminology that everyone can understand. So don't use big words like Pneumonoultramicroscopicsilicovolcanoconiosis, a lung disease caused by inhaling silca dust, say 'Silica Lung Disease' ~ Roger Payne*

30. *Effective communication is 20% what you know and 80% about what you feel about what you know. ~ **Jim Rohn***

31. *The reason why so few people are agreeable in conversations is that each is thinking more about what he intends to say than about what others are saying, and we never listen when we are eager to speak. ~ **Francois La Rochefoucauld 1613-1680***

32. *Intelligence, knowledge or experience are important and might get you a job, but strong communication skills are what will get you promoted. ~ **Mirelle Guiliano***

33. *There are four ways, and only four ways, in which we have contact with the world. We are evaluated and classified by these*

four things: WHAT WE DO, HOW WE LOOK, WHAT WE SAY, AND HOW WE SAY IT. ~ **Dale Carnegie 1888-1955**

34. *Ask most therapists, and they will tell you that good communication is at the heart of any successful relationship.* ~ **Sophie Winters**

35. *Attentive listening is the foundation of good therapy, leadership, parenting, friendship, and even meaningful politics. The need to be heard, understood, and truly known is universal.* ~ **Stephen Post and Jill Neimark**

36. *Communicate unto the other person that which you would want him to communicate unto you if your positions were reversed.* ~ **Aaron Goldman**

37. *For good or ill, your conversation is your advertisement. Every time you open your mouth you let men look into your mind. Do they see someone that is well clothed, neat, business wise, and intelligent?* ~ **Bruce Burton**

38. *Even when you choose your words well, if your tone of voice is hurried, hostile, or defensive, people may hear something very different from what you intended.* ~ **Rick Brinkman and Rick Kirschner**

39. *The most beautiful name in the world is the other person's name, remember and use two or three times in the conversation to create positive emotions.* ~ **Jay Saldivar**

40. *Follow this simple technique to enhance eye contact and*

communication: *Whenever you greet a colleague, look into their eyes long enough to notice the eye colour.* ~ **Ryan Cooper**

41. *We are always dependent on other people for our results and achievements, therefore it is important to being able to use effective communication skills.* ~ **Don Chandler**

42. *Write to be understood, speak to be heard, read to grow. Words should be used as tools of communication and not as a substitute for action.* ~ **Anonymous**

43. *The way you communicate reveals everything about you. Words are the clothes your thoughts wear.* ~ **Amanda Patterson**

44. *If you just communicate, you just get by. But if you communicate skilfully, you can work wonders.* ~ **Jim Rohn**

45. *Keep it short and simple (KISS). Abraham Lincoln's Gettysburg Address took only two minutes and 246 words, most of them of one or two syllables. Before Lincoln, then-famous orator Edward Everett's spoke for two hours and 13,607 words, many of them multi-syllabic. Simplicity is more memorable.* ~ **David Kusnet**

46. *To speak little is natural. Therefore a gale does not blow a whole morning nor does a downpour last a whole day.* ~ **Lao Tzu 604-531 BC**

47. *The worst distance between people is a simple misunderstanding.* ~ **John Powell**

48. Words are singularly the most powerful force available to humanity. We can choose to use this force constructively with words of encouragement, or destructively, using words of despair. Words have energy and power to help, to hurt, to humiliate and to humble. ~ **Yehuda Berg**

49. Any problem, big or small, within a family, always seems to start with bad communication. Someone isn't listening. ~ **Emma Thompson**

50. Good communication is as stimulating as black coffee, and just as hard to sleep after. ~ **Anne Morrow Lindbergh**

51. The way some people communicate they need a high five, in the face, with a chair. ~ **Anonymous**

52. Communication leads to a community, that is, to understanding and intimacy and mutual valuing. ~ **Rollo May**

53. A lack of communication leads to a lack of trust that leaves room for doubt. ~ **Annie Amari**

54. The two words information and communication are often used interchangeably, but they signify quite different things. Information is giving out; communication is getting through. ~ **Sydney Harris**

55. Body language is communication on another level. It can be subtle or blatant; it can be consciously sent and unconsciously received; it can be carefully practiced and displayed, but more often than not is uncontrollable; and it can let you down by revealing your true beliefs and behaviours. ~ **David Needham**

56. You can have brilliant ideas, but if you can't get them across, your ideas won't get you anywhere. ~ **Lee Lacocca**

57. We try to hide our emotions but we forget that our eyes speak ~ **Anonymous**

58. Someone once asked me 'Why do you insist on taking the hard road?' I replied 'Why do you assume there are always two roads' ~ **David Counter**

59. I never lose and argument. I either win, or I learn. ~ **Anonymous**

60. The biggest single problem with communication is often the illusion that it has actually taken place ~ **George Bernard Shaw 1856-1950**

61. Words are spoken, but the biggest factor when communicating is the perception that it has taken place......when in fact it hasn't. ~ **Roger Payne**

62. The most important thing in communication is hearing what isn't said. ~ **Peter F. Drucker**

63. Don't underestimate anyone. They might know more than they say, think more than they speak, and notice more than you realise. ~ **Anonymous**

64. *If you talk to a man in a language he understands, it will go to his head. If you talk to him in his own language, that goes to his heart* ~ **Nelson Mandela**

65. *Before you speak, think, is it necessary? Is it true? Is it kind? Will it hurt anyone? Will it improve on the silence?* ~ **Sri Syatha Sai Baba**

66. *Communication to any form of relationship is like OXYGEN to life. Without it...it DIES.* ~ **Tony Gaskins**

67. *When you forget yourself and your fears, when you get beyond self-consciousness because your mind is trying to think about what you are trying to communicate, you become a better communicator.* ~ **Peggy Noonan**

68. *The way you communicate reveals everything about you. Words are the clothes your thoughts wear.* ~ **Amanda Patterson**

69. *The more we elaborate our means of communication, the less we communicate.* ~ **J. B. Priestley**

70. *Many attempts at communication are nullified by saying too much.* ~ **Robert Greenleaf**

71. *The quieter you become, the more you can hear.* ~ **Anonymous**

72. *Never ASSUME: it means to accept something without*

proof of it being true, or accepting it without question. ~ **Michael Weldon**

73. *Of all of our inventions for mass communication, pictures still speak the most universally understood language. ~* **Walt Disney**

74. *Communication leads to community, that is, to understand, intimacy and mutual valuing. ~* **Rollo May**

75. *Write to be understood, speak to be heard, read to grow. ~* **Lawrence Clark Powell**

76. *The less people know, the more they seem to yell. ~* **Seth Godin**

77. *Assumption and lack of communication are the number one relationship killers at home or at work. We all perceive things differently. We may be together but we all live entirely different lives and we have different view on the same things. Understand this before you get angry and begin shouting at someone for not believing what you believe. ~* **Egypt.thegoodvibe.co**

78. *Storytellers, by the very act of telling, communicate learning that changes lives and the world: telling stories is a universally accessible means through which people make meaning. ~* **Chris Cavanaugh**

79. *Communication and Trust are two main ingredients for a successful RELATIONSHIP. ~* **Anonymous**

80. *Developing excellent COMUNICATION skills is absolutely essential for effective leadership. The leader must be able to share knowledge and ideas to transmit a sense of urgency and enthusiasm to others. If a leader cannot get a message across clearly and motivate other to act quickly on it, then having the message does not even mater.* ~ **Gilbert Amelio**

9
BODY LANGUAGE

Body language is a very powerful non-verbal communication tool. It was the first form of communication when our early ancestors, Homo erectus, appeared in Africa nearly two million years ago. So we had body language before we had speech, and apparently up to 80% of what you understand in a conversation is read through the body, not the spoken word.
~ Deborah Bull ~

1. *Body language is more powerful than words. In 1/10th of a second it has already read your face. ~ **Anonymous***

2. *Your body language shapes who you are in the eyes of others. ~ **Amy Cuddy***

3. *The language of your body is the key that can unlock your soul and your thoughts. ~ **Konstantin Stanislavski***

4. *Actresses can be in all shapes and sizes, but it is a profession, and as an actor your body is one of your tools, so you have to make sure it sends the right messages. ~ **Rebel Wilson***

5. *In the world of good communication the human body can*

*give clear signals even if we are not. ~ **Dan Murphy***

6.   *Would you look at that? Legs crossed and pouting lips. If that's not a sexual signal I don't know what is. ~ **Cher***

7.   *Its estimated that over 60% of human communication is non-verbal body language. Some 30% is your tone, so that means that 90% of communication isn't coming out of your mouth. ~ **Merl Hitch***

8.   *The actions of the body is far more memorable than any words. ~ **Anonymous***

9.   *Body Language is the key to personal success. ~ **Brian Adams***

10.   *Body Language is about being effective, not being proper. ~ **Don Adams***

11.   *The mood was terrible. You could see it in their eyes. Their body language said it all – were defeated. Then at half time the coach put me on and told me to rev them up. I was hoping I could give us some energy and bring us back. I dug deep, had a huddle and gave them my best leadership talk, told them all about being a team and never giving in regardless, and we won by two goals. I was never so shocked in all my life. ~ **Monro Arams***

12.   *30% of all communication problems are due to tone of voice. It's not what you say, but how you say it that creates all the problems. ~ **Tim Brooks***

13. *Bad communication corrupts good manners. I hope that before I die I hear that good communication corrects bad manners.* ~ **Benjamin Banneker**

14. *I have to work hard at talking positively to myself. If I don't, it's just real hard to get through the day, and I get really down, and just want to cry. My whole body language changes and I get more slumped over. If I can convince myself to be positive everything changes. There's a smile on my face and I walk with a spring in my feet.* ~ **Delta Burk**

15. *The words alone, lonely, and loneliness are three of the most powerful words in the English language......those words say that we are human and that our bodies reflect how we feel; they are like the words hunger and thirst, but all of them are not simply words about the body, they are words that reflect our soul.* ~ **Donald Miller**

16. *A shoe is not only a design, it's a part of your body language, the way you walk. The way you move is dictated by your shoes.* ~ **Christine Louboutin**

17. *Body language, although a part of our communication since the cave man, is a recent breakthrough in science. Your body language, your facial expression, your energy will come through to your audience long before you speak.* ~ **Peter Guber**

18. *A group of psychiatrists claim to have found 23 body language signals that indicate lying. For you to see all 23 at once they recommend you see a politician being interviewed on*

television. ~ **Conan O'Brian**

19. *The earliest language was body language and since this language is the language of questions, if we limit the questions, and we only pay attention to, or place values on spoken or written language, then we are ruling out a large area of the human language.* ~ **Paulo Preire**

20. *When speaking aloud, you punctuate frequently with body language. Your listener hears commas, full stops, question marks, exclamation points as you shout, whisper, pause, wave your arms, roll your eyes, wrinkle your brow. When writing, punctuation plays the part of body language. It helps the reader hear you in the way you want to be heard.* ~ **Russell Baker**

21. *In reality, even if you cannot 'speak the language', you can still understand much of which is being said if you use your eyes.* ~ *Aron Welsh*

22. *A great attitude toward your approach to an interview — demonstrated by your good posture—is everything.* ~ **Cindy Ann Peterson**

23. *Life is not all 'high emotion.' Some of the most interesting things happen when arachnids (spiders) are expressing themselves with gestures and other forms of body language.* ~ **David Attenborough**

24. *I have three tools at my disposal - my whistle, my body language and my talk. It is a question of how I marry them up to try to get the players around to my way of thinking.* ~ **Alan**

Lewis

25. *Body language is more fascinating to me than actual language.* ~ **Michele Yeo**

26. *Watch how you communicate with a woman. Because you're always communicating, even when you're not talking - with your body language, your facial expressions, your eyes* ~ **Orlando Bloom**

27. *Part of being out there, campaigning, talking to people, is being able to read body language.* ~ **Gary Johnson**

28. *We're losing social skills, the human interaction skills, how to read a person's mood, to read their body language, how to be patient until the moment is right to make or press a point. Too much exclusive use of electronic information dehumanises what is a very, very important part of community life and living together.* ~ **Vincent Lucas**

29. *When you're on set all day, and you don't look people in the eye, it's really relaxing. Normally when you talk to someone, a lot of the conversation is in the body language and in the eye contact and stuff. And if you don't do that, if you just listen to the words, it's quite relaxing, because there's just one thing to focus on.* ~ **Ryan Cartright**

30. *The most important thing in communication is hearing what isn't said.* ~ **Peter F. Drucker**

31. *Behaviour in the human being is sometimes a defence, a way of concealing motives and thoughts, but body language often unravels all that and you see the hidden truth. ~* **Abraham Maslow**

32. *What you do speaks so loud that I cannot hear what you say. ~* **Ralph Waldo Emerson 1803-1882**

33. *The human body is the best picture of the human soul. ~* **Ludwig Wittgenstein**

34. *Although you can practice covering up body language, every time you try to do it you are taking the exam and you need 10 out of 10 to pass. ~* **Anonymous**

35. *The body never lies. ~* **Martha Graham**

36. *Nonverbal communication forms a social language that is in many ways richer and more fundamental than our words. ~* **Leonard Mlodinow**

37. *There are four ways, and only four ways, in which we have contact with the world. We are evaluated and classified by these four contacts: what we do, how we look, what we say, and how we say it. ~* **Dale Carnegie**

38. *A great attitude toward your approach to an interview — demonstrated by your good posture — is everything. ~* **Cindy Ann Peterson**

39. *Every kind of language is a specialised form of bodily gesture, and in this sense, it may be said that the dance is the mother of all languages... an original language of total bodily gesture.*

This 'original' language is thus the one and only real language, which everybody who is in any way expressing himself is using all the time. What we call speech and the other kinds of language are only parts which have undergone specialised development. ~ **R.G. Collingwood**

40. *When the eyes say one thing, and the tongue another, a practiced man relies on the language of the first.* ~ **Ralph Waldo Emerson**

41. *The limits of my language means the limits of my world.* ~ **Ludwig Wittgenstein**

42. *You have to think an awful lot about your motivations or people's behavioural intentions or what their body language can indicate or what's really going on or what makes people sometimes do, sometimes, the irrational things they do.* ~ **Ron Silver**

43, *To effectively communicate, we must realize that we are all different in the way we perceive the world and use this understanding as a guide to our communication with others.* ~ **Anthony Robbins**

44. *In terms of nonverbal communication, by not seeing the full face - whether it's bangs in the eyes of a woman or a man or a*

beard - there can be some who perceive the individual is hiding something. ~ **Judith Rasband**

45. *We're losing social skills, the human interaction skills, how to read a person's mood, to read their body language, how to be patient until the moment is right to make or press a point. Too much exclusive use of electronic information dehumanises what is a very, very important part of community life and living together.* ~ **Vincent Nichols**

46. *Body language is essential for an actress, even if you don't use your body in an athletic way. Just to be free, to use it like your voice. A body can be small and have incredible violence. A body talks.* ~ **Anne Parillau**

47. *Nonverbal communication forms a social language that is in many ways richer and more fundamental than our words.* ~ **Leonard Mlodinow**

48. *The captains of England and Australia can barely exchange pleasantries these days without a body-language expert immediately declaiming on the angle of their handshakes.* ~ **Lawrence Booth**

49. *Experienced trial attorneys tend to rely on instinct when picking a jury. You get an idea of the kind of people that you are looking for and pay careful attention to their answers and body language.* ~ **James Diamond**

50. *The ability to simplify means to eliminate the unnecessary so that the necessary may speak.* ~ **Hans Hofmann**

51. The only human being whose body language and voice will always match is a baby. ~ **Anonymous**

52. Words are singularly the most powerful force available to humanity. We can choose to use this force constructively with words of encouragement, or destructively using words of despair. Words have energy and power with the ability to help, to heal, to hinder, to hurt, to harm, to humiliate and to humble. ~ **Yehuda Berg**

53. There are some people who could hear you speak a thousand words and still not understand you. And there are others who will understand without you even speaking a word. ~ **Yasmin Mogahed**

54. If personality is an unbroken series of successful gestures, then there was something gorgeous about him (The Great Gadsby). ~ **F. Scott Fitzgerald 1896-1940**

55. Your body communicates as much as your mouth so make sure you don't contradict it. ~ **Allan Ruddock**

56. Listen to a person when they are LOOKING at you not just when they are talking to you. ~ **Rachel Walchin**

57. I listen to your words, I also see body language. ~ **Michael Chang**

58. Looking into someone's eyes changes the whole conversation. ~ **Anonymous**

*59. The ability to speak several languages is an asset, but the ability to keep your mouth shut in any one of them is priceless. ~ **Anonymous***

*60. If you wish to find the truth, do not listen to the words coming to you. Rather see the body language of the speaker, it speaks the facts that are not audible. ~ **Don Turner***

*61. Of all the things you wear your expression is the most important. ~ **Anonymous***

*62. Know your powers - the powers of your words, your silence, your mind, your body language and your body itself – CONTROL THEM. ~ **Sonya Teclat***

*63. SMILE, even if you don't feel like it. Your body language helps determine your state of mind. ~ **Gitte Falkenberg***

*64. People don't tell me what I need to hear. Instead I listen to the unsaid words, observe quietly, reading the unspoken words between the lines, The words they think they can hide from me. This kind of listening is an art all to itself. ~ **Ann Mayer***

*65. Don't listen to their words, just watch them. Then let go of the people who dull your shine, poison your spirit, and brig you drama. Cancel your subscription to their issues. ~ **Dr Steve Maraboli***

*66. You don't have to know how to control your thoughts, you just have to learn how to stop them controlling you. ~ **Kevin***

Halden

67. When the eyes say one thing, and the mouth say another, a practiced man will rely on the language of the first. ~ **Ralph Waldo Emerson**

68. Body language as a non-verbal communication is essential to any relationship. Being completely oblivious to body language reduces the chances of any lasting relationship. ~ **Tracy Procter**

69. In the middle of a tight game you simply can't risk shouting out you leave it all to body language. ~ **Hank Walden**

70. When I walk around the workshop I can pick up on who is having a good day and who is having a bad day before I get to them. ~ **Bill Hall**

71. Get in touch with the way the other person is feeling: Approximately 55% Body Language, 38% Tone and 7% words. ~ **Steffi Galway**

72. Just remember, the language of gestures is far more powerful than the language of the spoken word. Bring the balance within you and project that balance. ~ **Anonymous**

73. Women's body language speaks eloquently, though silently, of her subordinate status in the hierarchy of status. ~ **Sandra Bartly**

74. If you adopt the body language of a power player, it will

greatly facility your ability to be a power player. ~ **Anonymous**

75. *Women all over the world are far better at reading body language than men. As a matter of fact it is associated with the female hormone oestrogen. Women are better at figuring out tone of voice, reading your face, posture and gestures.* ~ **Helen Fisher**

76. *A women's body is a dark and monstrous mystery; between her breasts a heavy whirlpool swirls and two rivers crash in a thunderous roar, and woe betide the man who slips and falls!* ~ **Nikos Kazantzakis**

77. *The human body is an instrument which only gives off music when it is used as a body. Always an orchestra, and just as the music traverses the walls, so sensuality traverses the body and reaches up to pure ecstasy.* ~ **Anais Nin**

78. *You have to think an awful lot about your motivations or people's behavioural intentions or what their body language can indicate or what's really going on or what makes people sometimes do, sometimes, the irrational things they do.* - **Ron Silver**

79. *Deafness has left me acutely aware of both the duplicity that language is capable of and the many expressions the body cannot hide.* ~ **Terry Galloway**

80. *To assess the quality of the thoughts of people, don't listen to their words, but watch their actions.* ~ **Amit Kalantri**

10

ACTIVE LISTENING

To listen means to pay close attention to what is being said 'behind' the words. You listen not only to the 'music,' but also to the 'tone' of the different instruments being played. Your listening not just for what someone knows, but also for what he or she is. Ears operate at the speed of sound, which is far slower than the speed of light the eyes take in. Generative listening is the art of developing deeper silences in yourself, so you can slow your mind's hearing to your ears natural speed, and hear beneath the words to their meaning.
~ Peter Senge ~

1.   *One of the most sincere forms of respect is actually listening to what another has to say without interrupting. ~* **Bryan H. McGill**

2.   *There is a voice that doesn't use words. It's called 'Listening!' ~* **Jalal ad-Din Rumi**

3.   *Most people do not listen with the intent to understand, they listen with the intent to reply. ~* **Stephen Covey**

4.   *Listening (the first competence of leadership) is not a skill, it is a discipline. All you have to do is keep your mouth shut. ~* **Peter F. Drucker**

5.   *Effective questioning brings insight, which fuels curiosity, which cultivates wisdom. The first part is to LISTEN.* ~ **Chip Bell**

6.   *The word LISTEN contains the same letters as the word SILENT. There is surely a reason for that.* ~ **Alfred Brendel**

7.   *The most basic of all human needs is the need to understand and be understood. The best way to understand people is to listen to them.* ~ **Ralph G. Nichols**

8.   *Effective listeners remember that 'words have no meaning, people have meaning.' The assignment of meaning to a term is an internal process; meaning comes from inside us. And although our experiences, knowledge and attitudes differ, we often misinterpret each other's messages while under the illusion that a common understanding has been achieved.* ~ **Larry Barker**

9.   *It is the province of knowledge to speak and it is the privilege of wisdom to listen.* ~ **Oliver Wendell Holmes 1841-1945**

10.   *Many 'ACTIVE LISTENING' seminars are, in actuality, little more than a shallow theatrical exercise in appearing like you're paying attention to another person. The requirements: lean forward, make eye contact, nod, grunt, or murmur to demonstrate you're awake and paying attention, and paraphrase something back every 30 seconds or so. As one executive I know wryly observed, many inhabitants of the local*

zoo could be trained to go through these motions, minus the paraphrasing. ~ **Robert R. Cooper**

11.   *The key to success is to get out into the store and listen to what the associates have to say. It's terribly important for everyone to get involved. Some of our best ideas come from clerks and stock boys.* ~ **Sam Walton**

12.   *One friend, one person who is truly understanding, who takes the trouble to listen to us as we consider a problem, can change our whole outlook on what we're discussing.* ~ **Dr. E. H. Mayo**

13.   *It's a rare person who wants to hear what he doesn't want to hear.* ~ **Dick Cavett**

14.   *The right to be heard does not automatically include the right to be taken seriously.* ~ **Hubert Humphrey**

15.   *I remind myself each morning that nothing I say today will teach me anything, so if I am going to learn it would be best if I listen instead.* ~ **Larry King**

16.   *One advantage of talking to yourself is that you know at least somebody's listening.* ~ **Franklin P. Jones**

17.   *You cannot truly listen to anyone and do anything else at the same time.* ~ **M. Scott Peck**

18.   *It is the province of knowledge to speak. And it is the privilege of wisdom to listen.* ~ **Oliver Wendell Holmes 1841-**

1935

19. *Listening looks easy, but it's not simple. Every head is a world where there is traffic and traffic jams are everywhere.* ~ **Cuban Proverb**

20. *Man's inability to communicate is a result of his failure to listen effectively.* ~ **Carl Rogers**

21. *There's a big difference between showing interest and really taking interest and it all begins with listening.* ~ **Michael P. Nichols**

22. *Too often we underestimate the power of a touch, a smile, a kind word, a listening ear, an honest compliment, or the smallest act of caring, all of which have the potential to turn a life around.* ~ **Leo Buscagila**

23. *This is the problem with dealing with someone who is actually a good listener. They don't jump in on your sentences, saving you from actually finishing them, or talk over you, allowing what you do manage to get out to be lost or altered in transit. Instead, they wait, so you have to keep going* ~ **Sarah Dessen**

24. *The greatest compliment that was ever paid me was when someone asked me what I thought, and attended to my answer.* ~ **Henry David Thoreau 1817-1862**

25. *Many attempts to communicate are nullified by saying too much.* ~ **Robert Greenleaf**

*26. Listening, not imitation, may be the sincerest form of flattery. ~ **Dr Joyce Brothers***

*27. Wisdom is the reward for a lifetime of listening when you'd have preferred to talk. ~ **D.J. Kaufman***

*28. Intelligent questions outrank really easy answers because somewhere in the middle goes 'listening'. ~ **Anonymous***

*29. The best time to hold your tongue is the time you feel you must say something or bust. ~ **Josh Billings***

*30. Everything in writing begins with language. Language begins with listening. ~ **Jeanette Winterson***

*31. Listening is a magnetic and strange thing, a creative force. The friends who listen to us are the ones we move toward. When we are listened to, it creates us, makes us unfold and expand. ~ **Karl Menninger***

*32. There are people who, instead of listening to what is being said to them, are already listening to what they are going to say themselves. ~ **Albert Guinon 1863 1923***

33. In a society where multitasking appears to be normal, information overload is common. So give yourself TIME to LISTEN, don't READ and LISTEN, don't TYPE and LISTEN, just LISTEN to EXACTLY what is said. Biologically, your brain can't recollect multiple sources of information all at once, and EVOLUTION has given it a simple way of dealing with overloading; it RANDOMLY DELETES whole chunks of information into a BIOLOGICAL RUBBISH BIN, never to be remembered. So instead of recalling 'A woman, without her man, is nothing.' You could end up with, 'A woman without her, man is nothing.' ~ **Roger Payne**

34. *You cannot truly listen to anyone and do anything else at the same time.* ~ **Scott Peck**

35. *To listen closely and reply well is the highest perfection we are able to attain in the art of true conversation.* ~ **Francois De La Rochefoucauld 1613-1680**

36. *Be a good listener. Your ears will never get you in trouble.* ~ **Frank Tyger**

37. *I think the one lesson I have learned is that there is no substitute for paying attention.* ~ **Diane Sawyer**

38. *Knowledge speaks, but wisdom listens.* ~ **Jimi Hendrix**

39. *To say that a person feels listened to means a lot more than just their ideas get heard. It's a sign of respect. It makes people feel valued.* ~ **Deborah Tannen**

40. *The way to stay fresh is you never stop travelling, you never stop listening. You never stop asking people what they think.* ~ **Rene McPherson**

41. *The best salespeople are great listeners. That's how you find out what the buyer wants.* ~ **Larry Wilson and Spencer**

Johnson

42. Just being available and attentive is a great way to use listening as a leadership tool. Some employees will come in, talk for twenty minutes, and leave having solved their problems entirely by themselves. ~ **Nicholas V. Luppa**

43. I would say that listening to the other person's emotions might be the most important thing I've learned in twenty years of business. ~ **Heath Herber**

44. Of all the skills of leadership, listening is the most valuable and one of the least understood. Most captains of industry listen only sometimes, and they remain ordinary leaders. But a few, the great ones, never stop listening. That's how they get word before anyone else of unseen problems and opportunities. ~ **Peter Nulty**

45. Listening is the only way to discover some really great stories. ~ **Don Friedman**

46. Most people in the world don't really use their brains to think. And people who don't think are the ones who don't listen either. ~ **Haruki Murakami**

47. A good listener tries to understand what the other person is saying. In the end he may disagree sharply, but because he disagrees, he wants to know exactly what it is he is disagreeing with. ~ **Kenneth A. Wells**

48. We listened to what our customers wanted and acted on

what they said. Good things happen when you pay attention. ~ **John F. Smith**

49. *There is as much wisdom in listening as there is in speaking--and that goes for all relationships, not just romantic ones. ~* **Daniel Dae Kim**

50. *I remind myself each morning: Nothing I say this day will teach me anything. So if I'm going to learn anything I must do it by listening. ~* **Larry King**

51. *When you are listening to someone completely, attentively, then you are listening not only to the words, but also the feeling and intent of what is being conveyed, to the whole of it, not just part of it. This way you get the ALL of the message, not just SOME of it. ~* **Jiddu Krishnamurti 1895- 1986**

52. *Long before I wrote stories, I listened for stories. Listening for them is something more acute than listening to them. I suppose it's an early form of participation in what goes on. Listening children know stories are there. When their elders sit and begin, children are just waiting and hoping for one to come out, like a mouse from its hole. ~* **Edora Welty**

53. *One thing is for sure - we can always have a challenge understanding what people mean if we do not know how to effectively listen. To listen properly is much the same as forgetting to start the engine of your car and expecting it to move forward. ~* **Byron Pulsifer**

54. *An appreciative listener is always stimulating. ~* **Agatha**

Christie 1890-1976

55.   *We have two ears and only one tongue in order that we may hear more and speak less.* ~ **Diogenes Laértlus 180-240 AD**

56.   *People love to talk but hate to listen. Listening is not merely not talking, though even that is beyond most of our powers; it means taking a vigorous, human interest in what is being told us. You can listen like a blank wall or like a splendid auditorium where every sound comes back fuller and richer.* ~ **Alice Duer Muer**

57.   *The older I grow, the more I listen to people who don't talk much.* ~ **Germain G. Glidden**

58. *Listen with your eyes as well as your ears.* ~ **Graham Speechly**

59.   *Friends are those rare people who ask how we are, and then wait to hear the answer.* ~ **Ed Cunningham**

60. *LISTEN, pause, SPEAK, then LISTEN AGAIN. Your ears have value, learn to use it.* ~ **Anonymous**

61. *The quieter you become the most you hear.* ~ **David Hockney**

62. *We don't learn from talking, we learn from listening.* ~ **Anonymous**

63. *When we fear what other people think about us, we are*

*frequently more focused on 'being interesting' and less focused on 'taking an interest.' That's why many people talk a great deal when they are anxious and why many people never feel heard. If both people and conversation are trying to be interesting, there is no one left to genuinely listen. ~ **John Yokoyama***

64. *Self-Control: If A = Success, then A= X+Y+Z, 'X' being work, 'Y' being play, and 'Z' keeping your mouth shut. ~ **Albert Einstein 1879-1955***

65. *You have to be willing sometimes to listen to some remarkable bad opinions. Because if you say to someone, 'That's the silliest thing I've ever heard; get on out of here!'—then you'll never get anything out of that person again, and you might as well have a puppet on a string or a robot. ~ **John Bryan***

66. *There is no such thing as a worthless conversation, provided you know what to listen for; questions are the breath of life for a conversation. ~ **James Nathan Miller***

67. *To be listened to is, generally speaking, a unique experience for most people. It is enormously stimulating. It is small wonder that people who have been demanding all their lives to be heard so often fall speechless when confronted with one who gravely agrees to lend an ear. Man clamours for the freedom to express himself and for knowing that he counts. But once offered these conditions, he often becomes frightened. ~ **Robert C. Murphy***

68. *When you talk you are simply repeating what you already know. But if you listen you might actually learn something new. ~ **Dalai Lama***

69. *One friend, one person who is truly understanding, who takes the trouble to listen to us as we consider a problem, can change our whole outlook on the world.* ~ **E. H. Mayo**

70. *Listen and be silent; how many people do you know that love to hear themselves talk? Listening is the key to learning, and we are never too old to learn.* ~ **Susan Wellington**

71. *Don't do for someone what they can do for themselves; leadership often means listening to what is (and isn't) being said and asking the right questions.* ~ **Anonymous**

72. *You can tell a great deal about a person's character simply by listening to the things they laugh at.* ~ **Earl Gray**

73. *The world is giving you answers each day. Just learn to listen.* ~ **Anonymous**

74. *You can ask 'why' all you want but it doesn't mean a damn thing unless you actually listening to the answer.* ~ **Rachel Meechin**

75. *Most of the successful people I've known are the ones who do more listening than talking.* ~ **Bernard Baruch**

76. *How, when, and where you say something can actually be more important than the message itself.* ~ **Anne Bruce & James S. Pepitone**

77. *For most of my life I've been a listener. At least in the*

beginning, I think the reason I listened so intently was to have a chance of hearing the train before it ran over me. ~ **Steve Rasnic Tem**

78. *Do the things you used to talk about doing but never did. Know when to let go and when to hold on tight. Stop rushing. Don't be intimidated to say it like it is. Stop apologising all the time. Learn to say no, so your yes has some oomph. Spend time with the friends who lift you up, and cut loose the ones who bring you down. Stop giving your power away. Be more concerned with being interested than being interesting. Be old enough to appreciate your freedom, and young enough to enjoy it. Finally, know who you are and listen more than talk.* ~ **Kristin Armstrong**

79. *In our rush to be heard and understood, we focus way too much on ourselves doing the talking. We are the critical factor in communication, it is true. But our listening is much more important than our talking, because our listening determines whether we learn anything, and actual communication occurs.* ~ **Harvey Robbins & Michael Finley**

80. *Spend your leisure time in cultivating an ear attentive to discourse, for in this way you will find that you learn with ease what others have found out with difficulty.* ~ *Socrates* **436-338 BC**

.

11
ASKING QUESTIONS

Most teachers waste their time asking questions which are intended to discover what a pupil does not know, whereas the true art of questioning has for its purpose to discover what the pupil does know or is capable of knowing.

~ Albert Einstein 1879-1955 ~

1.   *How do you get the right answers? By asking the right questions, of course. The questions you ask define the areas in which you want answered, so take your time and even asking questions about unrelated subjects can be a useful strategy for breaking the ice and getting great solutions. ~* **Jamie McKenzie**

2.   *Remember, the quality of a question is not judged by its complexity but by the complexity of thinking it provokes. ~* **Joseph O'Connor**

3.   *Ask, and it shall be given you; seek; and you shall find; knock and it shall be opened unto you. For every one that asketh receiveth; and he that seeketh findeth; and to him that knocketh it shall be opened. ~* **Matthew 7:7-8**

4.   *There are no right answers to wrong questions. ~* **Ursula K. Le Guin**

5.   The art and science of asking questions is the source of all knowledge. ~ **Thomas Berger**

6.   If I had to do it again, I'd ask more questions and interrupt fewer answers. ~ **Robert Brault**

7.   Questions are places in your mind where answers fit. If you haven't asked the right question, the answer has nowhere to go. It hits your mind and bounces right off. You have to ask the right question to open up the space for the answer to fit. ~ **Clayton Christiensen**

8.   You don't have to know everything in the world. We aren't supposed to. It makes you boring in mixed company if you can't be interested in asking questions of other people. ~ **Angela Johnson**

9.   Ask the RIGHT questions if you're want to find the CORRECT answers, and keep probing until you do. But don't expect the answer you want to be there every time. ~ **Vanessa Redgrave**

10.   Question everything, assume nothing. Learn the truth. ~ **Anonymous**

11.   It is the nature, and the advantage, of strong people that they can bring out the crucial questions and form a clear opinion from them. The weak always have to decide between alternatives that are not necessarily their own. ~ **Dietrich Bonhoeffer**

12. *Judge a man by his questions rather than his answers.* ~ **Voltaire (Francois Marie Arouet) 1694 -1798**

13. *It is not the answer that enlightens, but the question.* ~ **Jean Baptiste Perrin 1870-1942**

14. *Remember, ignorance is only a temporary affliction remedied by asking the right questions.* ~ **Colin Wright**

15. *He who asks a question is a fool for five minutes; he who does not ask a question remains a fool forever.* ~ **Chinese proverb**

16. *Take risks. Ask BIG questions. Don't be afraid to make mistakes; if you don't make mistakes, you're not reaching far enough.* ~ **David Packard**

17. *Want to be more innovative. Start by asking more 'WHY' questions.* ~ **Jason Silver**

18. *Who questions much, shall learn much, and retain much.* ~ **Francis Bacon 1561-1626**

19. *Knowledge is having the right answer. Intelligence is asking the right question.* ~ **Anonymous**

20. *Although there is such a thing as the occasional stupid question, one doesn't often hear them because stupid people rarely ask questions, and intelligent people bite their tongues first.* ~ **Anonymous**

21.   *If you do not ask the right questions, you don't get the right answers. A question asked in the right way often points to its own answer.* ~ **Edward Hodnett**

22.   *The best scientists and explorers have the attributes of kids! They ask questions and have a sense of wonder. They have curiosity so they ask. 'Who, what, where, why, when, and how questions!' They never stop asking questions just like a five year old.* ~ **Sylvia Earle**

23.   *Successful people ask better questions, and as a result, they get better answers.* ~ **Tony Robbins**

24.   *Teaching. It's 10% asking kids' questions. It's 90% inspiring kids to ask you questions that you can't answer.* ~ **Anonymous**

25.   *It is better to know some of the questions than all of the answers.* ~ **James Thurber**

26.   *If you have any doubt about how learning happens, engage in sustained enquiry: study, ponder, consider alternative enquiries, then arrive at your best belief grounded in evidence.* ~ **John Dewy**

27.   *Don't be afraid of the answers, be afraid of not asking the questions.* ~ **Jennifer Hudson**

28.   *Life is still an unanswered question, but let's believe in the dignity and importance of the question.* ~ **Tennessee Williams**

29. *Politicians - If they can get you asking the wrong questions, they don't have to worry about right answers.* ~ **Thomas Pynchon**

30. *The one who asks questions doesn't lose his way.* ~ **African Proverb**

31. *Ignorance is only a temporary affliction quickly remedied by asking a question.* ~ **Colin Wright**

Life is an unanswered question, but let's believe in the dignity and importance of the question. ~ **Tennessee Williams**

32. *The important thing is not to stop questioning.* ~ **Albert Einstein 1879-1955**

33. *A prudent question is one half of wisdom.* ~ **Francis Bacon 1521-1626**

34. *A timid question will always receive a confident answer.* ~ **Lord Darling 1849-1946**

35. *Questioning is the ability to organise our thinking around what we don't know, not around what we do know.* ~ **Anonymous**

36. *Question: We all know the speed of light (299,702 kilometres per second); so what is the speed of dark?* ~ **Terry Pratchett**

37. *A sudden bold and unexpected question doth many times*

surprise a man and lay him open. ~ **Francis Bacon 1521 1626**

38. *An educated man is one who has finally discovered that there are some questions to which nobody has the answer. ~* **Anonymous**

39. *Every clarification breeds new questions. ~* **Arthur Bloch**

40. *You don't have to have a special talent. You simply have to be passionately curious. ~* **Anonymous**

41. *Beware of the man who knows the answer before he understands the question. ~* **Anonymous**

42. *Reason can answer questions, but imagination has to ask them. ~* **Ralph Gerard**

43. *A wise man can learn more from a foolish question than a fool can from an intelligent answer. ~* **Bruce Lee**

44. *Change direction with your questions but don't stop asking them. Curiosity has its own reason for existing. ~* **David Brown**

45 *One cannot help but be in awe when someone contemplates the mysteries of eternity, of life, of the marvellous structure of reality when all you asked them was their thoughts on government policy. ~* **Edmund Burke**

46. *Ignorance is a temporary affliction, remedied only by asking the right question. ~* **Colin Wright**

47. In general, questions are fine; you can always seize upon the parts of them that interest you and concentrate on answering those. And one has to remember when answering questions that asking questions isn't easy either, and for someone who's quite shy to stand up in an audience to speak takes some courage. ~ **Vikram Seth**

48. The one real object of education is to have everyone in the condition of continually asking questions. ~ **Mandell Creighton**

49. Without asking a question it is doubtful you'll get the right answer. ~ **Chinese Proverb**

50. Better to ask a question than remain ignorant. ~ **Roman proverb**

51. You can tell whether a man is clever by his answers. You can tell whether a man is wise by his questions. ~ **Arthur Miller**

52. Millions of people have seen apples fall but only Newton asked the question why? ~ **Bernard Mannes Baruch 1870-1965**

53. You may THINK you know the answer, but if you ask the question then you WILL know the answer. Confirmation is just as important as Contradiction. ~ **Andrew Blyth**

54. What is the one thing RIGHT NOW that you are sure of? Now that is known as a probing question. ~ **Anonymous**

55. Life is extremely complicate so don't try to find answers.

The moment you do life will change the questions. ~ **Anonymous**

56. *It is not the answer that enlightens, but the question. ~* **Eugene Ionesco**

57. *The five essential entrepreneurial skills for success are concentration, discrimination, organization, innovation and communication. ~* **Michael Faraday**

58. *Take risks, ask really challenging questions, if you don't get the answers you looking for then rephrase the question. Every answer you get you learn one way or another. The moment you stop asking questions is the moment you stop learning. ~* **Roger Payne**

60. *There are many questions that we have to ask ourselves. That is how new ideas are born. ~* **Anonymous**

61. *Asking questions doesn't mean you don't know your job, asking questions means you want to improve the quality of your work. ~* **Robert Allen**

62. *The key to wisdom is this – constant and frequent questioning, for by doubting we are led to question, by questioning we arrive at the truth. ~* **Peter Abelard**

63. *It is better to debate a question without settling it than to settling a question without debating it. ~* **Joseph Joubert**

64. *Always ask simple, 'Who, When, Why, What, Where, How,*

questions. Listen carefully and quietly for the reply and DO NOT interrupt the answer. Confirm with 'Is that what you meant?' question before asking anything else. ~ **Jean Bradley**

65. My investment of time, as an educator, in my judgment, is best served teaching people how to think about the world around them. Teach them how to pose a question. How to judge whether one thing is true versus the other. ~ **Neil deGrasse Tyson**

66. Every man ought to be inquisitive through every hour of his great adventure down to the day when he shall no longer cast a shadow in the sun. For if he dies without a question in his heart, what excuse is there for his continuance. ~ **Frank Moore Colby**

67. We get wise by asking questions, and even if these are not answered, we get wise, for a well packed question carries its answer on its back as a snail carries its shell. ~ **James Stephens**

68. The art and science of asking questions is the source of all knowledge. ~ **Thomas Berg**

69. That is the essence of science: ask an impertinent question, and you are on the way to a pertinent answer. ~ **Jacob Bronowski**

70. One of the greatest gifts you have is not being afraid to question. ~ **Ruby Dee**

71. Questioning is the ability to organise our thinking around what we don't know. ~ **Anonymous**

72. *To be able to ask a question clearly is two thirds of the way to getting it answered.* ~ **John Ruskin 1819-1900**

73. *For true success ask yourself these four questions: Why? Why not? Why not me? Why not now?* ~ **James Allen 1864-1912**

74. *The uncreative mind can spot wrong answers, but it takes a very creative mind to spot wrong questions.* ~ **Anthony Jay**

75. *In a world of constant change, the fundamentals are more important than ever.* ~ **Jim Collins**

76. *Communication is the cornerstone of effective project management, and yet most of it is done ad hoc, driven by individuals, personalities, and preferences, rather than by needs, protocols, processes, and procedures.* ~ **Carl Pritchard**

77. *Effective communication is built on the cement of trust. And trust is based on trustworthiness, not politics.* ~ **Steven R. Covey**

78. *Effective communication is an essential component of professional success whether it is at the interpersonal, inter-group, intra- group, organisational or external level.* ~ **Mike Myatt**

79. *Whether the communication is written or verbal, formal or informal, the question must be asked as to whether or not it was effective.* ~ **Carl Pritchard**

80. Choose one of these: Brief, Short, To The Point, Succinct, Concise. What do they all have in common? They all describe how you should ask a question. ~ **Roger Payne**

A wise man can learn more from a foolish question than a fool can from an intelligent answer.
*~ **Bruce Lee***

12

INTEGRITY

Integrity is the quality of being honest and having strong moral principles and moral uprightness. It is generally considered to be a personal choice to hold oneself to consistent moral and ethical standards.
~ Anonymous ~

1.   *Integrity is not a conditional word. It doesn't blow in the wind or change with the weather. It is your inner image of yourself, and if you look in there and see a man who won't cheat and lie, then you know he never will. ~* **John D. MacDonald**

2.   *A life lived with integrity even if it lacks the trappings of fame and fortune is a shining star in whose light others may follow in the years to come. ~* **Denis Waitley**

3.   *To give real service you must add something which cannot be bought or measured with money, and that is sincerity and integrity. ~* **Douglas Adams**

4.   *Have the courage to say no. Have the courage to face the truth. Do the right thing because it is right. These are the magic keys to living your life with integrity. ~* **W. Clement Stone**

5.   *Integrity without knowledge is weak and useless, and*

knowledge without integrity is dangerous and dreadful. ~ **Samuel Johnson**

6.   *No one can be happy who has been thrust outside the pale of truth. And there are two ways that one can be removed from this realm: by lying, or by being lied to. ~* **Seneca 4 BCE-65 CE**

7.   *When people cheat in any arena, they diminish themselves. They threaten their own self-esteem, and their relationship with others, by undermining the trust they have in their ability to succeed and their ability to be true. ~* **Cheryl Hughes**

8.   *Integrity is choosing your thoughts and actions based on values rather than personal gain. ~* **Chris Karcher,**

9.   *I never had a policy; I have just tried to do my very best each and every day. ~* **Attributed to Abraham Lincoln 1809-1865**

10.   *There are some things that money cannot buy like honesty, manners, morals and integrity. ~* **James Faber**

11.   *Perhaps the surest test of an individual's integrity is his refusal to do or say anything that would damage his self-respect. ~* **Thomas S. Monson**

12.   *Achievement of your happiness is the only moral purpose of your life, and that happiness, not pain or mindless self-indulgence, is the proof of your moral integrity, since it is the proof and the result of your loyalty to the achievement of your values. ~* **Ayn Rand**

13. *Character is doing the right thing when nobody's looking. There are too many people who think that the only thing that's right is to get by, and the only thing that's wrong is to get caught. ~* **J.C. Watts**

14. *The only ethical principle which has made science possible is that the truth shall be told all the time. If we do not penalize false statements made in error, we open up the way for false statements by intention. And a false statement of fact, made deliberately, is the most serious crime a scientist can commit. ~* **Dorothy L. Sayers 1893-1957**

15. *If you have integrity, nothing else matters; if you don't have integrity, nothing else matters. ~* **Alan Simpson**

16. *Selfishness is not living as one wishes to live, it is asking others to live as one wishes to live. ~* **Oscar Wilde 1854-1900**

17. *The right type of leader is democratic. He must not consider himself a superior sort of personage. He must actually feel democratic; it is not enough that he try to pose as democratic—he must be democratic, otherwise the veneer, the sheen, would wear off, for you can't fool a body of intelligent workingmen for very long. He must ring true. ~* **Thomas Coleman Du Pont**

18. *There is no pillow as soft as a clear conscience. ~* **French Proverb**

19. *Don't try to be different. Just be good. To be good is different enough. ~* **Arthur Freed**

20. *Do not repeat anything you will not sign your name to.* ~ **Anonymous**

21. *People with good intentions make promises. Only people with good character keep them.* ~ **Anthony Walcott**

22. *The measure of a man's real character is what he would do if he knew he never would be found out.* ~ **Thomas Babington Macaulay 1800-1859**

23. *Integrity is the concept of consistency of actions, values, methods, principles, expectations and outcomes. It can be regarded as the very opposite of hypocrisy.* ~ **Anita Osborne**

24. *Try not to become a man of success but rather try to become a man of true value.* ~ **Albert Einstein 1879-1975**

25. *Character is higher than intellect.* ~ **Ralph Waldo Emerson 1803-1882**

26. *The only exercise some people get is jumping to conclusions, running down their friends, sidestepping responsibility, and pushing their luck! What kind of person is that?* ~ **Anonymous**

27. *Honesty is the first chapter in the book of wisdom.* ~ **Thomas Jefferson 1743-1826**

28. *Every job is a self-portrait of the person who does it. Autograph your work with excellence.* ~ **Ted Key**

29. *Quality means doing it right when no one is looking.* ~ **Henry Ford 1863-1947**

30. *Laws control the lesser man. Right conduct controls the greater one.* ~ **Chinese Proverb**

31. *The integrity of men is to be measured by their conduct, not their professions.* ~ **Junius 1769-1772 (Pseudonym)**

32. *Nothing is at last sacred but the integrity of your own mind.* ~ **Ralph Waldo Emerson 1883- 1902**

33. *Lacking Integrity is like parachuting. If your main parachute fails then opening your reserve parachute only slows you down slightly, it doesn't stop you having a crash landing from which you are unlikely to recover.* ~ **Roger Payne**

34. *Let me be thankful first, because I never was robbed before; second, because although they took my purse, they did not take my life; third, although they took my all, it was not much; and fourthly, because it was I who was robbed, and not I who robbed.* ~ **Matthew Henry 1662-1714**

35. *This above all to thine own self be true, and it must follow, as the night follow the day, thou canst not then be false to any man.* ~ **William Shakespeare 1564-1610**

36. *Integrity is the lifeblood of democracy. Deceit is a poison in its veins.* ~ **Edward Kennedy**

37. *Dignity consists not in possessing honours, but in the consciousness that we deserve them.* ~ **Aristotle 384-382 BC**

38. *You do not wake up one morning a bad person. It happens by a thousand tiny surrenders of self-respect to self-interest.* ~ **Robert Brault**

39. *Nothing more completely baffles one who is full of tricks and duplicity than straight forward and simple integrity in another.* ~ **Charles Caleb Colton 1718-1832**

40. *You can outdistance that which is running after you, but not what is running inside you.* ~ **Rwandan Proverb**

41. *We grow with years more fragile in body, but morally stouter, and can throw off the chill of a bad conscience almost at once* ~ **Logan Pearsall Smith 1865-1946**

42. *Let us be grateful to the mirror for revealing to us our appearance only.* ~ **Samuel Butler 1835- 1932**

43. *To be persuasive we must be believable; to be believable we must be credible; to be credible we must be truthful.* ~ **Edward R. Murrow**

44. *In judging ourselves, we cannot be too severe; in judging others, we cannot be too candid; we should judge ourselves by our motives, but others by their actions.* ~ **William Nevins**

45. *Every time I've done something that doesn't feel right, it's ended up not being right.* ~ **Mario Cuomo**

46. *Real integrity is doing the right thing, knowing that nobody's going to know whether you did it or not.* ~ **Oprah Winfrey**

47. *My goal in life is to be as good of a person my dog already thinks I am.* ~ **Anonymous**

48. *We judge ourselves by what we feel capable of doing, while others judge us by what we have already done.* ~ **Henry Wadsworth Longfellow 1807-1882**

49. *Don't be impressed by followers, money, diplomas, masters' degrees or titles. Be impressed by humility, integrity, kindness, and generosity.* ~ **C.E.D.**

50. *The chief lesson I have learned in a long life is that the only way you can make a man trustworthy is by trusting him; and the surest way to make him untrustworthy is to distrust him and show your distrust.* ~ **Henry L. Stimson**

51. *I don't have to attend every argument I'm invited to.* ~ **Anonymous**

52. *Goodness is the only investment that never fails.* ~ **Henry David Thoreau 1817-1862**

53. *You don't carry in your countenance a letter of recommendation.* ~ **Charles Dickens 1812-1870**

54. *The only correct actions are those that demand no*

*explanation and no apology. ~ **Red Auerbac***

55. *Character is doing the right thing even when it costs more than you want to pay. ~ **Michael Josephson***

56. *I have fancied myself a rebel, but at every critical moment of my life, I have been exactly the child my parents raised. ~ **Robert Brault***

57. *Integrity without knowledge is weak and useless, and knowledge without integrity is dangerous ~ **Samuel Johnson 1708 -1794***

58. *People who fight fire with fire end up with only the ashes of their own integrity. ~ **Michael Josephson***

59. *Live in such a way that you would not be ashamed to sell your parrot to the town gossip. ~ **Will Rogers***

60. *Challenges are what make life interesting and overcoming them is what makes life meaningful. ~ **Joshua J. Marine***

61. *For most people, blaming others is a subconscious mechanism for avoiding accountability. In reality the only thing in your way is YOU! ~ **Anonymous***

62. *As a leader, you not only have to do the right thing, but be perceived to be doing the right thing. A consequence of seeking a leadership position is being put under intense public scrutiny, being held to high standards, and enhancing a reputation that is constantly under threat. ~ **Jeffrey Sonnenfeld and Andrew***

Ward

63. The highest compact we can make with our fellow is, 'Let there be truth between us two forever more.' ~ **Ralph Waldo Emerson 1803 1882**

64. Show class, have pride and display character. If you do, winning takes care of itself. ~ **Paul Bryant**

65. Being a male is a matter of birth. Being a man is a matter of age. Being a gentleman is a matter of choice. ~ **Van Diesel**

66. You may not be able to control every situation and its outcome, but you can control your attitude and how you deal with it. ~ **Anonymous**

67. Things turn out for the best for people who make the best out of the way things turn out. ~ **Anonymous**

68. People with good intentions make promises, people with good character keep them. ~ **Anthony Rutledge**

69. Trust is rebuilt by focusing not on what the other person did or did not do but on critiquing one's own behaviour, improving one's trustworthiness, and focusing attention not on words and promises but on actions, attitudes, and ways of being. ~ **Kenneth Cloke and Joan Goldsmith**

70. Once your integrity is bought into question, even over a small matter, you can never get it back. Pirates of old used to call it 'the black spot' and it will remain on the palm of your

hand forever. ~ **Roy West**

71.   *The chief lesson I have learned in a long life is that the only way you can make a man trustworthy is by trusting him; and the surest way to make him untrustworthy is to distrust him and show your distrust.* ~ **Henry L Simpson**

72. *What convinces is conviction. Believe in the argument you're advancing. If you don't you're as good as dead. The other person will sense that something isn't there, and no chain of reasoning, no matter how logical or elegant or brilliant, will win your case for you.* ~ **Lyndon B. Johnson**

73. *Goodness is about character, integrity, honesty, kindness, generosity, moral courage, and the like. More than anything else, it is about how we treat other people. The greatness of any man is not in how much wealth he acquires, but in his integrity and his ability to affect those around him positively.* ~ **Bob Marley**

74. *The worst disease in the world today is corruption. And there is a cure: transparency.* ~ **Bono**

75. *If we elect the same corrupt politicians every time, that's a very clear message that we don't want a change.* ~ **Sukant Ratnakar**

76. *When greeted upon his return to power by cries of 'Algérie Française!' (Algeria Is French) [De Gaulle] answered his countrymen, 'Je vous ai compris' (I have understood you). Indeed he had. But he did not say he would keep Algeria French.*

*No leader can lie, or condone official lying, without turning totalitarian. But he may, and often must, tell what one political scientist call 'the truth, the partial truth, and nothing but the truth.' ~ **Brock Brower***

77. *Goodness is about character integrity, honesty, kindness, generosity, moral courage, and the like. More than anything else, it is about how we treat other people. The greatness of a man is not in how much wealth he acquires, but in his integrity and his ability to affect those around him positively. ~ **Denis Prager***

78. *I think leadership is more than just being able to cross the t's and dot the i's. It's about character and integrity and work ethic. ~ **Steve Largent***

79. *Be Impeccable With Your Word. Speak with integrity. Say only what you mean. Avoid using the word to speak against yourself or to gossip about others. Use the power of your word in the direction of truth and honesty. ~ **Don Miguel Ruiz***

80. *We live in a world where 'the end justifies the means' has become an acceptable school of thought. Where sales people over promise and under deliver, all in the name of making their quota for the month. Applicants exaggerate in job interviews because they desperately need a job, and CEOs overstate their projected earnings because they don't want the board of directors to replace them. None of them care about integrity. ~ **Amy Rees Anderson***

Integrity without knowledge is weak and useless, and knowledge without integrity is dangerous
~ **Samuel Johnson 1708 -1794**

13

LOYALTY

Successful team leaders go out of their way to build trust amongst their team, and when this is achieved a by-product called loyalty is born. Loyalty ensures that should a crisis occur then the team will go the extra mile to overcome it. It is also demonstrated in their day to day work which tends to be of a high standard. The only way you can get it in the first place is by earning it. You can't force loyalty on anyone but you can build it by making it a major focus of your team. A team that at its core is loyal and trustworthy is almost unbeatable.

~ *Ray Thornton* ~

1.   *Loyalty isn't grey. It's black and white. You're either completely loyal, or not loyal at all.* ~ **Sharnay**

2.   *Loyalty is hard to find in the workplace, trust is easy to lose, and your actions speak louder than any words you say.* ~ **Anonymous**

3.   *If put to the pinch, an ounce of loyalty is worth a pound of cleverness.* ~ **Elbert Hubbard 1856-1915**

4.   *If having a soul means being able to feel love and loyalty and gratitude, then animals are better off than a lot of humans.* ~ **James Herriot**

5.   *The only people I owe my loyalty to are those who never made me question theirs.* ~ **Anonymous**

6.   *There is something wrong with your character if opportunity controls your loyalty.* ~ **Anonymous**

7.   *The highest spiritual quality, the noblest property of mind a man can have, is this of loyalty ... a man with no loyalty in him, with no sense of love or reverence or devotion due to something outside and above his daily life, with its pains and pleasures, profits and losses, is as evil a case as man can be.* ~ **Algernon Charles Swinburne 1837-1909**

8.   *Loyalty cannot be blueprinted. It cannot be produced on an assembly line. In it cannot be manufactured at all, for its origin is the human heart the centre of self-respect and human dignity. It is a force which leaps into being only when conditions are exactly right for it and it is a force very sensitive to betrayal.* ~ **Maurice Frank**

9,   *Some people take loyalty way too far. I have boundaries when it comes to loyalty. Yes, I am loyal, but not to a fault. I cannot and will not compromise myself for other peoples' senseless behaviour. I have common sense, a great deal of wisdom, and I value my life. Loyalty shouldn't cost you your integrity, freedom or your life.* ~ **Stephanie Lahart**

10.   *Trust and Loyalty are earned not simply given. There is no halfway with either. If you give your loyalty and trust to a team and you expect all it members, including the team leader, to*

*trust you and be loyal to you. ~ **Jeffrey Gitomer***

11.   *Be loyal to those who are not there. In doing so you build the trust of those who are not present for they will come to know. ~ **Stephen Covey***

12.   *Our earliest ancestors probably learned that loyalty was a valuable survival tool. In the jungle, the desert, or the open plains, loyalty to your tribe increased your chances of surviving harsh weather and an unreliable supply of food and water. ~ **Dianne M. Durkin***

13.   *The foundation stones for a team's success are honesty, character, integrity, trust, and loyalty. ~ **Zig Ziglar***

14.   *I have loyalty that runs in my bloodstream, when I lock into someone or something, you can't get me away from it because I commit thoroughly. That's in friendship, that's a deal, that's a commitment. Don't give me paper I can get the same lawyer who drew it up to break it. But if you shake my hand, that's for life. ~ **Jerry Lewis***

15.   *EMPLOYEE loyalty begins with EMPLOYER loyalty. Your employees should know that if they do their job they were hired to do with a reasonable amount of competence and efficiency, you will support them, no questions. ~ **Harvey Mackay***

16.   *Most ethical principles are pretty unambiguously good. Honesty, fairness, compassion - sure they have their downsides (being 'honest to a fault'), but that's more a by-product of something good than it is something evil in and of itself. Then*

*there's loyalty. While ostensibly a positive trait, we are much more apt these days to hear about loyalty in the context of problems - loyalty to a country or religion leading to fanatical acts of chauvinism or violence, loyalty to family or friends leading to nepotism and cronyism in government, or loyalty to co-workers or a company leading to cover-ups of financial chicanery or unethical dealings. ~ **Michael Blanding**

17. *Loyalty and friendship, which is to me the same, created all the wealth that I've ever thought I'd have. ~ **Ernie Banks***

18. *Loyalty is a characteristic trait. Those who have it, give it free of charge. ~ **Ellen J. Barrier***

19. *Be more concerned with your character than your reputation, because your character is what you really are, while your reputation is merely what others think you are. ~* **Anonymous**

20. *Confidentiality is a virtue of the loyal, as loyalty is the virtue of faithful. ~ **Cheryl Cole***

21. *Within the hearts of men, loyalty and consideration are esteemed greater than success. ~ **Bryant H. McGill***

22. *Loyalty is what makes us trust, Trust is what makes us stay, Staying is what makes us love, and love is what gives us hope. ~* **Glenn van Dekken**

23. *An honest enemy is better than a friend who lies. Pay less attention to what people say and more to what people do. Their*

*actions will show you the truth. ~ **Ellis Thompson***

24. *There is something wrong with your character if 'opportunity' controls your loyalty. ~ **Sean Simonds***

25. *No more important duty can be urged upon those who are entering the great theatre of life than simple loyalty to their best convictions. ~ **Edwin Hubbell Chapin 1814-1880***

26. *I am stuck in a generation where loyalty is just a tattoo on the forearm, love is just a flippant quote to get into bed with someone, and lying is the new truth. ~ **Anonymous***

27. *I place an enormous premium on loyalty. If someone betrays me, I can forgive them rationally, but emotionally I have found it impossible to do so. ~ **Richard E. Grant***

28. *Loyalty is something you give regardless of what you get back, and in giving loyalty, you're getting more loyalty; and out of loyalty flow other great qualities. ~ **Charles Jones***

29. *Trust is earned, respect is given, and loyalty is demonstrated. Betrayal of any of those is to lose all three and friendships will melt away like butter on a hot day. ~ **Anonymous***

30. *The greater the loyalty of a group toward the group, the greater is the motivation among the members to achieve the goals of the group, and the greater the probability that the group will achieve its goals. ~ **Rensis Likert***

31.   *We are all in the same ship in a stormy sea, and we owe each other loyalty if we don't want that ship to sink. ~ **G.K. Chesterton 1874-1936***

32.   *I like messy people: people who don't fit in a box or stay between the lines, but whose integrity is greater than any rule book and whose loyalty is stronger than blood. ~ **Jim Wren***

33.   *The scholar does not consider gold and jade to be precious treasures, but loyalty and good faith, now that's a different thing altogether. ~ **Confucius 551-479 BC***

34.   *There are men and women who make the world better by being the people they are. They have the gift of kindness, courage, loyalty and integrity. It matters little to them whether they are behind the wheel of a truck, running a business or bringing up a family. They teach the truth by living it. ~ **James A Garfield***

35.   *If a man asks me for my loyalty I will judge him on his honesty. If a man asks me for my honesty I will judge him on his loyalty. ~ **Raymond Demming***

36.   *True friendship and loyalty is one in which everything can be told, and nothing will be judged. ~ **Anonymous***

37. *Loyalty often drives corruption. Corporate scandals, political machinations, and sports cheating highlight how loyalty's pernicious nature manifests in collusion, conspiracy, cronyism, nepotism, and other forms of cheating. Yet loyalty is also touted as an ethical principle that guides behaviour. ~ **John***

Hildreth

38. *Some people aren't loyal to you they are loyal to their need of you. Once their need changes so does their loyalty to you.* ~ **Julie Ford**

39. *Those who don't know the true value of loyalty can never appreciate the cost of betrayal.* ~ **Anonymous**

40. *There are only two options to being loyal, your either in or your out, there is no in between.* ~ **Pat Riley**

41. *Never push someones loyalty to the point where they don't give a damn any more.* ~ **Anonymous**

42. *Don't let your loyalty become slavery. If others don't appreciate you let them eat alone.* ~ **Julie Ford**

43. *My loyalty and friendship has no bounds, no matter where life takes us you'll always have my hand.* ~ **Ellie Williams**

44. *Loyalty is so rare these days, so if you have someone who remained loyal to you then appreciate them and remain loyal to them.* ~ **Anonymous**

45. *Where the battle still rages, there the loyalty of the soldier is proved.* ~ **Martin Luther 1483-1586**

46. *When a gifted team dedicates itself to unselfish trust and combines instinct with boldness and effort, it is ready to climb the cliff face.* ~ **Patan Jali**

47. RESPECT is earned, HONESTY is appreciated, TRUST is gain, LOYALTY is returned. ~ **Ben Barber Snr**

48. Loyalty is one of the cornerstones of your team leading skills. Like integrity, loyalty cannot be bought or sold, it cannot be traded, it has to be earned. Unfortunately once your team realise you are disloyal toward them then no matter what you do thereafter you can never win it back regardless what you promise. ~ **Al Bradford**

49. Even the richest man cannot buy a poor man's loyalty as he cannot know what will happen when it's truly tested. ~ **Anonymous**

50. Love is friendship that has caught fire. It is quiet understanding, mutual confidence, sharing and forgiving. It is loyalty through good and bad times. It settles for less than perfection and makes allowances for human weaknesses. ~ **Ann Landers**

51. I look for these qualities and characteristics in people. Honesty is number one, respect number two, and three would have to be loyalty. ~ **Sumner Altice**

52. If the King will not die for you, then he should not expect you to die for him. ~ **Jacqueline Carey**

53. Loyalty is dead, the experts proclaim, and the statistics seem to bear them out. On average, big corporations now lose half their customers in five years, half their employees in four,

and half their investors in less than one. We seem to face a future in which the only business relationships will be opportunistic transactions between virtual strangers. ~ **Frederick R. Reichheld**

54. Why would you want to be loyal to any company that draws a line between management and workers, between team leaders and team members? ~ **Glen Trowbridge**

55. Loyalty cannot be blueprinted. It cannot be produced on an assembly line. In fact, it cannot be manufactured at all, for its origin is the human heart — the centre of self-respect and human dignity. It is a force which leaps into being only when conditions are exactly right for it — and it is a force very sensitive to betrayal. ~ **Maurice Franks**

56. A successful life is not an easy life. It is built on strong qualities, sacrifice, endeavour, loyalty and integrity. ~ **Grant D. Searchfield**

57. You should be more concern with who is loyal behind your back as well as those who are loyal to your face. Loyalty should not depend on anyone's presence. ~ **Llewelyn Roberts**

58. Life has taught me that you can't control someone's loyalty. No matter how good you are to them, doesn't mean they'll treat you the same. No matter how much they mean to you it doesn't mean they value you the same. Sometimes the people you trust the most turn out to be the very people you can treat the least. ~ **Trent Shelton**

59. *When I give, it does not come with strings. I'm not keeping track of what you owe me. When I give, I choose to do so without ulterior motives. I give because I know what it's like to be without. To long for and be ignored; to speak and not be heard; to care for and have nothing returned. When I give it's because I know the value in what I have in my heart. And I refuse to let the world stop me from sharing that, But when things start being taken for granted, When you no longer appreciate my sincerity, I won't switch, I won't get angry, and I won't be spiteful. I'll just get smart, and change your role in my life. Because when I give, I'm all in. But when I'm done, there's no turning back. ~* **Rob Hill Sr.**

60. *The ability to inspire loyalty is a critical leadership quality. ~* **Geoffrey Hindley**

61. *Respect is earned. Honesty is appreciated. Trust is gained. Loyalty is returned. ~* **Anonymous**

62. *I may be stupid, as you say, to believe in honour and friendship and loyalty without price. But these are virtues to be cherished, for without them we are no more than beasts roaming the land. ~* **David Gemmell**

63. *Loyalty was a funny thing. So was love. They both bit you when you least expected it. ~* **Jodi Lynn Anderson**

64. *Nothing is more noble, nothing more venerable, than loyalty. ~* **Marcus Tullius Cicero 106-43 BC**

65. *Leadership is a two-way street, loyalty up and loyalty down.*

*~ **Admiral Grace Murry Hopper***

*66. The only true test of loyalty is fidelity in the face of ruin and despair. ~ **Eric Felten***

*67. The highest spiritual quality, the noblest property of mind a man can have, is this of loyalty ... a man with no loyalty in him, with no sense of love or reverence or devotion due to something outside and above his poor daily life, with its pains and pleasures, profits and losses, is as evil a case as man can be. ~ **Algernon Charles Swinburne 1837 -1909***

*68. I belong to the people I love, and they belong to me. They and the love and loyalty I give them, form my identity far more than any word or group ever could. ~ **Veronica Roth***

*69. Generally, most men are only as loyal as their options. ~ **Bill Maher***

*70. Our modern, rootless times do seem to be a particularly inhospitable environment for loyalty. We come and go so relentlessly that our friendships can't but come and go too. What sort of loyalty is there in the age of Facebook, when friendship is a costless transaction, a business of flip reciprocity? Friendship held together by nothing more perm-anent than hyperlinks is hardly the stuff of selfless fidelity. ~ **Eric Felten***

*71. Every contact we make with a customer influence whether or not they will come back. We have to be great every time or we'll lose them. ~ **Kevin Stiriz***

72. *Loyalty means I am down with you right or wrong. But I will tell you if you are wrong and help you get it right ~ **Anonymous***

73. *The strength of a family, like the strength of an army, is in its loyalty to each other. ~ **Mario Puzo***

74. *Don't be a fool for too long. When you realise you are being taken for granted it's time to make a move. Life isn't meant to be settling for less than you are worth. ~ **Tony Gaskin***

76. *All men are loyal, but their objects of allegiance are at best approximate. ~ **John Barth***

77. *The highest compact we can make with our fellow is – 'Let there be truth between us two forever more.' ~ **Ralph Waldo Emerson 1803 – 1882***

78. *Never esteem anything as of advantage to you that will make you break your word or lose your self-respect. ~ **Marcus Aurelius 161-180 AD***

79. *An onion shared with a close friend tastes like roast lamb. ~ **Egyptian proverb***

80. *When you look at lobbyists and the our lawmakers it's obvious that the lobbyists want something for their money, and that is the pecuniary advantage their client gets when a law is passed that benefits them, not the public. This is corruption in its worst form. Laws should be passed for the benefit of the public, not the few. We need a government that is loyal to us not to a multitude of wealthy companies ~ **Andy Déclassé***

14

PLANNING

Planning means looking ahead and 'chalking out' future courses of action to be followed. It is a preparatory step, a systematic activity which determines when, how and who is going to perform a specific task. Planning takes into consideration available team members and resources your team has, or will require, so you get effective co-ordination, contribution and the precise requirements you will need. It is the basic team leader or manager function which includes formulation of one or more detailed plan to achieve optimum balance of needs and requirements with the available resources.

~ *Roger Payne* ~

1.   *On the whole students don't plan to fail their grades. They all can learn, just not on the same day or in the same way. We on the other hand expect them to learn on demand. We have set the benchmark and the method of achieving it. And when the student fails to achieve it in the way we have said, we blame them, when we should be blaming ourselves.* ~ ***Albert Einstein 1879- 1955***

2.   *Good luck is usually the result of good planning.* ~ ***Anonymous***

3. *There is no such thing as planning for every eventuality. You are not infallible, so some things will inevitably go wrong. Don't let it unsettle you, simply adapt and move on. You will succeed in the end if you are patient enough. ~ **Roger Payne***

4 *A good plan implemented today is better than a brilliant plan implemented tomorrow. ~ **General George S. Patton***

5. *Planning is bringing the future into your present so you can do something about it NOW. ~ **Alan Lakein***

6. *To achieve greatness two things are needed; a plan, and not quite enough time. ~ **Leonard Bernstein***

7. *A first rate Organizer is never in a hurry. He is never late. He always keeps up his sleeve a margin for the unexpected. ~ **Arnold Bennet 1867-1931***

8. *Whatever failures I have known, whatever errors I have committed, whatever follies I have witnessed in private and public life have been the consequence of action without thought. ~ **Bernard M. Baruch 1870-1965***

9. *Few people have any next, they live from hand to mouth without a plan, and are always at the end of their line. ~ **Ralph Waldo Emerson 1803-1882***

10. *Plan more than you can do, then do it. Bite off more than you can chew, then chew it. Hitch your wagon to a star, keep your seat, and there you are. ~ **Anonymous***

11.   *Plan well before you take the journey. Remember the carpenter's rule: Measure twice, cut once.* ~ **Anonymous**

12.   *Thoroughness characterizes all successful men. Genius is the art of taking infinite pains. All great achievement has been characterised by extreme care, infinite painstaking thought, right down to the minutest detail.* ~ **Albert Hubbard**

13.   *He, who every morning plans the transactions of the day, and follows that plan, carries a thread that will guide him through a labyrinth of the most busy life.* ~ **Victor Hugo 1802-1885**

14. *A good plan is like a road map: it shows the final destination and usually the best way to get there.* ~ **H. Stanley Judd**

15.   *The will to succeed is important. But what is more important is the will to plan and prepare.* ~ **Bobby Knight**

16.   *Nobody ever wrote down a plan to be broke, fat, lazy, or stupid. Those things are what happen when you don't have a plan.* ~ **Larry Winget**

17.   *You can do irrefutably impossible things with the right amount of planning and support from intelligent and hardworking people and a pizza.* ~ **Scott M. Gimple**

18. *The four steps to consistent achievement: Plan Purposefully, Prepare Prudently, Proceed Positively, and Pursue*

Persistently. ~ **Anonymous**

19. *To accomplish great things, we must not only act but also dream. Not only plan but also believe.* ~ **Anatole France 1844-1964**

20. *It is not the strongest of the species that survive, not the most intelligent, but the one most responsive to change.* ~ **Charles Darwin 1809-1892**

21. *Never look back unless you are planning to go that way.* ~ **Henry David Thoreau 1843-1916**

22. *It's easy to come up with new ideas; the hard part is letting go of what worked for you two years ago, but will soon be out of date.* ~ **Roger von Oech**

23. *There are some people who live in a dream world, and there are some who face reality; and then there are those who turn one into the other.* ~ **Douglas H. Everett**

24. *Always plan ahead as it wasn't raining when Noah built the Ark.* ~ **Richard Cushing**

25. *An intelligent plan is the first step to success. The man who plans knows where he is going, knows what progress he is making, and has a pretty good idea when he will arrive.* ~ **Basil S. Walsh**

26. *He is the best man who, when making his plans, fears and reflects on everything that can happen to him, but in the*

moment of action is bold. ~ **Herodotus 484 – 425 BCE**

27. *Failed plans should not be interpreted as a failed vision. Visions don't change, they are only refined. Plans rarely stay the same, and are scrapped or adjusted as needed. Be stubborn about the vision, but flexible with your plan.* ~ **John C. Maxwell**

28. *Before you build a better mousetrap, it helps to know if there are any mice out there.* ~ **Anonymous**

29. *Succession planning (continual planning) helps build the strength of a team to ensure long term growth and stability.* ~ **Teala Wilson**

30. *First comes thought; then organization of that thought, into ideas and plans; then transformation of those plans into reality. The beginning, as you will observe, is in your imagination.* ~ **Napoleon Hill 1883-1970**

31. *Do not plan for ventures before finishing what's at hand.* ~ **Euripides 480-406 BC**

32. *Divide your movements into easy-to-do sections. If you fail, divide again.* ~ **Peter Nivio Zarleng**

33. *Don't be a time manager, be a priority manager. Cut your major goals into bite-sized pieces. This way each small priority or requirement on the way to ultimate goal becomes a mini goal in itself.* ~ **Denis Waitley**

34. *Planning is a process of choosing among those many options. If we do not choose to plan, then we choose to have others plan for us.* ~ **Richard I. Winwood**

35. *Every well-built house started in the form of a definite purpose plus a definite plan in the nature of a set of detailed blueprints.* ~ **Napoleon Hill 1883-1970**

36. *Walk with the dreamers, the believers, the courageous, the cheerful, people with their heads in the clouds and their feet on the ground. They are the true salt of the earth and the winners of most of life's races because they plan in their minds.* ~ **Wilfred Peterson**

37. *Everything someone does on a daily basis should be traceable back to an annual or quarterly plan.* ~ **Richard E. Griggs**

38. *The reason most people never reach their goals is that they don't clearly define them. Winners can tell you where they are going, what they will do along the way, and who will be sharing the adventure with them. When you can do that you'll be a winner too.* ~ **Dennis Waitley**

39. *It is a bad plan that has no room for modification.* ~ **Publilius Syrus 85-43 BC**

40. *First you write down your goal; your second job is to break down your goal into a series of steps, beginning with steps which are absurdly easy.* ~ **Fitzhugh Dodson**

41. *There are three kinds of people. Those who pan for things to happen. Those who watch things happen. And those who wonder if they will happen. Which are YOU?* ~ **Anonymous**

42. *For the happiest life, days should be rigorously planned, nights left open to chance.* ~ **Mignon McLaughlin**

43. *Reduce your plan to writing. The moment you complete this, you will have definitely given concrete form to the intangible desire.* ~ **Napoleon Hill 1883-1970**

44. *If you plan properly you should never have to say 'I am prepared for the worst, but hope for the best.'* ~ **Benjamin Disraeli 1804-1881**

45. *I have always thought that one man of tolerable abilities may work great changes, and accomplish great affairs among mankind, if he first forms a good plan, and, cutting off all amusements or other employments that would divert his attention, make the execution of that same plan his sole study and business.* ~ **Benjamin Franklin 1706-1790**

46. *Failure inevitably occurs because of doing things without thinking about them, or thinking about things without doing them.* ~ **Andy Leamond**

47. *If you plan to win as I do, the game never ends.* ~ **Stan Mikita**

48. *You can't plow a field simply by turning it over in your mind.* ~ **Gordon B. Hinckle**

49. *If you don't design your own life plan, chances are you'll fall into someone else's plan. And guess what they have planned for you? Not much.* ~ **Jim Rohn**

50. *If you employed study, thinking, and planning time daily, you could develop and use the power that can change the course of your destiny.* ~ **W. Clement Stone**

51. *If you have accomplished all that you have planned for yourself, you have not planned enough.* ~ **Edward Everett Hale 1822-1909**

52. *In complex situations, we may rely too heavily on planning and forecasting and underestimate the importance of random factors in the environment. That reliance can also lead to delusions of control.* ~ **Hillel J. Einhorn**

53. *Sometimes we need to stop analysing the past and start planning the future.* ~ **Alan Lakein**

54. *Planning ahead is a measure of class. The rich and even the middle class plan for generations, but the poor can plan ahead only a few weeks or days.* ~ **Gloria Steinam**

55. *It is a mistake to look too far ahead. Only one link in the chain of destiny can be handled at a time.* ~ **Winston Churchill 1874-1965**

56. *If you hear a good idea, capture it; write it down. Don't trust*

your memory. Then on a cold wintry evening, go back through your journal, the ideas that changed your life, the ideas that saved your marriage; the ideas that bailed you out of bankruptcy, the ideas that helped you become successful, and the ideas that made you millions. What a good review going back over the collection of ideas that you gathered over the years. So be a collector of good ideas for your business, for your relationships, for your future. ~ **Jim Rohn**

57. Whatever failures I have known, whatever errors I have committed, whatever follies I have witnessed in private and public life have been the consequence of action without thought. ~ **Bernard Baruch**

58. It's not the plan that is important, it's the planning. ~ **Dr Graeme Edwards**

59. Life is a long preparation for something that never happens. ~ **William Butler Yeats 1865-1939**

60. Long range planning works best in the short term. ~ **Doug Evelyn**

61. Success doesn't just happen, it's planned for. ~ **Anonymous**

62. No battle plan has ever survived contact with the enemy ~ **Helmeth von Moltke 1800-1891**

63. Planning is not simply a leadership task, it is a team task. It is only by using everyone's knowledge and experience can you

possibly get enough ideas to make a good plan. Don't waste that talent and your time by ignoring them. ~ **Jerry McWilliams**

64. *Planning without action is futile, action without planning is fatal.* ~ **Anonymous**

65. *Don't be a time manager, be a priority manager. Cut your major goals into bite-sized pieces. Each small priority or requirement on the way to ultimate goal become a mini goal in itself.* ~ **Denis Waitley**

66. *Plan well before you take the journey. Remember the carpenter's rule: Measure twice, cut once.* ~ **Anonymous**

67. *Besides the obvious, adaptability is the key to planning. The bigger the task the greater the planning required and the greater the risk of a problem occurring. Be prepared, have contingencies in place as part of your original plan to counter these problems. Remember the old Army saying: Prior Planning and Preparation Prevents Piss Poor Performance.* ~ **Dean Arrowsmith**

68. *The wise man bridges the gap by laying out the path by means of which he can get from where he is to where he wants to go.* ~ **J.P. Morgan**

69. *When planning for a year, plant corn. When planning for a decade, plant trees. When planning for life, train and educate people.* ~ **Anonymous**

70. *If you employed study, thinking, and planning time daily,*

you could develop and use the power that can change the course of your destiny. ~ **W. Clement Stone**

71. *Nobody ever wrote down a plan to be broke, fat, lazy, or stupid. Those things are what happen when you don't have a plan.* ~ **Larry Winget**

72. *There are some people who live in a dream world, and there are some who face reality; and then there are those who turn one into the other.* ~ **Douglas H. Everett**

73. *Plan for what it is difficult while it is easy. Do what is great while it is small.* ~ **Sun Tzu 544-496 BC**

74. *Planning without action is futile, action without planning is fatal.* ~ **Anonymous**

75. *When you're dying of thirst it's too late to think about digging a well.* ~ **Anonymous**

76. *The person who doesn't know where his next dollar is coming from usually doesn't know where his last dollar went.* ~ **Peter Osborne**

77. *We always plan too much and think too little.* ~ **Joseph Schumpeter**

78. *Preparation is the be-all of good trial work. Everything else - felicity of expression, improvisational brilliance - is a satellite around the sun. Thorough preparation is that sun.* ~ **Louis Nizer**

79. *Plan much more than you can do, then do it. Bite off much more than you can chew, then chew it. Hitch your wagon to a star, keep your seat, and there you are.* ~ **Anonymous**

80. *Planning is the only way to keep yourself on track. Plan your moments to be joyous. Plan your days to be filled with peace. Plan your life to an experience that is filled with personal growth and learning and awareness. When you know where you are going, the universe will clear a path for you to follow.* ~ **Lyniana Vanzant**

15
PREPERATION

Champions do not become champions when they win the event, but in the hours, weeks, months and years they spend preparing for it. The victorious performance itself is merely the demonstration of their championship character.

~ *Alan Armstrong* ~

1.   *Spectacular achievement is always preceded by lots of unspectacular preparation.* ~ **Robert H Schuller**

2.   *I believe luck is preparation meeting opportunity. If you hadn't been prepared when the opportunity came along, you wouldn't have been lucky.* ~ **Oprah Winfrey**

3.   *Opportunity is a haughty goddess who wastes no time with those who are unprepared.* ~ **George S. Clason 1874-1957**

4.   *If I miss a day of practice, I know it. If I miss two days, my manager knows it. If I miss three days, my audience knows it.* ~ **André Previn**

5.   *The best preparation for tomorrow is doing your best today.* ~ **H. Jackson Brown, Jr.**

6.   *There's only one way to assure consistently good work.*

*That is consistently thorough preparation. ~ **Andrew Loomis***

*7. Success depends upon previous preparation. ~ **Confucius 551-479 BC***

*8. Opportunity does not waste time with those who are unprepared. ~ **Idowu Koyenikan***

*9. You have to prepare physically, mentally, emotionally and spiritually to conquer any mountain. ~ **Lailah Gifty Akita***

*10. Musicians do not get on stage without hearing the song singing inside of them. Poets do not write as if they are jotting down a sermon, they see everything in their subconscious before presenting it to the conscious, which they later turn to readable materials. Artist do not draw and paint without painting in dream states, trance, or see an art form that others do not see. Being creative does not calls for being any supernatural entity, but in creating with the entities inside of you. ~ **Michael Bassey Johnson***

*11. Leaders don't venture without vision. They don't pray without plans. They don't climb without clues. They are always prepared. ~ **Israelmore Ayivor***

*12. You don't get lucky without preparation, and there's no sense in being prepared if you're not open to the possibility of a glorious accident. ~ **Twyla Tharp***

*13. You can't prepare for the details of every single possible thing that might come your way, because the future is uncertain. But you can prepare the best you can. ~ **Auliq Ice***

14. *A discovery is said to be an accident meeting a prepared mind. ~* **Albert Szent-Gyorgyi**

15. *If a person accepts that they will stumble, fall, and even be struck down every now and then, then that is a constructive view because the person will be prepared. Preparedness is not the same as fatalism. ~* **Gudjon Bergmann**

16. *Plan and prepare for what it is difficult while it is easy, do what is great while it is small. ~* **Sun Tzu 544-496 BC**

17. *Live your dreams by setting and taking action on your goals; this will prepare you to live the life that you once only dreamed of. ~* **Catherine Pulsifer**

18. *You cannot move forward in any project, or task, career, relationship or changing a habit unless you plan. And having finalised the plan you practice each part until it is perfect, then you swing into action and achieve your goal. ~* **Byron Pulsifer**

19. *Expect the best. Prepare for the worst. Capitalize on what comes. ~* **Zig Zigler**

20. *We all need to plant seeds in order to spring to life. Similarly, you can't climb a mountain starting at the top. It takes preparation, tools, skills and a set path to follow one step at a time. ~* **Catherine Pulsifer**

21. *The past is behind: learn from it. The future is ahead: prepare for it. The present is here: live it! ~* **Thomas S. Monson**

22.   *Preparation for life is so important. Luck is what happens when preparedness meets opportunity. Opportunity is all around us. Are you prepared?* ~ **Earl Nightingale**

23.   *The meeting of preparation with opportunity generates the offspring we call luck.* ~ **Anthony Robbins**

24.   *Confidence is preparation. Everything else is beyond your control.* ~ **Richard Kline**

25.   *When an employee is PREPARED, EQUIPPED, and ARMED with the RIGHT HABITS to address almost any situation, delivering exceptional customer service becomes easy.* ~ **Robert Stevenson 1772-1850**

26.   *Preparation is what allows the teacher to truly inspire. Preparation is in knowing exactly how the lesson plan will flow. It's knowing what questions to ask and how to draw the answer out, then lead the student into the next question.* ~ **Shawn L.**

27.   *Prepare while others are daydreaming.* ~ **William Arthur Ward**

28.   *It's not the will to win that matters - everyone has that. It's the will to prepare to win that matters.* ~ **Paul 'Bear' Bryant**

29.   *Life is like a combination lock; your job is to find the right numbers, in the right order, so you can have anything you want. It's all a matter of preparation.* ~ **Brian Tracy**

30. *One's goals will quickly be considered unrealistic if one's not adequately prepared to meet them.* ~ **Jessica Minty**

31. *If I had eight hours to chop down a tree, I'd spend six sharpening my axe.* ~ **Abraham Lincoln 1809-1865**

32. *Prepare a definite plan for carrying out your goal and begin at once, whether you're ready or not, to put this plan into action.* ~ **David Joyce**

33. *Spectacular achievement is always preceded by spectacular preparation.* ~ **Robert H. Schuller**

34. *For the want of a nail, the shoe was lose; for the want of a shoe the horse was lose; and for the want of a horse the rider was lost, being overtaken and slain by the enemy, all for the want of care about a horseshoe nail.* ~ **Benjamin Franklin 1706-1790**

35. *The general who wins the battle makes many calculations in his temple before the battle is fought. The general who loses makes but few calculations beforehand.* ~ **Sun Tzu 544-496 BC**

36. *Doing your preparation in advance and then letting your brain process the information while you sleep helps to cement this information in your memory making it easier to access the next day.* ~ **Tricia Alach**

37. *True stability results when presumed order and presumed disorder are balanced. A truly stable system expects the unexpected, is prepared to be disrupted, waits to be*

transformed. ~ **Tom Robbins**

38. *In the field of observation, chance favours only the prepared minds.* ~ **Louis Pasteur 1822-1895**

39. *The best preparation for the future is the present well seen to, and the last duty done.* ~ **George MacDonald**

40. *You can't push anyone up the ladder unless he is ready to climb himself.* ~ **Andrew Carnegie 1835-1919**

41. *First ask yourself: What is the worst that can happen? Then prepare to accept it. Then proceed to improve on the worst.* ~ **Dale Carnegie 1888-1955**

42. *The secret of success in life is for a man to be ready for his opportunity when it comes.* ~ **Benjamin Disraeli 1804-1881**

43. *It's not the will to win that matters, because everyone has that. It's the will to prepare to win that matters.* ~ **Paul Bryant**

44. *One important key to success is self-confidence. An important key to self-confidence is preparation and planning.* ~ **Arthur Ashe**

45. *The wise man bridges the gap by laying out the path by means of which he can get from where he is to where he wants to go.* ~ **J. P. Morgan**

46. *Confidence doesn't come out of nowhere. It's a result of something...hours and days and weeks and years of constant*

work and dedication. ~ **Roger Staubach**

47. *The meeting of preparation with opportunity generates the offspring we call luck.* ~ **Tony Robbins**

48. *Preparation eradicates cowardice, which we define as the failure to act in the midst of fear.* ~ **Veronica Roth**

49. *Long range planning does not deal with future decisions, but with the future of present decisions.* ~ **Peter F. Drucker**

50. *Before anything else, preparation is the key to success.* ~ **Alexander Graham Bell 1847-1922**

51. *Man can live about forty days without food, about three days without water, about eight minutes without air...but only for one second without hope.* ~ **Hal Lindsey**

52. *Preparation is the key to leadership success. The more prepared you are the less your struggle to make it happen and the more your effectiveness!* ~ **Israelmore Ayivor**

53. *The commander must decide how he will fight the battle before it begins. He must then decide who he will use the military effort at his disposal to force the battle to swing the way he wishes it to go; he must make the enemy dance to his tune from the beginning and not vice versa.* ~ **Field Marshal Montgomery 1887-1976**

54. *Talent is cheaper than table salt. What separates the talented individual from the successful one is a lot of hard work.*

~ Stephen King

55. *I learned that the only way you are going to get anywhere in life is to work hard at it. Whether you're a musician, a writer, an athlete, or a businessman, there is no getting around it. If you do, you'll win—if you don't, you won't. ~* **Bruce Jenner**

56. *It is not what you do for your children, but what you have taught them to do for themselves. ~* **Ann Landers**

57. *Noah built the Ark, then he, his wife, their three sons and their wives, plus two of every creature in the world got on it, only then did it start raining. That must surely tell you something. ~* **Anonymous**

58. *Whether it is a call to action for blood drives, disaster relief, or just community outreach, the Red Cross does an extraordinary job at not only meeting the immediate needs of a community, but also the preparation and planning for long-term support. ~* **Daruis Rucker**

59. *Be prepared. Never allow your government to take you for granted. Your vote, your voice and your actions are the greatest fear any government has, for without them they will not look after the people, they will look after their own interests. ~* **Anonymous**

60. *Go to the ant you sluggard; consider its ways and be wise. It has no commander, no overseer or ruler. Yet it stores its food in summer and gather its food at harvest. ~* **Proverb 6:6**

61. *Be mindful of the future but not at the expense of the moment.* ~ **Que Gon Jinn**

62. *You can expect a pretty pathetic performance if you haven't prepared for the future.* ~ **Anonymous**

63. *If you believe you can accomplish everything by 'cramming' at the eleventh hour, by all means, don't lift a finger now. But you may think twice about beginning to build your ark once it has already started raining.* ~ **Max Brooks**

64. *The general who wins the battle makes many calculations in his temple before the battle is fought. The general who loses makes but few calculations beforehand.* ~ **Sun Tzu 544-496 BC**

65. *If planning is the guide telling you how to get things done, preparation is finding all the necessary tools that ensures you can do it.* ~ **Daniel Bray**

66. *The will to win is worthless if you do not have the will to prepare.* ~ **Thane Yost**

67. *Talent is cheaper than table salt. What separates the talented individual from the successful one is a lot of hard work.* ~ **Stephen King**

68. *Some athletes have a certain amount of natural talent, thereafter they must work hard like the rest of us. Staying on top means working hard.* ~ **Paul Coffey**

69. *Execution is the ability to mesh strategy with reality, align*

*people with goals, and achieve the promised results. ~ **Larry Bossidy***

70. *Life is like a combination lock; your job is to find the right numbers, in the right order, so you can have anything you want. ~ **Brian Tracy***

71. *I get up every morning determined to both change the world and to have one hell of a good time. Sometimes, this makes planning the day difficult. ~ **E. B. White***

72. *The best preparation for tomorrow is doing your best today. ~ **H. Jackson Brown, Jr.***

73. *The meeting of preparation with opportunity generates the offspring we call luck. ~ **Tony Robbins***

74. *Meticulous planning and preparation will enable everything a man does to appear spontaneous. ~ **Mark Caine***

75. *Long-range planning and preparations does not deal with future decisions, but with the future of present decisions. ~ **Peter F. Drucker***

76. *A community is like a ship; everyone ought to be prepared to take the helm. ~ **Henrik Ibsen***

77. *I always had a philosophy which I got from my father. He used to say, 'Listen. God gave to you the gift to play football. This is your gift from God. If you take care of your health, if you are in good shape all the time, with your gift from God no one will stop you, but you must be prepared. ~ **Pele***

78. *Talent alone won't make you a success. Neither will being in the right place at the right time, unless you are ready. The most important question is: 'Are you ready?'* ~ **Johnny Carson**

79. *Education is a social process. Education is growth; Education is not a preparation for life, Education is life itself. Don't waste it.* ~ **John Dewy**

80. *If it's really stupid and it works, then it ain't really stupid is it?* ~ **Anonymous**

16

GOAL SETTING

People are remarkably bad at remembering long lists of goals. I learned this at a professional level when trying to get my high-performance coaching clients to stay on track; the longer their lists of to-dos and goals, the more overwhelmed and off-track they got. Clarity comes with simplicity and few of them knew what they were doing. The simple definition of goal setting is the process of identifying something that you want to achieve, and establishing how you will get there and how long it will take you.

*~ **Brendon Burchard** ~*

1.   *The reason most people never reach their goals is that they don't define them, learn about them, or even seriously consider them as believable or achievable. Winners who goal set can tell you where they are going, what they plan to do along the way, and who will be sharing the adventure with them. ~ **Denis Waitley***

2.   *When you set a goal it must be Specific, Measurable, Appropriate, Realistic, and Time Bound. ~ **Anonymous***

3.   *Failures do what is tension relieving, while winners do what is goal achieving. ~ **Dennis Waitley***

4.   *Most 'impossible' goals can be met simply by breaking them down into bite size chunks, writing them down, believing them, and then going full speed ahead as if they were routine.* ~ **Don Lancaster**

5.   *Goals: There's no telling what you can do when you get inspired by them, and there's no telling what you can do when you believe in them, and there's no telling what you can do when you act on them.* ~ **Jim Rohn**

6.   *You have to set goals that are almost out of reach. If you set a goal that is easily attainable and without much work or though you are struck with something below your true talent and potential.* ~ **Steve Garvey**

7.   *Every ceiling, when reached, becomes a floor, upon which one walks as a matter of course and prescriptive right.* ~ **Aldous Huxley 1894-1963**

8.   *It is a paradoxical but profoundly true and important principle that the most likely way to reach a goal is to be aiming not at the goal itself, but at some more ambitious goal beyond it.* ~ **Arnold Tonybee**

9.   *Some men give up their designs when they have almost reached the goal; while others, on the contrary, obtain a victory by exerting, at the last moment, more vigorous efforts than before.* ~ **Polybius 264-146 BC**

10.   *Life can be pulled by goals just as surely as it can be pushed by drives.* ~ **Viktor Frankl**

11.   *The real value of setting goals is not recognition or reward, it's the person we become by finding the discipline to achieve it.* **~ Cass Smiley**

12.   *Our plans miscarry because they have no aim. When a man does not know what harbour he is making for, no wind is the right wind.* **~ Seneca 4 BC-65 AD**

13.   *Set your goals high, and don't stop till you get there.* **~ Bo Jackson**

14.   *Giving up on your goal because of one setback is like slashing the three other tyres on your car because you've got one flat.* **~ Anonymous**

15.   *However brilliant an action may be, it should not be accounted great when it is not the result of a great purpose.* **~ Francois de la Rochefoucauld 1613-1680**

16.   *What did you do TODAY to bring you one step nearer your GOAL?* **~ Anonymous**

17.   *The trouble with not having a goal is that you can spend your life running up and down the field and never score.* **~ Bill Copeland**

18.   *Our goals can only be reached through a vehicle of a plan, in which we must fervently believe, and upon which we must vigorously act. There is no other route to success.* **~ Stephen A. Brennan**

19. Action without planning is fatal, but planning without action is futile. ~ **Anonymous**

20. You must have long term goals to keep you from being frustrated by short term failures. ~ **Charles C. Noble**

21. When chasing your goal and obstacles arise you don't necessarily have to climb them, you go around them. But you do not change your decision to get there. ~ **Zig Ziglar**

22. The most important key to achieving great success is to decide upon your goal and launch, get started, take action, move, as inaction breeds stagnation. ~ **Brian Tracy**

23. The will to win, the desire to succeed, the urge to reach your potential...these are the keys that will unlock door to personal excellence. ~ **Confucius 551-479 BC**

25. My philosophy of life is that if we make up our mind what we are going to make of our lives, then work hard toward that goal, we never lose somehow we win out. ~ **Ronald Reagan**

26. Write it down. Written goals have a way of transforming wishes into wants; cant's into cans; dreams into plans; and plans into reality. Don't just think it – ink it! ~ **Anonymous**

27. A difficult time can be more readily endured if we retain the conviction that our existence holds a purpose – a cause to pursue, a person to love, a goal to achieve. ~ **John Maxwell**

28. *One way to keep momentum going is to have constantly greater goals.* ~ **Michael Korda**

29. *Failures do what is tension relieving, while winners do what is goal achieving.* ~ **Dennis Waitley**

30. *When a goal matters enough to a person, that person will find a way to accomplish what at first seemed impossible.* ~ **Nido Qubein**

31. *All who have accomplished great things have had a great aim, they have fixed their gaze on a goal which was high, one which sometimes seemed impossible.* ~ **Orison Swett Marden 1848-1924**

32. *If you want to be happy, set a goal that commands your thoughts, liberates your energy and inspires your hopes.* ~ **Andrew Carnegie**

33. *All successful people have a goal. No one can get anywhere unless he knows where he wants to go and what he wants to be or do.* ~ **Norman Vincent Peale**

34. *Setting goals is the first step in twining the invisible to the visible.* ~ **Tony Robbins**

35. *Remember, what you get by reaching your destination isn't nearly as important as what you become by reaching your goals, and what you will become is the winner you were born to be!* ~ **Zig Ziglar**

36. *Aim for the top. There is plenty of room there. There are so few at the top it is almost lonely there.* ~ **Samuel Insull**

37. *Goals are new, forward moving objectives. They draw you in and magnetize you towards them.* ~ **Mark Victor Hansen**

38. *Of all the things I've learned since those early days, setting goals has had the most profound effect on my life. Every aspect of my existence – my accomplishments, my income, my bank balance, my lifestyle, my donations, even my personality changed for the better.* ~ **Jim Rohn**

39. *You may get skinned knees and elbows, but it's worth it if you score a spectacular goal.* ~ **Mia Hamm**

40. *All who have accomplished great things have had a great aim, have fixed their gaze on a goal which was high, one which sometimes seemed impossible.* ~ **Orison Swett Marden**

41. *You must have long range goals to keep you from being frustrated by short range failures.* ~ **Charles C. Noble**

42. *Man is a goal seeking animal. His life only has meaning if he is reaching out and striving for his goals.* ~ **Aristotle 384-322 AD**

43. *I feel that the most important step in any major accomplishment is setting a specific goal. This enables you to keep your mind focused on your goal and off the many obstacles that will arise when you're striving to do your best.* ~ **Kurt Thomas**

44. *By recording your dreams and goals on paper, you set in motion the process of becoming the person you most want to be. Put your future in good hands - your own. ~ **Mark Victor Hansen***

45, *A goal is not the same as a desire, and this is an important distinction to make. You can have a desire you don't intend to act on. But you can't have a goal you don't intend to act on. ~ **Tom Morris***

46. *If you don't know where you're going any road will get you there. ~ **Alice in Wonderland***

47. *If it doesn't challenge you then it won't change you. ~ **Anonymous***

48. *Success doesn't happen overnight. Keep your eye on it and don't look back. ~ **Erin Andrews***

49. *A winner is someone who recognises his God given talents, works his tail off to develop them into skills, and uses these skills to accomplish his goals. ~ **Larry Bird***

50. *The real value of setting goals is not recognition or reward, it's the person we become by finding the discipline to achieve it. ~ **Cass Smiley***

51. *You'll never change your life if you don't change something you do every day. The secret of your success with be found in your daily life. ~ **Anonymous***

52. *Don't set your goals by what other people think is important, set them by what YOU think is important.* ~ **Anonymous**

53, *DECIDE! - COMMIT! - DO! - SUCCEED!* ~ **Robbie Aldwich**

54. *People with specific goals succeed. It's as simple as that.* ~ **Earl Nightingale**

55. *The KEY to goal setting is don't bite off more than you can chew. Don't make them too easy, but don't make them impossible either. When you achieve the first goal set then next one a little harder so that you climb the ladder of success a little at a time.* ~ **Dean Boscombe**

56. *A victory is half one when one gains the habit of getting and setting goals.* ~ **Og Mandino**

57. *A goal is a dream with a deadline.* ~ **Napoleon Hill 1883-1970**

58. *A dream written down with a date becomes a GOAL. A Goal broken down into steps becomes a PLAN. A Plan backed by ACTION makes your dreams come true.* ~ **Anonymous**

59. *If you want to go fast GO ALONE. If you want to go far GO TOGETHER.* ~ **Anonymous**

60. *Success is something earned, something worthwhile. It*

comes only to those who are determined and committed to their goals come what may. ~ **Lou Holtz**

61. *Discipline is the bridge between goals and success.* ~ **Jim Rohn**

62. *Shoot for the moon then even if you miss you'll be amongst the stars.* ~ **Les Brown**

63. *If the plan doesn't work then change the plan NOT THE GOAL.* ~ **Anonymous**

64. *The only thing standing between you and your goal is a load of crap you keep telling yourself as to why you can't achieve it.* ~ **Gale Watson**

65. *It always seems impossible until its done.* ~ **Nelson Mandela**

66. *What you get by achieving you goals is not as important as what you become by achieving your goals.* ~ **Henry David Thorea**

67. *Successful people maintain a positive focus in life no matter what is going on around them. Setting goals is the first step in turning the invisible into the visible. Set your goals high, and don't stop till you get there. Discipline is the bridge between goals and accomplishment.* ~ **Jack Canfield**

68. *Determine what you want and why you want it. Once you understand what's important you can utilize your passions and*

achieve anything. ~ **Brook Griffin**

69. *What you get by achieving your goals is not as important as what you become by achieving your goals.* ~ **Zig Zigler**

70. *The 10 life lessons Albert Einstein wrote down which will help you with your life goals: Follow your curiosity. Perseverance is priceless. Focus on the present. Your imagination is powerful, use it frequently. Don't be afraid to make mistakes, just don't make the same ones twice. Live in the moment. Create value in everything you do. Don't expect different results when you repeat the same thing. Knowledge comes from experience. Learn the rules and then play better each time.* ~ **Albert Einstein 1879-1975**

71. *An average person with average talents and ambition and an average education, can outstrip the most brilliant genius in our society, if that person has clear, focused goals.* ~ **Mary Kay Ash**

72. *Nothing in the world can take the place of persistence. Talent will not; nothing is more common than unsuccessful men with talent. Genius will not; unrewarded genius is almost a proverb. Education will not; the world is full of educated derelicts. Persistence and determination are omnipotent.* ~ **Calvin Coolidge 1872-1973**

73. *The reason most people never reach their goals is that they don't define them, or ever seriously consider them as believable or achievable. Winners can tell you where they are going, what they plan to do along the way, and who will be sharing the*

adventure with them. ~ **Denis Waitley**

74. *You have to set goals that are almost out of reach. If you set a goal that is attainable without much work or thought, you are stuck with something below your true talent and potential. ~* **Steve Garvey**

75. *Give a man a bow and arrow and tell him to, 'SHOOT!' and his first response would be, 'At what?' When there is no target there is no purpose for shooting. He could shoot the arrow anywhere and wherever the arrow ended up would be where the arrow ended up. Not much to it. On the other hand, if you gave him a target and challenged him to hit the bullseye – everything changes. You now gave him something to aim at, something to challenge his skills against, something to measure his progress with, and something that gives all of his effort – purpose. All by adding in a simple target. ~* **Anonymous**

76. *If you raise your standards but don't really believe you can meet them then you've already sabotaged yourself. You won't even try; you'll be lacking the sense of certainty that allows you to tap the deepest capacity that's within you. Our beliefs are like unquestioned commands, telling us how things are, what's possible and impossible and what we can and cannot do. They shape every action, every thought and feeling that we experience. As a result, changing our belief systems is central to making any real and lasting change in our lives. ~* **Anthony Robbins**

77. *One of life's fundamental truths states, 'Ask and you shall receive.' As kids we get used to asking for things, but somehow*

we lose this ability in adulthood. We come up with all sorts of excuses and reasons to avoid any possibility of criticism or rejection. If you need help setting your goals ask someone you trust, let them help you. You'll be amazed with what they can come up with. ~ **Jack Canfield**

78. *What I think a lot of, and all great marathon runners do, is envision crossing that finish line. Visualisation is critical. But for me, I set a lot of little goals along the way to get my mind off that overwhelming goal of 26.2 miles. I know I've got to get to 5, and 12, and 16, and then I celebrate those little victories along the way.* ~ **Bill Rancic**

79. *You can never guarantee you'll be the smartest person in the room, but there is no excuse for not being the most prepared.* ~ **Brendan Paddick**

80. *By taking the time to stop and appreciate who you are and what you've achieved - and perhaps learned through a few mistakes, stumbles and losses - you actually can clearly define everything about you. Self-acknowledgment and appreciation are what give you the insights and awareness to move forward toward higher goals and accomplishments.* ~ **Jack Canfield**

17
LATERAL THINKING
(Thinking outside the box)

Many highly intelligent people are poor thinkers; they lack the capacity to think laterally and only think vertically. Countless people of average intelligence are skilled thinkers, both vertically and laterally. The power of the car is separate from the way the car is driven.

~ Edward de Bono ~

1. *Just because you're a musician doesn't mean all your ideas are about music. Every once in a while I get an idea about plumbing, I get an idea about city government, and they come the way they come. ~* **Jerry Garcia**

2. *Whatever you can do or dream you can begin. Boldness has genius, and magic and power in it. Begin it now. ~* **Johann Wolfgang von Goethe 1749-1842**

3. *There is no doubt that creativity is the most important human resource of all. Without creativity, there would be no progress, and we would be forever repeating the same patterns. ~* **Edward de Bono**

4. *A mediocre idea that generates enthusiasm will go further*

than a great idea that inspires no one. ~ **Mary Kay Ash**

5.   *We often refuse to accept an idea merely because the tone of voice in which it has been expressed is unsympathetic to us. ~* **Friedrich Nietzche**

6.   *To develop a complete mind: study the science of art; study the art of science. Learn how to see. Realize that everything connects to everything else. ~* **Leonardo da Vinci 1452-1519**

7.   *Your vision will become clear only when you look into your heart. Who looks outside, dreams. Who looks inside awakens. ~* **Carl Jung 1875-1961**

8.   *Do not train children in learning by force and harshness, but direct them to it by what amuses their minds, so that you may be better able to discover with accuracy the peculiar bent of the genius of each. ~* **Plato 428 -348 BC**

9.   *Capital isn't that important in business. Experience isn't that important. You can get both of these things. What is important is ideas. ~* **Harvey Firestone**

10.   *Management has a lot to do with answers. Leadership is a function of questions. And the first question for a leader always is: 'Who do we intend to be?' Not 'What are we going to do?' but 'Who do we intend to be?' ~* **Max DePree**

11,   *Do not seek to follow in the footsteps of the men of old; seek what they sought. ~* **Matsuo Basho**

12.   *Vision without action is a daydream. Action with without vision is a nightmare.* ~ **Japanese Proverb**

13.   *Lateral thinking is really about being able to think around bends and up hills and down dales.* ~ **Howard Thomas**

14.   *One man may have an idea but it may take 10 others to see its potential and develop it.* ~ **Roger Davies**

15.   *People who refer to out-of-the-box thinking see the box ...Where as people who don't know the box even exists are the innovative thinkers.* ~ **Lisa Goldenberg**

16.   *Lateral thinking is being open to any possibility regardless where it comes from, its unrestricted thinking.* ~ **Anonymous**

17.   *One's mind, once stretched by a new idea, never regains its original dimensions.* ~ **Oliver Wendell Holmes**

18.   *Imagination is more important than knowledge. For while knowledge defines all we currently know and understand, imagination points to all we might yet discover and create.* ~ **Albert Einstein 1879-1955**

19.   *The definition of Tautology: This wallpaper is stating that it is a wallpaper, therefore the wallpaper's statement of this wallpaper stating it is a wallpaper states that it is a wallpaper. The statement that precedes this one is necessarily true because it is necessarily true. Therefore that statement, preceding this statement, is a statement that is necessarily true, ergo it is that it is, and that is necessarily true.* ~ **Anonymous**

20. *The uncreative mind can spot wrong answers, but it takes a creative mind to spot a wrong question.* ~ **Anthony Jay**

21. *You've got to think about big things while you're doing small things, so that all the small things go in the right direction.* ~ **Alvin Toffler**

22. *To accomplish great things we must dream as well as act.* ~ **Anatole France 1844-1924**

23. *The good ideas are all hammered out in agony by individuals, not spewed out by groups.* ~ **Charles Brower**

24. *With normal vertical thinking one may look for different approaches until one finds a promising one. With lateral thinking one goes on generating as many approaches as one can find even after you've found a promising one. The more you find the greater the chance of success.* ~ **Edward de Bono**

25. *In the creative state a man is taken out of himself. He lets down as it were a bucket into his subconscious, and draws up something which is normally beyond his reach. He mixes this thing with his normal experiences and out of the mixture he makes a work of art.* ~ **E.M. Forster**

26. *Determine that the thing can and shall be done and then we shall find the way.* ~ **Abraham Lincoln 1809-1865**

27. *Dreams are extremely important; you can't do it unless you can imagine it.* ~ **George Lucas**

*28. Cherish your visions and your dreams as they are the children of your soul, the blueprints of your ultimate achievements. ~ **Napoleon Hill 1883-1970***

*29. Instead of thinking outside the box why not get rid of the box? ~ **Anonymous***

*30. The grand aim of science is to cover the greatest number of empirical facts by logical deduction from the smallest number of hypothesis or axioms. ~ **Albert Einstein 1879-1955***

*31. I know you think you fully understand what you thought I said, but I'm not completely sure you realise that what you assume what you heard is not what I meant. ~ **Alan Greenspan***

*32. Imagination is the living power and prime agent of all human perception. ~ **Samuel Taylor Coleridge***

*33. The master of the art of living makes little distinction between his work and his play, his labour and his leisure, his mind and his body, his education and his recreation, his love and his religion. He hardly knows which is which; he simply pursues his vision of excellence in whatever he does, leaving others to decide whether he is working or playing. To him he is always doing both. ~ **Buddha 567-484 BC***

*34. When you think outside the box you see the invisible and can often do the impossible. ~ **Anonymous***

35. It is not enough to have a good mind, the main thing is to *use it well. ~ **Rene Descartes***

36. *Natural resources have dropped out of the competitive equation. In fact, a lack of natural resources may even be an advantage. Because the industries we are competing for, the industries of the future, are all based on brainpower. ~ **Lester Thurow***

37. *Lateral thinking is concerned not with playing with the existing pieces but with seeking to change those very pieces. It is concerned with the perception part of thinking. This is where we organise the external world into the pieces we can then 'process'. ~ **Edward de Bono***

38. *A new idea is delicate. It can be killed by a sneer or a yawn; it can be stabbed to death by a quip and worried to death by a frown on the right man's brow. ~ **Ovid***

39. *The gift of fantasy has meant more to me than my talent for absorbing positive knowledge. ~ **Albert Einstein 1879-1955***

40. *Ideas are like rabbits. You get a couple and learn how to handle them, and pretty soon you have a dozen. ~ **John Steinbeck***

41. *Discovery consists of seeing what everybody has seen and thinking what nobody has thought. ~ **Albert von Szent Gyorgyi 1893-1986***

42. *People only see what they are prepared to see. ~ **Ralph Waldo Emerson 1803-1882***

43. *I never came upon any of my discoveries through the process of rational thinking.* ~ **Albert Einstein 1879-1955**

44. *The third rate mind is only happy when it is thinking with the majority. The second rate mind is only happy when it's thinking when it's with the minority. The first rate mind is happy thinking on its own.* ~ **A.A. Milne**

45. *An idea that is not dangerous is unworthy of being called an idea at all.* ~ **Oscar Wilde**

46. *Every great advance in science has issued from a new audacity of imagination.* ~ **John Dewey**

47. *Focus should be to encourage and develop creativity in all children without the ultimate goal being to make all children inventors, but rather to develop a future generation of critical thinkers.* ~ **Faraq Mousa**

48. *The future belongs to those who see possibilities before they become obvious.* ~ **John Scully**

49. *If one advances confidently in the direction of his dreams, and endeavours to live the life which he has imagined, he will meet with success unexpected in common hours.* ~ **Henry David Thoreau 1817-1862**

50. *Advances in technology have a great deal to do with a bar of soap and a hot shower* ~ **Roger Payne**

51. *You cannot depend on your eyes when your imagination is out of focus.* ~ **Mark Twain 1835- 1910**

52. *We are dying from over thinking. Lateral or otherwise. We are slowly killing ourselves by thinking about everything. Think, think, think, you can never trust the human mind anyway. It's a death trap.* ~ **Anthony Hopkins**

53. *The real voyage of discovery consists of not in seeking new landscapes but in having new eyes.* ~ **Marcel Proust 1871-1921**

54. *People mistakenly assume that their thinking is done by their head; it is actually done by the heart which first dictates the conclusion, then commands the head to provide the reasoning that will defend it.* ~ **Anthony de Milo**

55. *To acquire knowledge one must study. To acquire ideas one must be free from restraint. To acquire wisdom one must observe.* ~ **Marilyn Vos Savant**

56. *If you never change your mind then why have one?* ~ **Edward De Bono**

57. *The most difficult subject can be explained to the most slow-witted man if he had not formed an idea about it already. But the simplest idea cannot be made clear to the most intelligent man if he is firmly persuaded that he knows already, without a shadow of doubt, what is laid before him.* ~ **Leo Tolstoy 1828-1910**

58. *When we do what we are naturally suited to do, our work takes on a higher quality of play, and it is that play that stimulates our brain and creates new things. ~* **Linda Niaman**

59. *I'll be more enthusiastic about encouraging thinking outside the box when there's evidence of any thinking going on inside it. ~* **Terry Pratchett**

60. *What you can do, or dream you can, begin it; boldness has genius, power and magic in it. ~* **Johann Wolfgang von Goethe 1749-1832**

61. *Today knowledge has power. It controls access to opportunity, ideas and advancement. ~* **Peter F. Drucker**

62. *Whether the concept of lateral thinking is pure hokum or a precious revelation is a matter of some controversy. People will always have new and exciting ideas either way. ~* **Anonymous**

63. *Nearly every man who develops an idea works it up to the point where it looks impossible, and then he gets discouraged. That's not the place to become discouraged. ~* **Thomas Edison**

64. *If at first the idea is not absurd, then there is no hope for it.~* **Albert Einstein 1879-1955**

65. *The ability to express an idea is well-nigh as important as the idea itself. ~* **Bernard Baruch**

66. *Thoughts lead on to purpose, purpose leads on to actions,*

actions form habits, habits decide character, and character fixes our destiny. ~ **Tryon Edwards 1809-1894**

67. Rightness is what matters in normal vertical thinking. Richness is what matters in lateral thinking, lots of richness. ~ **Edward De Bono**

68. Every child is an artist. The problem is how to remain an artist once we grow up. ~ **Pablo Picasso 1881-1973**

69. The expression 'think outside the box' is a mantra frequently quoted, especially in business meetings. Its intention is to supposedly encourage creativity, innovation, and imaginative thinking. However, in most cases the phrase is meaningless and instead becomes a rather misleading cliché. ~ **Anonymous**

70. Google is a wonderful tool but far too often we give the youth of today answers to remember rather than problems to solve. ~ **Roger Lewin**

71   THINKING is the secret for a happy and rewarding life. Not essentially critical or positive thinking, but just thinking on its own. Imaginative thinking is all about breaking free from conventional belief systems, questioning assumptions and public opinions, and seeing in every challenge a new opportunity. ~ **Thomas Edison 1847-1941**

72. An idea, like a ghost, must be spoken to a little before it will explain itself. ~ **Charles Dickens**

73. *Man can alter his life by altering his thinking.* ~ **William James 1842-1910**

74. *After years of telling corporate citizens to 'trust the system', many companies must relearn instead to trust their people and encourage them to use neglected creative capacities in order to tap the most potent economic stimulus of all: idea power.* ~ **Rosabeth Moss Kanter**

75. *Creativity requires the courage to let go of certainties.* ~ **Erich Fromm**

76. *Creativity exists in the present moment. You can't find it anywhere else.* ~ **Natalie Goldberg**

77. *The most important thing in science is not so much to obtain new facts as to discover new ways of thinking about them.* ~ **Sir William Bragg 1856-1942**

78. *Knowledge is being applied to knowledge itself. It is now fast becoming the one factor in production, sidelining both capital and labour.* ~ **Peter F Drucker**

79. *Without leaps of imagination, or dreaming, we lose the excitement of possibilities. Dreaming, after all, is a form of planning.* ~ **Gloria Steinem**

80. *INNOVATION is the specific tool of entrepreneurs, the means by which they exploit change as an opportunity for a different business or a different service. It is capable of being presented as a discipline, capable of being learned, capable of*

being practiced. Entrepreneurs need to search purposefully for the sources of innovation, the changes and their symptoms that indicate opportunities for successful innovation. And they need to know and to apply the principles of successful innovation. ~ **Peter F. Drucker**

18
BEING CREATIVE

Creativity differs from innovation and discovery. Creativity is about making something new, rather than merely applying or discovering something new. Creative solutions are insightful, they're novel, they're simple, they're elegant, and when you find one creative idea, more often than not it triggers other ideas. A key to being creative, is the ability to find associations between different fields of knowledge, especially ones that appear radically different at first. The process requires people with curiosity, energy, and the openness to see connections where others cannot.
~ Professor Richard Foster ~

1.   *There is no doubt that creativity is the most important human resource of all. Without creativity, there would be no progress, and we would be forever repeating the same patterns. ~ **Edward de Bono***

2.   *Creative activity could be described as a type of process where teacher and pupil are located in the same individual. ~ **Arthur Koestler***

3.   *Creativity is thinking up new things. Innovation is doing new things. ~ **Theodore Levitt***

4. *When we engage in what we are naturally suited to do, our work takes on the quality of play and it is play that stimulates creativity.* ~ **Linda Naiman**

5. *Creativity is dreaming new thing up. Innovations is doing new things with the creative ideas.* ~ **Clare Bell**

6. *We will discover the nature of our particular genius when we stop trying to conform to our own and other's people's models, learn to be ourselves and allow our natural channel to open.* ~ **Shakti Gawain**

7. *Imagination is not only the uniquely human capacity to envision that which is not – and therefore the fount of all invention and innovation – in its arguably most transformative and revelatory capacity it is the power that enables us to empathise with humans whose experiences we have never shared.* ~ **J.K. Rowling**

8. *To create one must first be inspired to dream of the possibilities to imagine the details and believe in the finished version.* ~ **Anonymous**

9. *Logic will get you from 'A' to 'B', imagination will take you anywhere.* ~ **Anonymous**

10. *Creativity is inventing, experimenting, growing, taking risks, breaking rules, making mistakes, and having fun.* ~ **Mary Lou Cook**

11. *Sometimes you have to make things up, to tell truths that*

alter outcomes. Without the power of the imagination we lack the power the power to alter outcomes, so if we can't imagine better outcomes in a better world, we cannot act to achieve these. ~ **Ruth Ozeki**

12. *Every artist dips his brush in his own soul, and paints his own nature into his pictures.* ~ **Henry Ward Beecher 1813-1887**

13, *I can't understand why people are frightened of new ideas. I'm frightened of the old ones.* ~ **John Cage**

14. *The key question isn't 'What fosters creativity?' Why in God's name isn't everyone creative? Where was the human potential lost? How was it crippled? I think therefore a good question might be not why do people create? But why do people not create or innovate? We have got to abandon that sense of amazement in the face of creativity, as if it were a miracle if anybody created anything.* ~ **Abraham Maslow**

15. *Nothing is done. Everything in the world remains to be done or done over. The greatest picture is not yet painted, the greatest play isn't written; the greatest poem is unsung. There isn't in the whole world a perfect railroad, or a good government, or a sound law. Physics, mathematics, and especially the most advanced and exact of the sciences are being fundamentally revised. Psychology, economics, and sociology are awaiting a Darwin, whose work in turn is awaiting an Einstein.* ~ **Lincoln Steffens**

16. *To turn really interesting ideas and fledgling technologies into a company that can continue to innovate for years, requires*

*a lot of discipline. ~ **Steve Jobs***

17.   *Creativity is... seeing something that doesn't exist already. You need to find out how you can bring it into being and that way you can be a playmate with God. ~ **Michele Shea***

18.   *The most potent muse of all is our own inner child. ~ **Stephen Nachmanovitch***

19.   *Daydreams are fertile ground for the imagination to soar. As you sit absorbed in a problem, notice when you get lost in a day dream. What were you just thinking of? Your unconscious is a rich source of images, ideas and experiences that lead to new connections, and fresh thinking. ~ **Linda Naiman***

20.   *Listen to anyone with an original idea, no matter how absurd it may sound at first. If you put fences around people, you get sheep. Give people the room they need. ~ **William McKnight***

21.   *Everyone who's ever taken a shower has had an idea. It's the person who gets out of the shower, dries off and does something about it who makes a difference. ~ **Nolan Bushnell***

22.   *All great deeds and all great thoughts have a ridiculous beginning. ~ **Albert Camus***

23.   *Daring ideas are like chessmen moved forward; they may be beaten, but they may start a winning game. ~ **Johann Wolfgang von Goethe 1739-1832***

24. *God is really just another artist. He invented the giraffe, the elephant and the cat. He has no real style. He just goes on trying other things.* ~ **Pablo Picasso 1881-1973**

25. *CREATE: verb: The act of banging your head on a desk until something pops out of your ears.* ~ **Alan Richards**

26. *A rock pile ceases to be a rock pile the moment a single man contemplates it, bearing within him the image of a cathedral.* ~ **Antoine de Saint Exupéry**

27. *The wastebasket is a writer's best friend.* ~ **Isaac Bashevis Singer**

28. *Improvisation frees us from being perfect, being in control, thinking ahead, and second guessing. It can feel like jumping into the abyss at first, but once you jump, fear turns into excitement, and your imagination kicks in.* ~ **Linda Naiman**
29. *To draw, you must close your eyes and sing.* ~ **Pablo Picasso 1881-1973**

30. *Creative clutter is better than idle neatness.* ~ **Anonymous** *Beware of minimising imagination by creating it to a game of pretend. Every single creation in existence, from the Great Wall of China to the first flight to the moon, was a by-product of imagination.* ~ **Anonymous**

31. *I shall become a master in this art only after a great deal of practice.* ~ **Erich Fromm**

32. *When the 'weaker' of the two brains (right and left) is*

stimulated and encouraged to work in cooperation with the stronger side, the end result is a great increase in overall ability and... often five to ten times more effectiveness. ~ **Professor Robert Ornstein**

33. *Because of their courage, their lack of fear, they (creative people) are willing to make silly mistakes. The truly creative person is one who can think crazy; such a person knows full well that many of his great ideas will prove to be worthless. The creative person is flexible; he is able to change as the situation changes, to break habits, to face indecision and changes in conditions without undue stress. He is not threatened by the unexpected as rigid, inflexible people are.* ~ **Frank Goble**

34. *Invention strictly speaking, is little more than a new combination of those images which have been previously gathered and deposited in the memory; nothing can come from nothing.* ~ **Sir Joshua Reynolds 1723-1792**

35. *To live a creative life, we must lose our fear of being wrong.* ~ **Joseph Chilton**

36. *'There is no use trying,' said Alice. 'One can't believe impossible things.' 'I daresay you haven't had much practice,' said the Queen. 'When I was your age, I always did it for half an hour a day. Why, sometimes I've believed as many as six impossible things before breakfast.'* ~ **Lewis Carroll (Alice in Wonderland) 1832-1898**

37. *Creativity is just connecting things. When you ask creative people how they did something they feel a little guilty because*

they didn't really do it, they just saw something. It seemed obvious to them after a while. That's because they were able to connect experiences they've had and synthesize new things. ~ **Steve Jobs**

38. *You see things and say 'Why?' I dream things and say 'Why Not?' ~* **George Bernard Shaw**

39. *The creative person is willing to live with ambiguity. He doesn't need problems solved immediately and can afford to wait for the right ideas. ~* **Abe Tannenbaum**

40. *A creative man is motivated by the desire to achieve, not the desire to beat someone else. ~* **Ayn Rand**

41. *An idea that is developed and put into action is more important than an idea that exists only as an idea. ~* **Edward de Bono**

42. *The life of the creative man is led, directed and controlled by boredom. Avoiding boredom is one of our most important purposes. ~* **Saul Steinberg**

43. *Creativity is the quality that you bring to the activity that you are doing. It is an attitude, an inner approach – how you look at things. Whatsoever you do, if you do it joyfully, if you do it lovingly, if your act of doing is not purely economical, then it is creative. ~* **Osho**

44. *Do not fear to be eccentric in opinion, for every opinion now accepted was once eccentric. ~* **Bertrand Russell 1872-1970**

45. *Every day is an opportunity to be creative the canvas is your mind, the brushes and colours are your thoughts and feelings, the panorama is your story, the complete picture is a work of art called, 'my life'. Be careful what you put on the canvas of your mind today – it matters.* ~ **Anonymous**

46. *It seems to be one of the paradoxes of creativity that in order to think originally, we must familiarize ourselves with the ideas of others.* ~ **George Kneller**

47. *The highest prize we can receive for creative work is the joy of being creative. Creative effort spent for any other reason than the joy of being in that light filled space, love, god, whatever we want to call it, is lacking in integrity.* ~ **Marianne Williamson**

48. *Held in the palms of thousands of disgruntled people over the centuries have been ideas worth millions – if they only had taken the first step and then followed through.* ~ **Robert M. Hayes**

49. *Some humans would do anything to see if it was possible to do it. If you put a large switch in some cave somewhere, with a sign on it saying 'End of the World Switch. PLEASE DO NOT TOUCH', the paint wouldn't even have time to dry.* ~ **Terry Pratchett**

50. *Nearly every man who develops an idea works it up to the point where it looks impossible, and then he gets discouraged. That's not the place to become discouraged.* ~ **Thomas A**

Edison 1837 -1941

51. *If we worked on the assumption that what is accepted as true really is true, then there would be little hope for advance.* ~ **Orville 1871-1948 and Wilbur Wright 1867-1912**

52. *All creative people want to do the unexpected.* ~ **Hedy Lamarr**

53. *Everyone has innate talent. What is rare is the courage to follow that talent into the dark places where it will lead you.* ~ **Erica Jong**

54. *Creativity is a wild mind and a disciplined eye.* ~ **Dorothy Parker**

55. *Creative people are curious, flexible, persistent and independent with a tremendous spirit of adventure and a love of play.* ~ **Henri Matisse**

56. *You don't have to be an artist to be creative. Creativity is a state of mind. Just ask keep asking why and thinking of ways that the current state of affairs can be changed. They don't always HAVE to be changed but at least you thought about it!* ~ **Anonymous**

57. *Frequently, we hear about innovate, creative minds. One of the most important qualities that these people possess, in my opinion, is that they are willing to be wrong. They recognize that being wrong is a part of the creative process.* ~ **T.B. Frost**

58. *Creativity opens our doors of perception. It's a gift to see the world through someone else's eyes. Or to see the world in a new light.* ~ **David Roberts**

59. *When you are being creative you are letting yourself be silently drawn by the strange pull of what you really love. It will rarely lead you astray.* ~ **Rumi**

60. *Making the simple complicated is commonplace. Making the complicate simple, awesomely simple, NOW THAT'S REAL CREATIVITY.* ~ **Charles Mingus**

61. *Imagination is the beginning of creation. You imagine what you desire, you will what you imagine, and at last, you create what you will.* ~ **George Bernard Shaw 1856-1950**

62. *Think left and think right and think low and think high. Oh, the thinks you can think up if only you try.* ~ **Dr Seuss**

63. *Creativity is more than just being different. Anybody can plan weird; that's easy. What's hard is to be as simple as Bach. Making the simple, awesomely simple, that's creativity.* ~ **Charles Mingus**

64. *Write while the heat is within you. The writer who postpones the recording of his thoughts uses an iron which has cooled to burn the hole with, therefore cannot inflame the minds of his audience.* ~ **Henry David Thoreau 1843-1916**

65. *Don't think. Thinking is the enemy of creativity. It's self-conscious, and anything self-conscious is lousy. You can't try to*

do things. You simply must do things. ~ **Ray Bradbury**

66. *Creativity is the power to connect the seemingly unconnected.* ~ **William Plomer**

67. *You see things; and you say, 'Why?' But I dream things that never were; and I say, 'Why not?'* ~ **George Bernard Shaw 1856-1950**

68. *Every artist was first an amateur, as was every inventor* ~ **Ralph Waldo Emerson1803-1882**

69. *Creativity takes courage.* ~ **Henri Matisse 1869-1954**

70. *You don't simply take a photograph, you make it.* ~ **Ansel Adams**

71. *Art enables us to find ourselves and lose ourselves at the same time.* ~ **Thomas Merton**

72. *Live in the moment, negotiate with your past, bath in opportunism and confidently invent your future.* ~ **Robert Wilkins**

73. *Sit down before fact as a little child, be prepared to give up every conceived notion, follow humbly wherever and whatever abysses nature leads, or you will learn nothing.* ~ **Thomas Huxley 1825-1895**

74. *When we engage in what we are naturally suited to do, our work takes on the quality of play and it is play that stimulates*

creativity. ~ **Linda Naiman**

75. *Curiosity about life in all of its aspects, I think, is still the secret of great creative people.* ~ **Leo Burnett**

76. *The world of reality has its limits, the world of imagination is boundless.* ~ **Anonymous**

77. *I began by tinkering around with some old tunes I knew. Then, just to try something different, I set to putting some music to the rhythm that I used in jerking ice-cream sodas at the Poodle Dog. I fooled around with the tune more and more until at last, lo and behold, I had completed my first piece of finished music.* ~ **Duke Ellington**

78. *Because of their courage, their lack of fear, they (creative people) are willing to make silly mistakes. The truly creative person is one who can think crazy; such a person knows full well that many of his great ideas will prove to be worthless. The creative person is flexible; he is able to change as the situation changes, to break habits, to face indecision and changes in conditions without undue stress. He is not threatened by the unexpected as rigid, inflexible people are.* ~ **Frank Goble**

79. *Creative novelty springs largely from the rearrangement of the existing knowledge, a rearrangement that is itself an addition to knowledge.* ~ **J. Kneller**

80. *Creativity is not the finding of a thing, but the making of something out of it after it is found.* ~ **James Russell Lowell**

19
BRAINSTORMING

Brainstorming is the name given to a situation when a group of people get together to come up with new ideas to solve a specific problem. Using rules which prevent fault-finding, people are able to think more freely and move into areas of thought they often wouldn't going into and so create numerous new ideas and possible solutions. The participants put forward ideas as they think of them and then everyone can build on that idea or develop their own. All the ideas are written down and only when the brainstorming session is over are the ideas evaluated.

~ *Roger Payne* ~

1.   Creativity is not the domain of one single person. Anyone can come up with an idea however outlandish it might seem. Someone else might add to it and suddenly it is not outlandish anymore. Some ideas come from left of field, others from right of field, and when they collide we have a new workable idea we can build on. ~ **Joshua Farnandez**

2.   Brainstorming rarely comes up with a new idea, what it does do is allow someone to recall old ideas and link them together to make a new idea. ~ **Brian Williams**

3.   Brainstorming allows people to freely recall information, then process, generate and disseminate that information, which can then be tested and used by the team to solve a problem that may be outside the ability of an individual. ~ **Anonymous**

4. *Brainstorming created a global platform that allowed more people to plug and play, collaborate and complete, sharing knowledge. It had never been used before in such a fashion, now it is the fashion.* ~ **Thomas Freedman**

5. *Thought is the wind, knowledge is the sail, and mankind is the vessel.* ~ **Augustus Hare 1834- 1903**

6. *Inspiration is for amateurs; those that like sitting in circles trying to come up with brilliant ideas by the dozen. The rest of us just show up and get on with our work. If you sit around for the clouds to part and a bolt of lightning to strike you in the brain, you aren't going to get a whole lot of work done. But if you just get to work, something will occur to you and something else you rejected will push you in another direction.* ~ **Chuck Close**

7. *It is the long history of humankind (and animal kind, too) those who learned to collaborate and improvise most effectively have prevailed.* ~ **Charles Darwin 1809-1902**

6. *It's easier to act your way into a new way of thinking than to think you way into a new way of acting.* ~ **Jerry Sternin**

9. *We've been brainstorming a ton of new ideas but we won't know the results until the middle of next spring.* ~ **Brynna Vogt**

10. *You might have some brilliant ideas but if you can't get them across your ideas won't get you anywhere.* ~ **Lee Lacocca**

11. *No problem can be solved by the same level of consciousness that created it.* ~ **Albert Einstein 1871-1955**

12. *All ideas are spontaneous and malleable, then you have to chase them and catch them. Finally you have to play with them to see what they actually do. Only then can you claim them to be your own and let someone else see them.* ~ **Mary Kay Ash**

13. *Your future is created by what you do today not what you do tomorrow* ~ **Alan Marshall**

14. *A new idea is like asking a hard question. To answer it is difficult.* ~ **W. H. Auden**

15. *The sorcery and charm of imagination, and the power it gives to the individual to transform his world into a new world of order and delight, makes it one of the most treasured of all human capacities.* ~ **Frank Barron**

16. *Do not seek to follow in the footsteps of the men of old; instead seek what they sought.* ~ **Matsuo Basho 1644-1694**

17. *We tend to think that our ideas are the creation of our own thoughts but the truth is that they are mostly the combination of our past experiences.* ~ **Anonymous**

18. *What is now proved was once only imagined.* ~ **William Blake**

19. *Many ideas grow better when transplanted into another mind than the one where they sprang up.* ~ **Oliver Wendell Holmes 1831-1945**

20. *All good ideas are all hammered out in agony by individuals, not spewed out by groups.* ~ **Charles Brower**

21. *Create lightning bolt ideas during brainstorming is like causing catastrophic disturbances in your atmosphere.* ~ **Ryan Lilly**

22. *Whenever man comes up with a better mousetrap, nature immediately comes up with a better mouse.* ~ **James Carswell 1830-1897**

23. *We should take care not to make the intellect our god; it has, of course, powerful muscles, but no personality. It cannot lead; it can only serve.* ~ **Albert Einstein 1879-1955**

24. *No idea is so outlandish that it should not be considered with a searching but at the same time steady eye.* ~ **Winston Churchill 1874-1965**

25. *The ideas that come out of most brainstorming sessions are usually superficial, trivial, and not very original. They are rarely useful. The process, however, seems to make uncreative people feel that they are making innovative contributions and that others are listening to them. That in itself is something.* ~ **A. Harvey Block**

26. *Genius is one percent inspiration, and ninety nine percent perspiration.* ~ **Thomas Edison 1837- 1941**

27. *Music is the art of thinking with sounds* ~ **Jules Combarie**

28. *Intelligence is something we are born with. Thinking is a skill that must be learned.* ~ **Edward de Bono**

30. *It is better to have enough ideas for some of them to be wrong, than to be always right by having no ideas at all.* ~ **Edward de Bono**

31. *Greater than the tread of mighty armies is an idea whose time has come.* ~ **Victor Hugo 1802-1885**

32. *You need chaos in your soul to give birth to a dancing star.* ~ **Friedrich Nietzsche 1844-1900**

33. *It is the essence of genius to make use of the simplest ideas.* ~ **Charles Peguy**

34. *The lightning spark of thought generated in the solitary mind awakens its likeness in another mind.* ~ **Thomas Carlyle 1795-1881**

35. *Your team is full of golden ideas, creativity and ingenuity. It's YOUR job to mine for gold.* ~ **Jonathan Michael Bowman**

36. *The world we have made as a result of the level of thinking we have done thus far creates problems we cannot solve at the same level of thinking at which we created them.* ~ **Albert**

Einstein 1871-1955

37. *Brainstorming is a creative process by which efforts are made to solve a specific problem spontaneously by a group of people who in most cases don't particularly want to be there, and for the most part are forced to listen to harebrained ideas put forward by other people that are modern day Luddites, and who have no creative thinking skills whatsoever.* ~ **Shane Cole**

38. *Creative novelty springs largely from the rearrangement of the existing knowledge, a rearrangement that is itself an addition to knowledge.* ~ **John Kneller**

39. *In the creative state a man is taken out of himself. He lets down as it were a bucket into his subconscious, and draws up something which is normally beyond his reach. He mixes this thing with his normal experiences and out of the mixture he sometimes makes a work of art.* ~ **E.M. Forster 1879-1970**

40. *If you have an apple and I have an apple and we exchange these apples then you and I will still each have one apple. But if you have an idea and I have an idea and we exchange these ideas, then each of us will have two ideas.* ~ **George Bernard Shaw 1856-1950**

41. *What you can do, or dream, you can begin it. Boldness has genius, power and magic in It.* ~ **Johann Wolfgang von Goethe 1749-1842**

42. *The ultimate solutions to problems are rational; the process of finding them is not.* ~ **W. Gordon**

43. *To CREATE as a TEAM one must first be INSPIRED to DREAM of the multiple POSSIBILITIES and then to IMAGINE the details and BELIEVE in the finished vision.* ~ **Anonymous**

44. *A moment's insight is sometimes worth a life's experience.* ~ **Oliver Wendell Holmes 1809-1894**

45. *Creative novelty springs largely from the rearrangement of the existing knowledge, a rearrangement that is itself an addition to knowledge.* ~ **J. Kneller**

46. *Creativity is to make, create, think or see what was never there before.* ~ **Anonymous**

47. *If you wish to advance into the infinite, explore the finite in all directions.* ~ **Johann Wolfgang von Goethe 1749-1832**

49. *How many people use the latest software on their desk computer yet don't know about the latest software for the computer in their head?* ~ **Ann Bralow**

50. *Why is it I always get my best ideas while shaving?* ~ **Albert Einstein 1879-1955**

51 *You cannot mandate ideas, you must provide the environment to let people become their best.* ~ **Anonymous**

52. *Don't let what you cannot do interfere with what you can do.* ~ **Anonymous**

53. *He who has imagination without learning has wings and no*

*feet. ~ **Joseph Joubert 1754-1824***

54. *Curiosity is one of the most permanent and certain characteristics of a vigorous mind. ~ **Samuel Johnstone 1696-1792***

55. *A person who can create ideas worthy of note is a person who has learned much from others. ~ **Konosuke Matsushita 1894-1989***

56. *I used to think anyone doing anything weird was weird. Now I know that it is the people that call others weird that are weird. ~ **Paul McCartney***

57. *If I have seen further it is by standing on the shoulders of giants. ~ **Isaac Newton 1643-1727***

58. *We are apt to think that our ideas are the creation of our own wisdom but the truth is that they are the result of the experience through outside contact. ~ **Konosuke Matsushita***

59. *It is much, much easier to tone down a wild idea than to think up a new one. ~ **Alex Osborne***

60. *Problems and solutions nest within a complex array of related systems and problems. ~ **Bob Weile***

61. *Change is not merely necessary to life, it is life. ~ **Alvin Toffler***

62. *We think in generalities, but we live in detail. ~ **Alfred***

Whitehead 1861-1947

63. Be not afraid of moving slowly, be afraid of standing still. ~ **Chinese Proverb**

64. The lightning spark of thought generated in the solitary mind awakens its likeness in another mind. ~ **Thomas Carlyle 1795-1881**

65. The mere formulation of a problem is often far more essential than its solution, which may be merely a matter of mathematical or experimental skill. To raise new questions, new possibilities, to regard old problems from a new angle requires creative imagination and marks real advances in science. ~ **Albert Einstein 1871-1955**

66. You learn more about developing new products by talking to your customers for a day than sitting in a circle for a week of brainstorming, a month of watching your competition, or a year of market research. ~ **Aaron Levie**

67. The creative adult is the inner child that survived the intellectual ravages of school ~ **Anonymous**

68. The whole difference between construction and creation is exactly this: that a thing constructed can only be loved after it is constructed; but a thing created is loved before it exists. ~ **Charles Dickens 1812-1870**

69. Every great advance in science has issued from a new audacity of imagination. ~ **John Dewy 1859-1952**

70. *The balance between benefits and defects is much more easily improved by removing defects than increasing benefits.* ~ **Alan Parr**

71. *Daring ideas are like chessmen moved forward; they may be beaten, but they may start a winning game.* ~ **Johann Wolfgang von Goethe 1749-1842**

72. *I'm not weird I just think differently, so what's wrong with a square circle that incorporates a rectangle? I call it a 'Squcirangle'.* ~ **Anonymous**

73. *I did anything alone. Whatever was accomplished in this country was accomplished collectively.* ~ **Golda Rei 1898-1978**

74. *We should take care not to make the intellect our god; it has, of course, powerful muscles, but no personality. It cannot lead; it can only serve.* ~ **Albert Einstein 1879-1955**

75. *People who don't take risks generally make about 2 big mistakes a year, people who do take risks generally make about 2 big mistakes a year.* ~ **Peter F. Drucker**

76. *It's not about breaking the rules. It is about abandoning the concept of rules altogether.* ~ **Paul Lemberg**

77. *Curiosity about life in all of its aspects, I think, is still the secret of great creative people.* ~ **Leo Burnett**

78. *I wonder who thought up the Bumblebee. Aerodynamically,*

*it shouldn't be able to fly, but the bumble bee doesn't know it so it goes on flying anyway. ~ **Mary Kay Ash***

79. *While we might not truly understand the nature of creativity and the imagination (at least, not yet), we can still continue to apply ourselves in order to benefit from the rewards that come from focused concentration and those brief moments of inspiration that hit us like lightning bolts. ~ **Anonymous***

80, *The mere formulation of a problem is far more often essential than its solution, which may be simply a matter of mathematical or experimental skill. To raise new questions, new possibilities, to regard old problems from a new angle requires creative imagination and marks real advances in science. ~ **Albert Einstein 1979-1955***

Creativity takes courage.
~ Henri Matisse 1869-1954

20

MINDSETS

Mindsets are beliefs about yourself and your most basic qualities. It's about your intelligence, your natural talents, and your personality. There are two types – fixed and growth. People with 'fixed' mindsets are convinced that what they were born with will never improve regardless what they do, so they don't try and improve on them. On the other hand people with a 'growth' mindset see these qualities as things that can be developed throughout their lives simply by the own efforts and dedication.

~ James Owen ~

1.   *Leadership is simply a mindset that shifts from being a follower to creating a positive workplace environment that attracts people to you. Any of us can demonstrate leadership in our work and in our lives. ~* **Robin S. Sharma**

2.   *Every day may not be a good day, but somewhere within that day there is always something good, find it and use it to make the next day better. ~* **Anonymous**

3.   *A business has to be involving, it has to be fun, and it has to exercise your creative instincts. ~* **Richard Branson**

4.   *Before the beginning of brilliance, there must be great*

chaos. Before a brilliant person begins something great, they must look foolish in the crowd. ~ **Fu His**

5.   Winning is not a sometime thing; it's an all-time thing. You don't win once in a while, you don't do things right once in a while, you do them right all the time. Winning is habit forming. Unfortunately, so is losing. ~ **Vince Lombardi**

6.   The only way of discovering the limits of the possible is to venture a little way past them ... into the impossible. ~ **Arthur C. Clarke**

7.   Its sort of a mental attitude about critical thinking and curiosity. It's about a mindset of looking at the world in a playful, curious and creative way. ~ **Adam Savage**

8.   Three quarters of your brain is unused, fill it. So before you speak, listen. Before you write, think. Before you spend, earn. Before you invest, investigate. Before you criticize, wait. Before you pray, forgive. Before you quit, try. Before you retire, save. Before you die, give. ~ **William A. Ward**

9.   Whatever the mind of man can conceive and believe, it can achieve. Thoughts are things! And powerful things at that, when mixed with definiteness of purpose, and burning desire, can be translated into riches. ~ **Napoleon Hill 1883-1970.**

10. Picture you brain forming brand new connections as you meet the challenges, so keep on going and fill the space. ~ **Carol Dweck**

11. *Architects often have a mindset when they solve a problem. You have a set of needs that you have to address. Often I feel that my projects have to have concrete applications that I have to address, yet I am quite prepared to rethink all of them to achieve my goal.* ~ **Pedro Reyes**

12. *After living with their dysfunctional behaviour for so many years, people become invested in defending their dysfunctions rather than changing them.* ~ **Marshall Goldsmith**

13. *You don't get what you wish for, you get what you work for.* ~ **Anonymous**

14. *Compared with what we ought to be, we are only half awake. Our inner fires are damp, our dreams are checked. We are making use of only a small part of our possible mental and physical resources.* ~ **William James 1842-1910**

15. *We all have prejudices we must dispel: the need to get away from thinking that 'I' am important and special and 'you' are not, and the frightened mindset that tells us that certain 'others' are of no consequence.* ~ **Ingrid Newkirk**

16. *When first starting to work with someone you try to get them in the same mindset that you were in when you were successful, and I realized the best thing you can ever do is realize that they are not you. They have a different persona and mindset, and you have to figure out what works best within your interpersonal communication with them.* ~ **Dan O'Brien**

17. *No matter what comes your way, shake it off and move*

*forward. When you have a positive attitude nothing can beat you. ~ **Anonymous***

18.   *The problem is not the problem; the problem is the attitude you have about the problem. ~ **Captain Jack Sparrow. (From 'Pirates of the Caribbean', 2000)***

19.   *My will shall shape the future. Whether I fail or succeed shall be no one's doing but my own. I am the force. I can clear any obstacle before me or I can be lost in the maze. My choice. My responsibility. Win or lose; only I hold the key to my destiny. ~ **Elaine Maxwell***

20.   *I WANT, I'LL TRY, and I NEED, are all terms for failure, whereas I AM, I WILL, and I HAVE, are all terms for success. Change your mindset and it will change your reality. ~ **David Roppo***

21.   *You can't build today's team with yesterday's strategy and be in business tomorrow. ~ **Adam Buschbacher***

22.   *Life's challenges are not supposed to paralyse you; they're supposed to help you discover who you are. ~ **Bernice Johnson Reagon***

23.   *The secret to change is to focus all of your energy not fighting the old, but on building the new. ~ **Socrates 471-399 BC***

24.   *I believe there is an inner power that builds winners and losers and the winner are the ones that listen to their hearts. ~*

Silvester Stallone

25. *You have to trust in something – your gut, destiny, life, karma, whatever. This approach has never let me down, and it has made all the difference in my life.* ~ **Steve Jobs**

26. *REGARDLESS WHAT YOU MIGHT BELIEVE YOUR MINDSET IS EVERYTHING.* ~ **Anonymous**

27. *Our life is what our thoughts make it.* ~ **Anonymous**
28. *People become really quite remarkable when they start thinking that they can do things. When they believe in themselves, they have the first secret of success.* ~ **Norman Vincent Peale 1898- 1993**

29. *Progress always involves risks. You can't steal second base and keep your foot on first.* ~ **Frederick B Wilcox**

30. *You can achieve anything you want in life if you have the courage to dream it, the intelligence to make a realistic plan, and the will to see that plan through to the end.* ~ **Sidney A. Friedman**

31. *The difference between ordinary and extraordinary is that little 'extra'.* ~ **Jimmy Johnson**

32. *The essential question is not, 'How busy are you?' but 'What are you busy at?'* ~ **Oprah Winfrey**

33. *Hope and fear cannot occupy the same space. Invite only one to stay.* ~ **Maya Angelou**

34. *IF IT DOESN'T CHALLENGE YOU IT WON'T CHANGE YOU.* ~ **Anonymous**

35. *How others see you is NOT important. How you see yourself IS.* ~ **Anonymous**

36. *Just remember, as long as the mind can envisage the fact that you can do something, you can do it, as long as you REALLY give 100%.* ~ **Arnold Schwarzenegger**

37. *Every great dream begins with a dreamer. Always remember, you have within you the strength, the patience, and the passion to reach for the stars to change the world.* ~ **Harriet Tubman (no known birth date) Died 1913**

38. *No one saves us but ourselves. No one can and no one may. We ourselves must walk the path.* ~ **Buddha 567-484 BC**

39. *One of the greatest discoveries of any generation is that they can alter their lives by altering their attitude.* ~ **William James 1842-1910**

40. *It's not what you do, it's how you do it. It's not what you see; it's how you look at it. It's not how your life is; it's how you live it.* ~ **Anonymous**

41. *Keep your thoughts positive because they become your WORDS. Keep your words positive because they become your BEHAVIOUR. Keep your behaviour positive because they become your HABITS. Keep your habits positive because they*

become your VALUES. Keep your values positive as they become your DESTINY. ~ **Mahatma Gandhi 1869-1948**

42. *Smart is something you become, not something you are.* ~ **Anonymous**

43. *The only place where 'success' comes before 'work' is in the dictionary.* ~ **Vidal Sassoon**

44. *Choosing to be positive and having a grateful attitude is going to determine how you will live your life.* ~ **Anonymous**

45. *If you work just for money, you'll never make it, but if you love what you're doing and you always put the customer first, success will be yours.* ~ **Ray Kroc**

46. *The important thing is not being afraid to take a chance. Remember, the greatest failure is to not try. Once you find something you love to do, be the best at doing it.* ~ **Debbi Fields**

47. *You can only grow if you feel awkward and uncomfortable when you try something new.* ~ **Brian Tracy**

48. *The key for making smart decisions is a mindset that actively monitors your thoughts and is open to shifting tides and new information. It is acutely aware that the interplay between our environment and its outcomes is ever in flux.* ~ **Noreena Hertz**

49. *Nothing will slow your progress like a negative mindset.* ~ **Anonymous**

50. *Once your mindset changes from negative to positive everything else on the outside changes with it.* ~ **Steve Maraboli**

51. *To change your life you have to change yourself. To change yourself you have to change your mindset* ~ **K. and W.**

52. *Contrary to popular belief it's not always that the smartest children in school that end up the brightest ones in the workplace. Attitudes often change and with them so do mindsets. Anyone who is truly determined enough can climb to the top of the tree regardless of their background.* ~ **Alex Anderson**

53. *Great works are performed, not by strength, but by perseverance.* ~ **Samuel Johnson 1709-1784**

54. *Would you like me to give you a formula for success? It's quite simple, really. Double your rate of failure.* ~ **Thomas J Watson 1874-1947**

55. *Test scores and measures of achievement tell you where a student is, but they don't tell you where a student could end up.* ~ **Carol Dweck**

56. *What lies behind us and what lies before us are tiny matters compared to what lies within us.* ~ **Ralph Waldo Emerson 1803-1882**

57. *We like to think of our champions and idols as superheroes*

who were born different from us. We don't like to think of them as relatively ordinary people who made themselves extraordinary. ~ **Carol Dweck**

58. Risk more than others think is safe. Care more than others think is wise. Dream more than others think is practical. Expect more than others think is possible. ~ **Claude T. Bissell**

59. I am the Master of my fate, the Captain of my soul and the General in charge of my thoughts. ~ **William Ernest Henley 1849-1903**

60. Regardless what kind of mindset you have it doesn't mean you cannot have creative thoughts. Everyone can be creative. Begin by asking a simple 'Why?' 'Who?' 'What?' 'Where?' or 'When?' This empowers you to think about a problem. If you take these questions to their natural conclusion you often meander over a wide spectrum of ideas before arriving at an answer that could light up the world. ~ **Roger Payne**

61. Imagine with all of your mind. Believe with all your heart. Achieve with all of your determination. ~ **Anonymous**

62. Most of the important things in the world have been accomplished by people who have kept on trying when there seemed no hope at all. ~ **Dale Carnegie 1888-1955**

63. He who wrestles with us, strengthens our nerves and sharpens our skills. Our antagonist is our helper. ~ **Edmund Burke 1729-1797**

64. *Your subconscious mind can do ANYTHING. You can't do anything unless you can picture it in yourself doing. Once you make the picture process conscious and deliberate, you begin to create the person you want to be. ~ **PreventDisease.com***

65. *Life isn't about finding yourself. Life is about creating yourself ~ **George Bernard Shaw 1856-1950***

66. *Children are born with gifts that are raw and full of potential and with the right nurturing they can do what today we believe is impossible. ~ **Anonymous***

67. *Try a thing you haven't done at least three times. Once, to get over the fear of doing it. Twice, to learn how to do it. And a third time, to figure out whether you like it or not. ~ **Virgil Garnett Thomson 1896-1989***

68 *Security is not the meaning of my life. Great opportunities are worth the risk. ~ **Shirley Hurstedler***

69. *Don't tell me how talented you are. Tell me how hard you work. ~ **Artur Rubenstein 1887-1982***

70. *Don't be too timid and squeamish about your actions. All life is an experiment. ~ **Ralph Waldo Emerson 1803-1882***

71. *The greatest mistake you can make in life is to be continually fearing you will make a mistake. ~ **Elbert Hubbard 1856-1915***

72. *Before the beginning of brilliance, there must be great*

*chaos. Before a brilliant person begins something great, they must look foolish in the crowd ~ **I. Ching***

73. *What did you learn today? What mistake did you make that taught you something? What did you try really hard at? ~ **Carol Dewck***

74. *When people undermine your dreams, predict your doom, or criticize you. Remember, they are telling you their story, not yours. ~ **Cynthia Occelli***

75. *To die is poignantly bitter, but the idea of having to die without having lived is unbearable. ~ **Erich Fromm***

76. *Every accomplishment starts with the decision to try. ~ **Anonymous***

77. *When the world says, 'Give up,' Hope whispers, 'Try just one more time.' ~ **Anonymous***

78. *Personal security is not the meaning of my life. Great opportunities are worth the risk. ~ **Shirley Hurstedler***

79. *Just because some people can do something with little or no training, it doesn't mean that other can't do it (and sometimes end up doing it better) it's all a matter of ones mindset. ~ **Carol Dweck***

80. *Life isn't about finding yourself. Life is about creating yourself. ~ **George Bernard Shaw***

21

BEING INNOVATIVE

Everyone can innovate. It generally refers to changing processes or creating more effective processes, products and ideas and it can be a catalyst for growth and success. Being innovative does not only mean developing new ideas and concepts. It can mean changing aspects of the way you do things within your team, and teams that innovate create more efficient work processes and have better productivity and performance. The innovation process is also having a great idea, executing it brilliantly, and communicating in a way that is both intuitive and fully celebrates the true magic of the initial concept.

~ Pete Foley ~

1.   *The innovation point is the pivotal moment when talented and motivated people seek the opportunity to act on their ideas and dreams. ~ **W. Arthur Porter***

2.   *Too much of our work amounts to the drudgery of arranging means toward ends, mechanically placing the right foot in front of the left and the left in front of the right, moving down narrow corridors toward narrow goals. Play widens the halls. Work will always be with us, and many works are worthy. But the worthiest works of all often reflect an artful creativity that looks more like play than work. ~ **James Ogilvy***

3.   *If the creator has a purpose in equipping us with a neck, he surely would have meant for us to stick it out.* ~ **Arthur Koestler**

4.   *Whether or not you can observe a thing depends upon the theory you use. It is the theory which decides what can be observed.* ~ **Albert Einstein1879-1955**

5.   *We don't know who discovered water, but we're certain it wasn't a fish.* ~ **John Culkin**

6.   *Innovation is not just about ideas, it's about making them happen.* ~ **Anonymous**

7.   *Every act of creation is first of all an act of destruction.* ~ **Pablo Picasso 1881-1973**

8.   *The uncreative mind can spot wrong answers, but it takes a very creative mind to spot wrong questions.* ~ **Anthony Jay**

9.   *Implementing best practice is copying yesterday, innovation is inventing tomorrow.* ~ **Paul Sloane**

10.   *In the modern world of business, it is useless to be a creative original thinker unless you can also sell what you create. Management cannot be expected to recognize a good idea unless it is presented to them by a good salesman.* ~ **David Ogilvy**

11.   *Ideas won't keep. Something must be done about them.* ~

Alfred North Whitehead 1861 - 1947

12.   *Ultimately innovative thinking is to think like God. If you're an atheist, pretend how God would do it.* ~ **Frank Lloyd Wright**

13.   *Innovators are mixers: they blend together ideas and people to come up with new recipes.* ~ **Charles Leadbetter**

14.   *Discoveries are often made by not following instructions but by going off the main road, by trying the untried.* ~ **Frank Tyger**

15.   *There are no dreams too large, no innovation unimaginable and no frontiers beyond our reach.* ~ **John S. Harrington**

16.   *Everyone has talent. What is rare is the courage to follow the talent to the dark place where it leads.* ~ **Erica Jong**

17.   *Simplicity will always stand out, while complexity will often get lost in the crowd.* ~ **Kevin Barnett**

18.   *The secret to creativity is knowing how to hide your sources.* ~ **Albert Einstein 1879-1955**

19.   *All human development, no matter what form it takes, must be outside the rules; otherwise we would never have anything new.* ~ **Charles Kettering 1876-1958**

20.   *Anyone can look for fashion in a boutique or history in a museum. The creative explorer looks for history in a hardware store and fashion in an airport.* ~ **Robert Wieder**

21.   *Vulnerability is NOT a weakness. That myth is profoundly dangerous. Vulnerability is the birthplace of innovation, creativity and change. ~ **Brene Brown***

22.   *The law of floatation was not discovered by contemplating the sinking of things, but by contemplating the floating of things which floated naturally, and then intelligently asking why they did so. ~ **Thomas Troward 1847-1916***

23.   *Intuition will tell the thinking mind where to look next. ~ **Jonas Salk***

24.   *The organizations of the future will increasingly depend on the creativity of their members to survive. Great Groups offer a new model in which the leader is an equal among Titans. In a truly creative collaboration, work is pleasure, and the only rules and procedures are those that advance the common cause. ~ **Warren Bennis***

25.   *Innovation it has been said, consists largely of rearranging what we know in order to find out what we do not know. Hence, to think creatively, we must be able to look afresh at what we normally take for granted. ~ **George Kneller***

26.   *I CAN is a hundred times better than IQ. ~ **Anonymous***

27.   *The reasonable man adapts himself to the world; the unreasonable one persists in trying to adapt the world to himself. Therefore all progress depends on the unreasonable man. ~ **George Bernard Shaw 1856-1950***

29. *The creation of something new is not accomplished by the intellect, but by the play instinct arising from inner necessity. The creative mind plays with the object it loves.* ~ Carl Jung

30. *The greatest invention in the world is the mind of a child.* ~ **Thomas Edison 1837-1941**

31. *The more original a discovery, the more obvious it seems afterwards.* ~ **Arthur Koestler**

32. *The man with a new idea is a crank - until the idea succeeds.* ~ **Mark Twain 1835-1910**

33. *Never wish that life was easier, wish that you were better.* ~ **Jim Pohn**

34. *If you don't try something new then you won't have the opportunity to succeed.* ~ **Katie Lime**

35. *The human body has two ends on it: one to create with and one to sit on. Sometimes people get their ends reversed. When this happens they need a kick in the seat of the pants and a slap on the face.* ~ **Roger von Oech**

36. *Some men look at things the way they are and ask why? I dream of things that are not and ask why not?* ~ **Robert Kennedy**

37. *The business world sees a measurable and growing intelligence gap with need for intellectual expertise constantly*

expanding. Available talent is decreasing even though the population is increasing. Being bombarded with information be it in Nintendo or Shogi and being able to process it, find patterns etc., is a vital skill. One way to increase this talent potential is through games. ~ **Leif Edvinso**n

38. *In every work of genius, we recognize our once rejected thoughts.* ~ **Ralph Waldo Emerson 1853-1852**

39. *Innovation is the process of turning ideas into manufacturable and marketable form.* ~ **Watts Humprey**

40. *If you always do what you always did, you will always get what you always got.* ~ **Albert Einstein 1879-1955**

41. *The innovation point is the pivotal moment when talented and motivated people seek the opportunity to act on their ideas and dreams.* ~ **W. Arthur Porter**

42. *Inspiration is for amateurs. The rest of us just show up and get to work.* ~ **Chuck Close**

43. *I begin with an idea and then it becomes something else.* ~ **Pablo Piccasso**

44. *Discovery consists of seeing what everybody has seen and thinking what nobody has thought.* ~ **Albert von Szent Gyorgy 1893-1986**

45. *To raise new questions, new possibilities, to regard old problems from a new angle, requires creative imagination and*

*marks real advance in science. ~ **Albert Einstein 1879-1955***

46. *A man is not idle because he is absorbed in thought. There is a visible labour and there is an invisible labour. ~ **Victor Hugo 1802-1805***

47. *Without change there is no innovation, creativity, or incentive for improvement. Those who initiate change will have a better opportunity to manage the change that is inevitable. ~ **William Pollard***

48. *To be creative you have to contribute something different from what you've done before. Your results need not be original to the world; few results truly meet that criterion. In fact, most results are built on the work of others. ~ **Lynne C. Levesque***

49. *Innovation is a wild mind behind a disciplined eye ~ **Dorothy Parker 1893-1967***

50. *Capital isn't so important in business. Experience isn't so important. You can get both these things. What is important is ideas. If you have ideas, you have the main asset you need, and there isn't any limit to what you can do with your business and your life. ~ **Harvey Firestone***

51. *Without the playing with fantasy no creative work has ever yet come to birth. The debt we owe to the play of imagination is incalculable. ~ **Carl Jung 1875-1971***

52. *Today is a new day. Even if you were wrong yesterday you can still get it right today. ~ **Dwight Howard***

53. *Man is a creature of hope and invention, both of which belie the idea that things cannot be changed. ~* **Tom Clancy**

54. *It isn't the incompetent who destroy an organization. The incompetent never get in a position to destroy it. It is those who achieved something and want to rest upon their achievements who are forever clogging things up. ~* **F.M. Young**

55. *Too much of our work amounts to the drudgery of arranging means toward ends, mechanically placing the right foot in front of the left and the left in front of the right, moving down narrow corridors toward narrow goals. Play widens the halls. Work will always be with us, and many works are worthy. But the worthiest works of all often reflect an artful creativity that looks more like play than work. ~* **James Olgilvy**

56. *An inventor is simply a person who doesn't take his education too seriously. You see, from the time a person is six years old until he graduates from college he has to take three or four examinations a year. If he flunks once, he is out. But an inventor is almost always failing. He tries and fails maybe a thousand times. It he succeeds once then he's in. These two things are diametrically opposite. We often say that the biggest job we have is to teach a newly hired employee how to fail intelligently. We have to train him to experiment over and over and to keep on trying and failing until he learns what will work. ~* **Charles Kettering 1876-1958**

57. *INVENTION, my dear friends is: 93% PERSPIRATION, 6% ELECTRICITY, 4% EVAPORATION, and 2% BUTTER SCOTCH*

RIPPLE. ~ **Willy Wonka (From 'Willy Wonka and the Chocolate Factory', 1971)**

58. *An invention has to make sense in the world it finishes in, not the world it started in.* ~ **Tom O' Riley**

59. *Learning and innovation go hand in hand. The arrogance of success is to think that what you did yesterday will be sufficient for tomorrow.* ~ **William Pollard**

60. *I was going to record talking. The foil was put on, then I shouted 'MARY HAD A LITTLE LAMB,' and the machine reproduced it perfectly.* ~ **Thomas Edison 1847-1941**

61. *Creativity is allowing yourself to make mistakes, art is knowing which ones to keep.* ~ **Scott Adams**

62. *There has been opposition to every innovation in the history of man, with the possible exception of the sword.* ~ **Benjamin Dana**

63. *In the modern world of business, it is useless to be a creative original thinker unless you can also sell what you create.* ~ **Anonymous**

65. *Management cannot be expected to recognize a good idea unless it is presented to them by a good salesman.* ~ **David Ogilvy**

66. *All work and no play doesn't just make Jill and Jack dull, it kills the potential of discovery, mastery, and openness to change*

and flexibility and it hinders innovation and invention. ~ **Joline Godfrey**

67. *When Alexander the Great visited Diogenes and asked whether he could do anything for the famed teacher, Diogenes replied: 'Only stand out of my light.' Perhaps someday we shall know how to heighten creativity. Until then, one of the best things we can do for creative men and women is to stand out of their light.* ~ **John W. Gardner**

68. *I do not fix problems. I fix my thinking and then the problems fix themselves.* ~ **Louise L. Hay**

69. *Once you have an innovation culture, even those who are not scientists or engineers - poets, actors, journalists - they, as communities, embrace the meaning of what it is to be scientifically literate. They embrace the concept of an innovation culture. They vote in ways that promote it. They don't fight science and they don't fight technology.* ~ **Neil Degrass Tyson**

70. *They always say time changes things, but you actually have to change them yourself.* ~ **Andy Warhol**

71. *It is the essence of genius to make use of the simplest ideas.* ~ **Charles Peguy**

72. *Innovation is taking a number of existing things and putting them together to make something new.* ~ **Tom Freston**

73. *Whether or not you can observe a thing depends upon the*

theory you use. It is the theory which decides what can be observed. ~ **Albert Einstein**

74. *I can't understand why people are frightened of new ideas. I'm frightened of the old ones.* ~ **John Cage**

75. *Without tradition, art is a flock of sheep without a shepherd. Without innovation, it is a corpse.* ~ **Winston Churchill 1874-1975**

76. *Failure is part of innovation, probably the most important part.* ~ **Curt Richardson**

77. *All work and no play doesn't just make Jill and Jack dull, it kills the potential of discovery, mastery, and openness to change and flexibility and it hinders innovation and invention.* ~ **Joline Godfrey**

78. *Most of us understand that innovation is enormously important. It's the only insurance against irrelevance. It's the only guarantee of long-term customer loyalty. It's the only strategy for out-performing a dismal economy.* ~ **Garry Hamel**

79. *The greater the contrast, the greater the potential. Great energy only comes from a correspondingly great tension of opposites.* ~ **Carl Jung 1875-1971**

80. *A creative mindset is in increasingly high demand: employers are vying for workers who are able to dream big and deliver big with the next must-have product. Creative thinking fuels innovation, it leads to new goods and services, creates jobs and delivers substantial economic rewards.* ~ **Jim Hunt**

22

TIME MANAGEMENT

Time management is the process of organising and planning how to effectively divide your time between specific activities. Effective time management enables you to work smarter, not harder, so that you get more done in less time regardless of the situation. Failing to manage your time damages your effectiveness and the effectiveness of your team, causing unnecessary disruption and stress.

~ *Roger Payne* ~

1. Don't be fooled by the Calendar. There are only as many days in the year as you make use of. One man only gets a week's value out of the year, while another man gets a full year's value out of a week. ~ **Charles Richards**

2. Ask yourself right now if what you are doing today is getting you closer to what you'll need tomorrow? ~ **Anonymous**

3. A man who wastes one hour of time has not discovered the value of life. ~ **Charles Darwin 1809-1882**

4. Lost wealth may be regain by hard work. Lost knowledge may be recovered by dedicated study, lost time can never be recovered. ~ **Anonymous**

5. *Don't ever say you don't have enough time. You have exactly the same amount of time as Albert Einstein, Hellen Keller, Pasteur, Michelangelo, Mother Teresa, Leonardo da Vinci, Thomas Jefferson, Lord Nelson, Attila the Hun. ~* **H. Jackson Brown**.

6. *A wise man does it once. A fool does it at last. Both do the very same things, just at different times. ~* **St John Alberg Acton 1834-1902**

7. *The secret of getting ahead is getting started. The secret of getting started is breaking your complex overwhelming tasks into smaller manageable tasks, and then start the first one. ~* **Mark Twain 1835-1910**

8. *The reason you're wasting so much time can be directly traced to your lack of concentration and inattention, besides the unnecessary diversions and distractions. ~* **Anonymous**

9. *People often complain about time when it's the lack of direction that is the problem. ~* **Zig Zigler**

10. *There is no such thing as too busy, learn to PRIORITISE, learn to DELEGATE. ~* **Roger Payne**

11. *This is the beginning of a new day. I have been given this day to use as I will. I can waste it or use it for good. What I do today is important, because I am exchanging a day of my life for it. When tomorrow comes, this day will be gone forever, leaving in its place something that I have traded for it. I want it to be gain, not loss; good not evil; success not failure, in order that I*

*shall not regret the price I paid for it. ~ **Anonymous***

*12.   You can't change the past, but you can ruin the present by worrying too much about the future. ~ **Anonymous***

*13.   Once you have mastered time, you will understand how true it is that most people overestimate what they can accomplish in a year – and underestimate what they can achieve in a decade! ~ **Anthony Robbins***

*14.   Determine never to be idle. No person will have occasion to complain of the want of time who never loses any. It is wonderful how much can be done if we are always doing. ~ **Thomas Jefferson 1743-1826***

*15.   Don't be fooled by the calendar. There are only as many days in the year as you make use of. One man gets only a week's value out of a year while another man gets a full year's value out of a week. ~ **Charles Brinckerhoff Richards 1833-1919***

*16.   The next time you find yourself in an argument, rather than waste time defending your position, see if you can see the other point of view first. ~ **Richard Carlson, PH.D***

*17.   Well-arranged time is the surest mark of a well arranged mind. ~ **Sir Issac Pitman 1813-1897***

*18.   He who every morning plans the transaction of the day and follows out the plan, carries a thread that will guide him through the labyrinth of the most busy life. ~ **Victor Hugo 1802-1885***

*19. You DON'T get paid BY the hour. You get paid for the VALUE you bring to that hour***. ~ Jim Rohn**

*20. Money, I can only gain or lose. But time I can only lose. So, I must spend it carefully. ~ **Anonymous***

*21. Vision without action is merely a dream. Action without vision just passes the time. Vision with action can change the world. ~ **Joel A. Barker***

*22. Don't spend a dollar's worth of time on a ten cent decision. ~ **Peter Turla***

*23. Everything requires time. It is the only truly universal condition. All work takes place in time and uses up time. Yet most people take for granted this unique, irreplaceable, and necessary resource. Nothing else, perhaps, distinguishes effective executives as much as their tender loving care of time. ~ **Peter F. Drucker***

*24. How you spend your time is more important than how you spend your money. Money mistakes can be corrected, but time is gone forever. ~ **David Norris***

*25. Be willing to make decisions on time. That's the most important quality in a good leader. Don't fall victim to what I call the 'ready – aim – aim – aim – aim syndrome.' You must be willing to fire. ~ **T. Boone Pickens***

26. Until we can manage time, we can manage nothing else. ~

Peter F. Drucker

27. Time has no meaning in itself unless we choose to give it significance. ~ **Leo Buscaglia**

28. How did it get so late so soon? ~ **Dr. Seuss**

29. Isn't it curious, there's never enough time to do it right, but there's always enough time to do it over. ~ **Jack Bergman**

30. Guard well your spare moments. They are like uncut diamonds. Discard them and their value will never be known. Improve them and they will become the brightest gems in a useful life. ~ **Ralph Waldo Emerson 1803-1882**

31. If you spend too much time thinking about a thing, you'll never get it done. ~ **Bruce Lee**

32. If you want to make good use of your time, you've got to know what's most important and then give it all you've got. ~ **Lee Iacocca**

33. Never let yesterday use up today. ~ **Richard H. Nelson**

34. A man must be master of his hours and days, not their servant. ~ **William Frederick Book 1873- 1940**

35. Welcome to the school of stupidity. Today we will learn that rudeness and time management are one and the same thing. ~ **Anonymous**

36. *Half our life is spent trying to find something to do with the time we have rushed through life trying to save.* ~ **Will Rogers**

37. *Time equals life; therefore, waste your time and waste of your life, or master your time and master your life.* ~ **Alan Lakein**

38. *You may delay, but time will not.* ~ **Benjamin Franklin 1706-1790**

39. *Review our priorities, ask the question; what's the best use of our time right now?* ~ **Alan Lakein**

40. *This time, like all times, is a very good one, if we but know what to do with It.* ~ **Ralph Waldo Emerson 1803-1882**

41. *In truth, people can generally make time for what they choose to do; it is not really the time but the will that is lacking.* ~ **Sir John Lubbock 1834 1919**

42. *The idea is to make decisions and act on them, to decide what is important to accomplish, to decide how something can best be accomplished, to find time to work at it and to get it done.* ~ **Karen Kakascik**

43. *There is nothing as useless as doing efficiently that which should not be done at all.* ~ **Peter F Drucker**

44. *The key is NOT to prioritise what's on your schedule but to schedule what's on your priorities.* ~ **Stephen Covey**

45. Do not confuse motion and progress. A rocking horse keeps moving but does not make any progress. ~ **Alfred A. Montapert**

46. You cannot run at full throttle when applying your mind to all of the different things running through your head. Focusing is the key to manifesting your desires. ~ **Steve Richardson**

47. Being busy means doing stuff. Being productive means getting stuff done. ~ **Anonymous**

48. Time is a great teacher, but unfortunately it kills all its pupils. ~ **Louis Hector Berlio 1803-1869**

49. Why kill time when one can employ it? ~ **English Proverb**

50. Don't force someone to make time for YOU. If they want to they will. ~ **Anonymous**

51. It's not enough to be busy, so are the ants. The question is, what are we busy about? ~ **Henry David Thoreau 1817-1862**

52. Time management means, find out where you're wasting it, create management goals, implement management plans, prioritise ruthlessly, delegate or outsource, establish routines and stick to them, set times limits for tasks, make sure your systems are organised, and don't waste times waiting. ~ **Alex Proud**

53. Yesterday's gone. Tomorrow has not yet come. We have only today. Let us begin. ~ **Mother Teresa**

54. *A wise person does it at once, a fool does it last. Both do the same thing; only at different times and most likely with different results.* ~ **Baltasar Gracian 1601-1658**

55. *Don't get sidetracked stomping on ants when you have elephants to feed.* ~ **Peter Turla**

56. *Set priorities for your goals. A major part of successful living lies in the ability to put first things first. Indeed, the reason most major goals are not achieved is that we spend our time doing second things first.* ~ **Robert J. Mckain**

57. *Lost time is never found again.* ~ **French Proverb**

58. *The time for action is now. It's never too late to do something.* ~ **Carl Sandburg**

59. *Time management is an oxymoron. Time is beyond our control, and the clock keeps ticking regardless of how we lead our lives. Priority management is the answer to maximising the time we have.* ~ **John C. Maxwell**

60. *To choose time is to save time.* ~ **Francis Bacon**

61. *You will never find time. If you want time, you must make It.* ~ **Charles Bixton 1823-1871**

62. *Half our life is spent trying to find something to do with the time we have rushed through life trying to save.* ~ **Will Rogers**

63. *Time is what we want most, but what we use the worst.* ~ **William Penn 1644-1718**

64. *We can no more afford to spend major time on minor things than we can to spend minor time on major things.* ~ **Jim Rohn**

65. *Everything requires time. It is the only truly universal condition. All work takes place in time and uses up time. Yet most people take for granted this unique, irreplaceable, and necessary resource. Nothing else, perhaps, distinguishes effective executives as much as their tender loving care of time.* ~ **Peter F. Drucker**

66. *Sometimes you will never know the value of a moment until you have lost it.* ~ **Dr Seuss**

67. *Time is the most valuable in in your life. You and you alone will determine how that coin will be spent. Be careful that it isn't spent on frivolities that bring you nothing.* ~ **Anonymous**

68. *Be mindful of how you approach time. Watching the clock is not the same as watching the sun rise.* ~ **Sophia Bedford-Pierce**

69. *You don't truly have success until you have time to do what matters most.* ~ **Nicole Banders**

70. *Time has a wonderful way of showing everyone what really matters.* ~ **Anonymous**

71. *Time is much more valuable than money. You can always*

*get more money but you cannot get more time. ~ **Jim Rohn***

72. *Any time women come together with a collective intention, it's a powerful thing. Whether it's sitting down making a quilt, in a kitchen preparing a meal, in a club reading the same book, or around the table playing cards, or planning a birthday party, when women come together with a collective intention, magic happens. ~ **Phylicia Rashard***

73. *Yesterday is CANCELLED ~ Check: Tomorrow is a PROMISSORY NOTE. Today is the only cash you have, SO SPEND IT WISELY. ~ **Kay Lyons***

74. *Most of us spent far too much time on what is perceived to be urgent and not enough time on what is really important. ~ **Stephen Covey***

75. *Meticulous planning will enable everything a man does to appear spontaneous. ~ **Mark Caine***

76. *Each time a man stands up for an ideal, or acts to improve the lot of others, or strikes out against injustice, he sends forth a tiny ripple of hope, and crossing each other from a million different centres of energy and daring, those ripples build a current that can sweep down the mightiest walls of oppression and resistance. ~ **Robert Kennedy***

77. *The common man is not concerned about the passage of time, the man of talent is driven by it. ~ Arthur **Schopenhauer 1788 – 1860***

78. The surest way to be late is to have plenty of time in the first place. ~ **Leo Kennedy**

79. The higher your energy level, the more efficient your body. The more efficient your body, the better you feel and the more you will use your talent to produce outstanding results. ~ **Tony Robbins**

80. The first rule of any technology used in a business is that automation applied to an efficient operation will magnify the efficiency. The second is that automation applied to an inefficient operation will also magnify it. ~ **Bill Gates**

23

PERFORMANCE MANAGEMENT

As work environments continue to evolve and develop, team leaders need to find ways to simplify how they manage their greatest asset – their people. The old system of the once or twice yearly interviews was often seen by the team member as hostile and unproductive for numerous reasons and did little to improve the relationship between the team leader and the team member. By using an ongoing method of continual feedback that improves team member skills it ensures the team leader, the team member and the team benefit.

~ Roger Payne ~

1.   *To be a great manager inspire your people to follow YOU, NOT YOUR RULES. ~* **Jeffery Gitomer**

2.   *The test of any organisation is not genius. It is the capacity to make common people achieve uncommon results. ~* **Peter F. Drucker**

3.   *To fear change is to fear being challenged, and to fear a challenge is to fear growth and new possibilities. ~* **Ty Howard**

4.   *Without change there is no innovation, creativity, or incentive to improve. Those who initiate change will have a better opportunity to manage the change, which is inevitable. ~*

William Pollard

5.   *The best method of performance management is to walk up to a team member and tell them how they are doing. It's called on the spot feedback. ~* **Dr Christopher Less**

6.   *The one statement NO team member has ever made, 'WOW! I'm really looking forward to my performance appraisal today.' ~* **Anonymous**

7.   *The most basic problem that performance appraisals don't do is they don't accurately assess and individuals performance. ~* **W. Edwards Deming**

8.   *Just remember the 6 most expensive words in business are 'We've always done it that way.' ~* **Catherine DeVrye**

9.   *The three rules of work: Out of clutter you'll find simplicity. Out of discord you find harmony. In the middle of difficulty lies opportunity. ~* **Alfred Einstein 1879-1955**

10.   *Trust gives you the permission to give people direction, get everyone aligned, and give them the energy to go get the job done. Trust enables you to execute with excellence and produce extraordinary results. As you execute with excellence and deliver on your commitments, trust becomes easier to inspire, creating a flywheel of performance. ~* **Douglas Conant**

11.   *The real secret of performance management is to keep the five guys who hate you away from the four guys who haven't made up their minds. ~* **Casey Stengel**

12. *A BAD MANAGER can take a GOOD TEAM and quickly destroy it, causing the best employees to flee and the remainder to lose all motivation. ~* **Anonymous**

13. *To WIN in the marketplace you must first WIN in the workplace. ~* **Doug Conant**

14. *Whatever you do, do it well, do it so well that when people see you do it they will want to come back and see it again, and they will bring others to see it too. ~* **Walt Disney**

15. *Tell me and I will forget. Show me and I may remember. Involve me and I will understand. ~* **Chinese proverb**

16. *The bad news is that ignoring the performance of people is almost as bad as shredding their effort in front of their eyes....The good news is that by simply looking at something that somebody has done, scanning it and saying 'uh huh,' [you] dramatically improve people's motivations. ~* **Dan Airely**

17. *Yes – The truth is the 'once a year' are brutal and uncompromising. ~* **Stacy Wild**

18. *There is something that is much more scarce, something rarer than ability. It is the ability to recognise ability. ~* **Robert Half**

19. *Managers and Leaders owe it to the organisation and to their fellow workers not to tolerate nonperforming individuals in important jobs. ~* **Peter F Drucker**

20. *Appreciate everything your associates do for the business. Nothing else can quite substitute for a few well chosen, well timed, sincere words of praise like 'Well done', 'Good job' and 'Keep it up! They're absolutely free and worth a fortune.* ~ **Sam Walton**

21, *I consider my ability to arouse enthusiasm among my team the greatest asset I possess. The way to develop the best that is in a person is by appreciation and encouragement.* ~ **Charles Schwab**

22. *I have yet to find a man, however exalted his station, who did not do better work and put forth greater effort under a spirit of approval than under a spirit of criticism.* ~ **Charles Schwab**

23. *One of the most tried and true forms of management is regular feedback.* ~ **Dr Christopher Lee**

24. *It is no use saying, 'We are doing our best.' You have to succeed in doing what is necessary.* ~ **Winston Churchill 1874-1965**

25. *When feedback is included in regular ongoing performance management throughout the year, the employee, the team leader and the organisation are better off.* ~ **Shane Arnold**

26. *To handle yourself, use your head. To handle others, use your heart.* ~ **Eleanor Roosevelt 1884- 1962**

27. *To get better and yield better result for your business,*

*performance management must be a year round process without end. ~ **Tricia Wilson***

29. *PERFORMANCE is a mixture of 'ABILITY' or what you're capable of doing, 'MOTIVATION' is your determination to do it and 'ATTITUDE' is how resolute you are to see it through. ~ **Lou Holtz***

30. *Regular feedback is the best performance management system as it allows the individual the time to alter their performance in line with how their team leader sees it. ~ **Ray Bart***

31. *Teaching is the only major occupation of man for which we have not yet developed tools that make the average person capable of competence and performance. In teaching we rely solely on the 'naturals', the ones who somehow know how to teach. ~ **Peter F Drucker***

32. *The essence of competitiveness is liberated when we make people believe that what they think and do is important – and then get out of their way while they do it. ~ **Jack Walsh***

33. *One of the most effective methods of assessment is regular feedback ~ **Dr Christopher Lee***

34. *An effective leader is also an effective listener. ~ **Artika Tyner***

35. *Leadership consists of nothing but taking responsibility for everything that goes wrong and giving your subordinates credit*

for everything that goes well. ~ **Dwight D. Eisenhower 1890-1969**

36. *Employees engage with employers and brands when they're treated as humans worthy of respect.* ~ **Meghan M. Biro**

37. *Performance Management isn't dead. What is dead is the old way of doing it. The proof in the pudding is the result you get by providing feedback on a regular basis so that the individual can change any bad habits as soon as they are picked up and not wait until the end of the year to be told about them.* ~ *Anita Bowness*

38. *Leadership is LIFTING a person's vision to a higher level, RAISING their performance to a higher standard, the BUILDING of a personality beyond its normal LIMITATIONS.* ~ **Peter F Drucker**

39. *If your actions inspire others to dream more, learn more, do more and become more, you are a leader.* ~ **John Quincy Adams 1767-1848**

40. *I start with the premise that the function of leadership is to produce more leaders, not more followers.* ~ **Ralph Nader**

41. *How far would Moses have gone if he had taken a poll in Egypt?* ~ **Harry S. Truman 1874 1972**

42. *Rank does not confer privilege or give power. It imposes responsibility.* ~ **Peter F Drucker**

43. *The world is a bell curve. Classroom test scores, employee performance in a company all fit neatly across the standard deviations of the famous curve bell.* ~ **Simon Sinek**

44. *The best executive is the one who has sense enough to pick good men to do what he wants done, and self-restraint to keep from meddling with them while they do it.* ~ **Theodore Roosevelt 1858-1919**

45. *Compromise: the art of sharing a pie in such a way that everyone thinks he has the biggest part.* ~ **Ludwig Erhard 1897-1977**

46. *If you are building a culture where honest expectations are communicated and peer accountability is the norm, then the group will address poor performance and attitudes.* ~ **Henry Cloud**

47. *A manager is responsible for the application and performance of knowledge.* ~ **Peter F Drucker**

48. *Leaders must be close enough to relate to others, but far enough ahead to motivate them.* ~ **John C. Maxwell**

49. *Difficult times disrupt your conventional ways of thinking and push you to forge better habits of thought and performance, one of which is to avoid doing performance assessments at the end of the year when you know it has a depressing effect on your employees. Do it as part of ongoing feedback throughout the year. A word here, another there, and watch the change in your team.* ~ **Robin S. Sharma**

50. *The man who starts out going nowhere, generally gets there.* ~ **Dale Carnegie 1888-1955**

51. *All organizations are perfectly designed to get the results they are now getting. If we want different results, we must change the way we do things.* ~ **Tom Northup**

52. *The fundamental task of management is to make people capable of joint performance through common goals, common values, the right structure, and the training and development they need to perform and to respond to change.* ~ **Peter F. Drucker**

53. *When I hear people complaining about how hard life is I always ask them, 'Compared to what?'* ~ **Sydney Justin Harris**

54. *No man will make a great leader who wants to do it all himself, or to get all the credit for doing it.* ~ **Andrew Carnegie 1835-1919**

55. *The leader has to be practical and a realist, yet must talk the language of the visionary and the idealist.* ~ **Eric Hoffer**

56. *The final test of a leader is that he leaves behind him in other men the conviction and the will to carry on.* ~ **Walter Lippmann 1879-1974**

57. *Your number one customers are your people. Look after employees first and then customers last.* ~ **Ian Hutchinson**

58. *We now accept the fact that learning is keeping ahead of change. So our most pressing task is to teach people how to learn.* ~ **Peter F Drucker**

59. *Executives owe it to the organisation and to their fellow workers not to tolerate nonperforming individuals.* ~ **Peter F Drucker**

60. *Good is somebody who delivered and allowed the company to overcome obstacles, without leaving a profound impact on its culture. Great is somebody who leads his company to achievements and performance and value that nobody was expecting it had.* ~ **Carlos Ghosn**

61. *I want to inspire people. I want them to look up to me and say, 'Because of you I didn't give up. I kept at it and succeeded.' Now that's what positive feedback can do!* ~ **Anonymous**

62. *Good leaders make people feel that they're at the very heart of things, not at the periphery. Everyone feels that he or she makes a difference to the success of the organization. When that happens people feel centred and that gives their work meaning.* ~ **Warren G. Bennis**.

63. *Selecting the right people with potential to excel and then developing those people through the coaching and mentoring process to achieve greatness is a primary responsibility of leadership. Effective leaders know precisely when to coach, when to mentor, and when to manage.* ~ **Dr. Rick Johnson**

64. *Performance Management is about human beings. Its task*

is to make people capable of joint performance, to make their strengths effective and their weaknesses irrelevant. ~ **Peter F Drucker**

65. One of the best forms of team member work reviews is to regularly assess the team member and tell them how to improve, then monitor the improvement. ~ **Anonymous**

66. When you take risks you learn that there will be times when you succeed and there will be times when you fail, and both are equally important. ~ **Ellen DeGeneres**

67. The way we measure productivity is flawed. People checking their BlackBerry over dinner is not the measure of productivity. ~ **Timothy Ferriss**

68. The first rule of any technology used in a business is that automation applied to an efficient operation will magnify the efficiency. The second is that automation applied to an inefficient operation will magnify the inefficiency. ~ **Bill Gates**

69. A particular shot or way of moving the ball can be a player's personal signature, but efficiency of performance is what wins the game for the team. ~ **Pat Riley**

70. There is nothing less productive than to make more efficient what should not be done at all. ~ **Peter F Drucker**

71. It is much more difficult to measure none performance than performance. Performance stands out like a ton of diamonds whereas none performance can almost always be

explained away. ~ **Harold Geneen**

72. *When feedback is included as part of ongoing performance discussions throughout the year the employee, the manager and the company are much better off.* ~ **Shauna McNight**

73. *Remember, inspirational quotes are still just quotes. It is the actions you perform after reading them that matter.* ~ **James Doyle**

74. *I would say that IQ is the strongest predictor of which field you can get into and hold a job in, whether you can be an accountant, lawyer, or nurse, for example. But once you are in that field, emotional intelligence emerges as a much stronger predictor of who will be most successful, because it is how we handle ourselves in our relationships that determines how well we do once we are in a given job.* ~ **Daniel Goleman**

75. *Effective leaders are not problem minded; they're opportunity-minded. They feed opportunities and starve problems. They think preventively.* ~ **Peter F Drucker**

76. *There is a good principle that create order, light and man. The is an evil principle that created chaos, darkness and women.* ~ **Pythagoras 557-497 BCE**

77. *A quiet word here and there on performance can bring miraculous results.* ~ **Dr Christopher Lee**

78 *When feedback is included is part of the regular ongoing performance throughout the year, the employee, the manager*

*and the organisation are far better off. ~ **Shawnia McKnight***

79. *Companies need to shift their approach by creating a culture where regular performance feedback are the norm not the exception. ~ **Melany Galant***

80. *One way or another every enterprise is learning and teaching institution. Training and development must be built into it on all levels, training and development that never stops. ~ **Peter F. Drucker***

24

JOB SATISFACTION

Your work is going to fill a large part of your life, and the only way to be truly satisfied is to do what you believe is great work. And the only way to do great work is to love what you do.
~Steve Jobs~

1.   *If it falls your lot to be a street sweeper, go out and sweep streets like Michelangelo painted pictures. Sweep streets like Handel and Beethoven composed music. Sweep streets like Shakespeare wrote poetry. Sweep streets so well that all the hosts of heaven and earth will have to pause and say, here lived a great street sweeper who swept his job well. ~ **Martin Luther King Jnr***

2.   *The secret of joy in work is contained in one word – excellence. To know how to do something really well is to enjoy it. ~ **Pearl S. Buck 1892-1973***

3.   *I have looked in the mirror every morning and asked myself: 'If today were the last day of my life, would I want to do what I am about to do today?' And whenever the answer has been 'No' for too many days in a row, I know I need to change something. ~ **Steve Jobs***

4.   *You can only become truly accomplished at something you*

*love. Don't make money your entire goal. Instead pursue the things you love doing and then do them so well that people can't take their eyes off of you. ~ **Anonymous***

5.   *There comes a time when you ought to start doing what you want. Look for then take a job that you love. You will look forward to getting out of bed in the morning. Personally I think you are out of your mind if you keep taking jobs that you don't like because you think it will look good on your resume. Isn't that a little like saving up sex for your old age? ~ **Warren Buffet***

6.   *Yes, I've made a great deal of dough from my fiction, but I never set a single word down on paper with the thought of being paid for it...I have written because it fulfilled me. Maybe it paid off the mortgage on the house and got the kids through college, but those things were on the side - I did it for the buzz. I did it for the pure joy of the thing. And if you can do it for the joy, you can do it forever. ~ **Stephen King***

7.   *I wanted to write about women and their work, and about valuing the work we, as women, choose to do. Too many women I knew disparaged their work. Many working mothers thought they ought to be home with their children instead, so they carried around too much guilt to enjoy much job satisfaction. ~ **Jennifer Chiaverini***

8.   *The really happy people are those who have broken the chains of procrastination, those who find satisfaction in doing the job at hand. They're full of eagerness, zest, and productivity. You can be, too ~ **Norman Vincent Peale 1898-1993***

9.   *A lot of companies chose to downsize, and maybe that was the right thing for them. We chose a different path. Our belief was that if we kept putting great products in front of customers, they would continue to open their wallets.* ~ **Steve Jobs**

10.   *I think people who are creative are the luckiest people on earth. I know that there are no shortcuts, but you must keep your faith in something greater than YOU, and keep doing what you love. Do what you love, and you will find the way to get it out to the world.* ~ **Judy Collins**

11.   *Pleasure in the job puts perfection in the work.* ~ **Aristotle 384-322 BC**

12.   *The law of work seems unfair, but nothing can change it; the more enjoyment you get out of your work, the more money you will make.* ~ **Mark Twain 1835-1910**

13.   *The people who make it to the top – whether they're musicians, or great chefs, or corporate honchos, are addicted to their calling ... [they] are the ones who'd be doing whatever it is they love, even if they weren't being paid.* ~ **Quincy Jones**

14   *Never continue in a job you don't enjoy. If you're happy in what you're doing, you'll like yourself, you'll have inner peace. And if you have that, along with physical health, you will have had more success than you could possibly have imagined.* ~ **Johnny Carson**

15.   *Job satisfaction often does not come from doing easy work but from the afterglow of satisfaction that comes after the*

achievement of a difficult task that demanded our best. ~ **Theodore Isaac Rubin**

16. The happiest people don't just get the best of everything, they make the best of everything. ~ **Anonymous**

17. For me, as far as playing jazz, no other art form, other than conversation, can give the satisfaction of spontaneous interaction. ~ **Stan Getz**

18. There are countless studies on the negative spill-over of job pressures on family life, but few on how job satisfaction enhances the quality of family life. ~ **Albert Bandera**

19. The only true measure of success is the ration between what we might have been and what we have become ~ **John Maxwell**

20. Odd, the years it took to learn one simple fact: that the prize just ahead, the next job, publication, love affair, marriage always seemed to hold the key to satisfaction but never, in the longer run, sufficed. ~ **Carolyn Gold Heilbrun**

21. One third of managers are victims of 'Information Fatigue Syndrome.' 49 % said they are unable to handle the vast amounts of information received. 33 % were suffering ill health as a direct result of information overload. 62 % admitted their business and social relationships had suffered because of it. 66 % reported tension with colleagues and diminished job satisfaction. 43 % think that important decisions are delayed and their abilities to make decisions are affected as a result of

having too much information. 86 % of the above didn't think that any of the above would change in the near future if at all. ~ **Jeff Davidson**

22. *I can't see myself leaving the club I grew up supporting....it's one of those things, the money's great but I still get paid reasonably well from the Lions and at the end of the day I think job satisfaction is the No.1 priority and I just love it up here. ~* **Jonathan Brown**

23. *Finish each day and be done with it. You have done what you could; some blunders and absurdities have crept in; forget them as soon as you can. Tomorrow is a new day; you shall begin it serenely and with too high a spirit to be encumbered with your old nonsense. ~* **Ralph Waldo Emerson 1803-1802**

24. *What is the recipe for successful achievement? To my mind there are just four essential ingredients: Choose a career you love, give it the best there is in you, seize your opportunities, and be a member of the team. ~* **Benjamin F Fairness 1890-1962**

25. *The only way to be truly satisfied is to do what you believe is truly great work. The only way to do truly great work is to love what you do. ~* **Steve Jobs**

26. *Work is love made visible. And if you can't work with love but only with distaste, it is better that you should leave your work and sit at the gate of the temple and take alms of the people who work with joy. ~* **Kihlil Gibran**

27. *Desire! That's the one secret of every man's career. Not education. Not being born with hidden talents, Desire.* ~ **Bobby Unser**

28. *Productivity and creativity are the true sources of personal workplace satisfaction. Freedom not dependency, provides the environment to achieve these goals.* ~ **Ron Paul**

29. *Happiness does not come from doing easy work but from the afterglow of satisfaction after the achievement for doing something extremely hard that demanded our best.* ~ **Theodore Isaac Rubin**

30. *Nowadays true job satisfaction and happiness should be about fulfilling your full potential, tapping into your own creativity and feeling that you make a difference.* ~ **Chris Humphries**

31. *In life you should 'own your personal satisfaction'. It is better than success because your success is measured by others, whereas satisfaction can only be measured by you.* *~Anonymous*

32. *Life is short, work where you're continuously accepted, respected, appreciated, encouraged, inspired, empowered and valued. If you're not then you're like 84% of the workforce.* ~ **Ty Howard**

33. *No person can be a truly great leader unless they take genuine joy of the success of those under them.* ~ **Anonymous**

34. *Pleasure in the job always puts satisfaction in the work.* ~ **Aristotle 284-322 BC**

35. *Without your enthusiasm for what you do your team will forget what you said, they will forget what you did, but it's unlikely they will ever forget how you made them feel.* ~ **Anonymous**

36. *Plenty of men can do good work for a spurt with immediate promotion in mind, but for promotion you want a man in whom good work has become a habit.* ~ **Henry L Doherty 1870-1939**

37. *The reward for having something well done is having done it.* ~ **Ralph Waldo Emerson 1803- 1882**

38. *Every job is a self-portrait of the person who does it. Either do a Michelangelo or a picture by numbers, the choice is yours.* ~ **Anonymous**

39. *You can only become truly accomplished at something you love. Don't make money your goal. Instead pursue the things you love doing and then do them so well that people can't take their eyes off of you.* ~ **Maya Angelou**

40. *Greed is a bottomless pit which exhausts the person in an endless effort to satisfy the need without ever reaching satisfaction.* ~ **Erich Fromm**

41. *The secret of joy in work is contained in one word – excellence. To know how to do something well is to enjoy it.* ~ **Pearl S. Buck**

42. *Dreams can come true, but there is a secret. They're realized through the magic of persistence, determination, commitment, passion, practice, focus and hard work. They happen a step at a time, manifested over years, not weeks ~* **Elbert Hubbard 1856-1915**

43. *Traditional employee engagement is still extremely important today, but it is much better when you are able to add social tools that will allow them collaborate, share and innovate. ~* **Anonymous**

44. *Satisfaction and happiness does not come from doing easy work. It comes after the achievement of a difficult task that demanded our best ~* **Theodore Isaac Rubin**

45. *Nowadays true job satisfaction and happiness is about fulfilling your full potential, tapping into your own creativity and feeling that you can make a difference. ~* **Chris Humphries**

46. *A job is not just a job anymore. It is who you are. And if you want to change who you are you have to change what you do. ~* **Anonymous**

47. *Learn to work the discomfort of discipline into the satisfaction of personal growth. ~* **Anthony Robbins**

48. *Desire! That's the one secret of every man's career. Not education. Not being born with hidden talents. Desire. ~* **Bobby Unser**

49. *I think everyone should experience defeat at least once during their career. You learn a lot from it. ~* **Lou Holtz**

50. *Only undertake what you can do in an excellent fashion. There are no prizes for average performance.* ~ **Brian Tracy**

51. *I have enjoyed great satisfaction from my climb of Everest and my trips to the poles. But there's no doubt that my most worthwhile things have been the building of schools and medical clinics.* ~ **Sir Edmund Hillary**

52. *Each of the professions means a prejudice. The necessity for a career forces everyone to take sides. We live in the age of the overworked, and the undereducated; the age in which people are so industrious that they become absolutely stupid.* ~ **Oscar Wilde 1854-1900**

53. *The biggest mistake that you can make is to believe that you are working for somebody else. Job security is gone. The driving force of a career must come from the individual. Remember: Jobs are owned by the company, you own your career!* ~ **Earl Nightingale**

54. *Nowadays job satisfaction and happiness is all about fulfilling your full potential, tapping into your own creativity and feeling that you make a difference.* ~ **Chris Humphries**

55. *Challenge is the pathway to engagement and progress in our lives. But not all challenges are created equal. Some challenges make us feel alive, engaged, connected, and fulfilled. Others simply overwhelm us. Knowing the difference as you set bigger and bolder challenges for yourself is critical to your sanity, success, and satisfaction.* ~ **Brendon Burchard**

56. *The ultimate victory in competition is derived from the inner satisfaction of knowing that you have done your best and that you have gotten the most out of what you had to give.* **~ Howard Cosell**

57. *Love your work, but never love the company you work for because you never know when it will stop loving you.* ~ ***Anonymous***

58. *Don't just work for the money because that only brings limited satisfaction ~***Ian Rowley***

59 *If you wish to achieve worthwhile things in your personal and career life, you must become a worthwhile person in your own self-development.* ~ **Brian Tracy**

60. *Nothing worthwhile comes easily. Work, continuous work and hard work, is the only way to accomplish results that last.* **~ Hamilton Holt 1872-1951**

61. *When defeat comes, accept it as a signal that your plans are not sound, rebuild those plans, and set sail once more toward your coveted goal.* ~ **Napoleon Hill 1883-1970**

62. *Our real problem is not our strength today; it is rather the vital necessity of action today to ensure our strength tomorrow.* **~ Calvin Coolidge 1872-1933**

63. *Only undertake what you can do in an excellent fashion. There are no prizes for average performance.* ~ **Brian Tracy**

64. *You got to like your work. You have got to like what you are doing, you have got to be doing something worthwhile so you can like it - because it is worthwhile, that it makes a difference, don't you see? ~ **Harland Saunders 1890-1980 (Mr KFC)***

65. *We know where most of the creativity, the innovation, the stuff that drives productivity lies - in the minds of those closest to the work. ~ **Jack Welsh***

66. *Analysing what you haven't got as well as what you have got is a necessary ingredient of a career. ~ **Orison Swett Marden 1848-1924***

67. *Are you bored with life? Then throw yourself into some work you believe in with all you heart, live for it, die for it, and you will find happiness that you had thought could never be yours. ~ **Dale Carnegie 1888-1955***

68. *Don't set compensation as a goal. Find work you like, and the compensation will follow. ~ **Harding Lawrence***

69. *The highest reward for a person's toil is not what they get for it, but what they become by it. ~ **John Ruskin 1819-1900***

70. *Great work is done by people who are not afraid to be great. ~ **Fernando Flores***

71. *Everyone enjoys doing the kind of work for which he is best suited ~ **Napoleon Hill 1883-1970***

72.   *In order that people may be happy in their work, these three things are needed: They must be fit for it: They must not do too much of it: And they must have a sense of success in it.* ~ **John Ruskin 1819-1900**

73.   *When you feel good about yourself you generally feel good about your work.* ~ **Anonymous**

74.   *Don't be afraid to give your best to what seemingly are small jobs. Every time you conquer one it makes you that much stronger. If you do the little jobs well, the big ones will tend to take care of themselves.* ~ **William Patten 1510-1598**

75.   *You don't have to change that much for it to make a great deal of difference. A few simple disciplines can have a major impact on how your life works out in the next 90 days, let alone in the next 12 months or the next 3 years.* ~ **Jim Rohn**

76.   *Love your job, but never fall in love with your company because you never know when it stops loving you.* ~ **Anonymous**

77.   *Nothing is really work unless you would much rather be doing something else.* ~ **James M. Barry 1860-1937**

78.   *Your profession is not what brings home your wealth. Your profession is what you were put on earth to do with such passion and such intensity that it becomes spiritual in calling.* ~ **Vincent Van Gogh 1953-1890**

79.   *Every man's work, whether it be literature or music or*

pictures or architecture or anything else, is always a portrait of himself. ~ **Elbert Hubbard 1856-1915**

80. *Judging by informal observation, most young people burn up their spare time buffing their emotional IQ and self-esteem with social media and non-stop texting. That's great for eye-thumb coordination, but what about the satisfaction of actually making something in a career that also makes money?* ~ **Seth Shostak**

25

APPLYING YOUR KNOWLEDGE
AND SKILLS

The function of any form of education should be to teach one to think, and to think critically. Intelligence plus character - that is the goal of true education at any level, but if you don't apply what you learn then learning loses most of its value. This is not to say that unapplied knowledge is useless. Some people get immense enjoyment out of learning for learnings sake. There is also the benefit of exercising your brain to increase its ability to absorb new information. On the whole, however, a huge proportion of the value of learning comes from applying what you've learned.

As the saying goes: Learning can be the most brutal of teachers. But you learn, by God do you learn ~ **C.S. Lewis 1898-1963**

1.   *The great Breakthrough in your life comes when you realize it that you can learn anything you need to learn to accomplish any goal that you set for yourself. This means there are no limits on what you can be, have or do. ~ **Andre Moreau***

2.   *To the man who only has a hammer, everything he encounters begins to look like a nail. ~ **Abraham Maslow***

3. *Perfection is achieved, not when there is nothing more to add, but when there is nothing left to take away.* ~ **Antoine de Saint Exupéry**

4. *Don't mistake silence for weakness. Smart people don't plan big out loud.* ~ **Anonymous**

5. *Anybody can become angry, that is easy, but to be angry with the right person and to the right degree and at the right time and for the right purpose and in the right way, that is not within everybody's power, AND IS NOT EASY.* ~ **Aristotle 384-322 BC**

6. *The test of a first rate intelligence is the ability to hold to opposing arguments in the mind at the same time and still retain the ability to function.* ~ **F. Scott Fitzgerald 1895-1940**

7. *Knowing others is intelligence: Knowing yourself is true wisdom. Mastering others is strength; mastering yourself is true power.* ~ **Lao Tzu 604-531 BC**

8. *Wise men have always found violent opposition from mediocrities. The later cannot understand it when a man does not thoughtlessly submit to hereditary prejudices, but honestly and courageously uses his intelligence and fulfils the duty to express the results of his thought in clear form.* ~ **Albert Einstein 1871-1955**

9. *One job of the unconscious is to act as a workshop for rough shaping ideas; crafting notions as new parts or tools become available; storing observations until something*

relevant appears in the landscape generally soaking, simmering, and incubating ideas. Gradually, while combing through its inventory, it finds bits and pieces that create a pattern. And when it slips knowledge of that pattern to the conscious mind, it's a surprise, like a telegram slid under the door. ~ **Diane Ackerman**

10. We are what we repeatedly do; excellence, then, is not an act but a habit. ~ **Aristotle 384-322 BC**

11. A wise man gets more use from his enemies than a fool from his friends. ~ **Baltasar Gracian 1601-1658**

12. There is no such thing as a great talent without great will power. ~ **Honore de Blalzac 1799-1850**

13. The measure of intelligence is your ability to change. ~ **Albert Einstein 1879-1955**

14. Can you avoid knowledge? You cannot! Can you avoid technology? You cannot! Things are going to go ahead in spite of ethics, in spite of your personal beliefs, in spite of everything. ~ **Jose M. R. Delgado**

15. Intelligence without ambition is a bird without wings. ~ **Salvador Dali**

16. Remember to watch your thoughts lest they become words. Watch your words; lest they become actions. Watch your actions; lest they become habits. Watch your habits; lest they become your character. Watch your character; lest it becomes

*your destiny. ~ **Lao Tze 605-531 BC***

17. *If you want to be more powerful in life then educate yourself. It's that simple. ~ **Anonymous***

18. *What we think, or what we know, or what we believe is, in the end of little consequence. The only consequence is what we learn and do with it. ~ **John Ruskin 1819-1900***

19. *The real voyage of discovery consists not in seeking new lands but seeing with new eyes. ~ **Marcel Proust 1871-1922***

20. *The best gift you can have is intelligence. If you know how to use it properly it opens doors for you that would otherwise remained shut. ~ **Anonymous***

21. *Try a thing you haven't done three times. Once to get over the fear of doing it twice to learn how to do it, do it a third time to figure out whether you like it or not. ~ **Virgil Garnett Thomson 1896-1989***

22. *There is far greater peril in buying knowledge than in buying meat and drink: the one you purchase of the wholesale or retail dealer, and carry them away in other vessels, and before you receive them into the body as food, you may deposit them at home and call in any experienced friend who knows what is good to be eaten or drunken, and what not, and how much, and when; and hence the danger of purchasing them is not so great. But when you buy the wares of knowledge you cannot carry them away in another vessel; they have been sold to you, and you must take them into the soul and go your way, either greatly*

harmed or greatly benefited by the lesson. ~ **Plato 428-348 BCE**

23. *The true sign of intelligence is not just knowledge but imagination and an enquiring mind.* ~ **Albert Einstein 1879-1955**

24. *We may be masters of our own thoughts, still we are the slaves of our own emotions.* ~ **Anonymous**

25. *In a global economy where the most valuable skill you can sell is your knowledge, a good education is no longer just a pathway to opportunity – it is a pre-requisite.* ~ **Barack Obama**

26. *Merely having an open mind is nothing; the object of opening the mind is like opening your mouth, know when to shut it again on something solid.* ~ **Gilbert Keith Chesterton 1874-1936**

27. *Some people say that artificial intelligence will make us feel inferior. But then anyone in their right mind will have an inferior complex every time they look at a flower.* ~ **Alan Kay**

28. *The highest form of intelligence is to observe yourself without judgement.* ~ **Jiddu Krishnamurti 1895-1986**

29. *Every lesson has its cost and it is always costlier when the lesson is not learned, for it will be repeated again at a higher cost.* ~ **Jensen Slaw**

30. *Go deeper past thoughts into silence, past silence into stillness, past stillness into the heart and love, passed the heart*

into the soul where you dream and wander and contemplate your life and what you want to do with it. ~ **Anonymous**

31.   *Great minds discuss ideas. Average minds discuss events. Small minds discuss people.* ~ **Eleanor Roosevelt 1884-1962**

32.   *The intelligence of that creature known as a crowd is the square root of the number of people in it.* ~ **Terry Pratchett**

33.   *Talent hits a target no one else can hit: genius is a target no one else can see.* ~ **Arthur Schopenhauer 1788-1860**

34.   *Knowledge is indivisible. When people grow wise in one direction, they are sure to make it easier for themselves to grow wise in other directions as well. On the other hand, when they split up knowledge, concentrate on their own field, and scorn and ignore other fields, they grow less wise -- even in their own field.* ~ **Isaac Asimov**

35.   *If the lessons of history teach us anything it is that nobody learns the lessons that history teaches us.* ~ **Anonymous**

36.   *The measure of intelligence is the ability to change.* ~ **Albert Einstein 1879-1955**

37.   *'How do you know so much about everything?' was asked of a very wise and intelligent man; and the answer was 'By never being afraid or ashamed to ask questions as to anything of which I was ignorant.'* ~ **John Abbott**

38.   *Knowledge is having the right answer. Intelligence is asking*

*the right question. ~ **Anonymous***

39. *I ain't one of those who believe that a half knowledge of a subject is useless, but it has been my experience that when a fellow has that half knowledge he finds it's the other half which would really come in handy. ~ **George Horace Lorimer 1867-1937***

40. *Great minds discuss ideas; Average minds discuss events; Small minds discuss people. ~ **Eleanor Roosevelt 1884-1962***

41. *Grades do not measure intelligence just the same as age doesn't measure maturity. ~ **Anonymous***

42. *The person who reads too much and uses his brain too little will fall into lazy habits of thinking but not doing. ~ **Albert Einstein 1879-1955***

43. *The world is a beautiful book, but is of little use to him that cannot read. ~ **Goldoni 1707-1793***

44. *It is the mark of an educated mind to be able to entertain a thought without accepting it. ~ **Aristotle 384-322 BC***

45. *Be smarter than other people, just don't tell them so. ~ **H. Jackson Brown***

46. *Being intelligent is not raising your voice but improving your argument. ~ **Anonymous***

47. *We learn something every day, and lots of times we find out*

that what we learned the day before was wrong. ~ **Bill Vaughan**

48. *Just the fact that some geniuses were laughed at does not imply that all who are laughed at are geniuses. They laughed at Columbus, they laughed at Fulton, they laughed at the Wright brothers. But they also laughed at Bozo the Clown.* ~ **Carl Sagan**

49. *Don't ever wrestle with a pig. You'll both get dirty, but only the pig will enjoy it.* ~ **Cale Yarborough**

50. *The average mind is happy because it can think. The above average mind is happy because it can continually think.* ~ **A. A. Milne 1882-1965**

51. *Granny Weatherwax smiled, "So you wanted magic. Watch." She put her hand into the struggling mass of bees and made a faint shrill piping noise at the back of her throat. There was a movement in the mass and a large bee, longer and fatter than the others, crawled onto on her hand. A few workers followed, stroking it and generally ministering to it.*
    "How did you do that?" said young Esk.
    "Ah," said Granny, "wouldn't you like to know."
    "Yes, I would. That's why I asked, Granny," said Esk severely.
    "Do you think I used magic?"
    Esk looked down at the queen bee, then up at the witch. "No, I think you just know a lot about bees."
    Granny grinned.
    "Exactly correct, that's one form of magic of course."
    "What, just knowing things?"
    "Knowing things that other people don't know," said

Granny. She carefully dropped the queen bee back among her subjects and closed the lid of the hive. ~ **Equal Rites**

52. Intelligence is like underwear. It's important that you have it but not necessary that you show it off. ~ **Anonymous**

53. As our circle of knowledge expands, so does the circumference of darkness surrounding it. ~ **Albert Einstein 1879-1955**

54. For you to insult me I must first value your opinion. ~ **Ann Bradley**

55. Thinking is probably the hardest work there is, which is why so few people engage in it. ~ **Henry Ford 1863-1947**

56. The true sign of intelligence is not knowledge but imagination. The function of education is to teach one to think intensively and to think critically. Intelligence plus character that is the goal of true education. The difference between stupidity and genius is that genius has its limits. ~ **Albert Einstein 1879-1955**

57. Genius is knowing to stay silent as others demonstrate their ignorance. ~ **Eric Lau**

58. I would much rather have people think I'm stupid, and shock them, than have people think I'm smart, and disappoint them. ~ **Mike Bronson**

59. I believe that imagination is stronger than knowledge. That myth is more potent than history. That dreams are more powerful than facts. That hope always triumphs over experience. That laughter is the only cure for grief. And I believe that love is stronger than death ~ **Robert Fulghum**

60. *Be a lifelong student. The more you learn, the more you earn and more self-confidence you will have.* ~ **Brian Tracy**

61. *If an Australian Aborigine drafted an I.Q. test, all of Western civilization would presumably flunk it.* ~ **Stanley Garn**

62. *Ignorance may be bliss, but it certainly is not freedom, except in the minds of those who prefer darkness to light and chains to liberty. The more true information we can acquire, the better for our enfranchisement.* ~ **Robert Hugh Benson 1871-1914**

63. *To certain people a man of intelligence is a more awkward customer than the most avowed rogue.* ~ **Georg Christoph Lichtenberg 1741-1799**

64. *Nourish the mind like you would your body for the mind cannot survive on junk food.* ~ **Jim Rohn**

65. *Eventually you realize that if you're going to talk sense, you're going to antagonize its opponents.* ~ **Robert Brault**

66. *Everyone is ignorant only on different subjects.* ~ **Will Rogers 1879-1935**

67. *Common sense is a flower that does not grow in everyone's garden.* ~ **Anonymous**

68. *The hunger and thirst for knowledge, the keen delight in the chase, the good humoured willingness to admit that the scent was false, the eager desire to get on with the work, the cheerful resolution to go back and begin again, the broad good sense, the unaffected modesty, the imperturbable temper, the gratitude for any little help that was given - all these will remain in my memory though I cannot paint them for others.* ~ **Frederic William Maitland**

69. *Be smarter than other people, just don't tell them so.* ~ **H. Jackson Brown**

70. *Carry out a random act of kindness, with no expectation of reward, safe in the knowledge that one day someone might do the same for you.* ~ **Princess Diana**

71. *Your intelligence is measured by those around you; if you spend your days with idiots you seal your own fate.* ~ **Mary M. Illigassch**

72. *There is no greater evidence of superior intelligence than to be surprised at nothing.* ~ **Josh Billings**

73. *Men are more readily contented with no intellectual light than with a little; and wherever they have been taught to acquire some knowledge in order to please others, they have most generally gone on to acquire more, to please themselves.* ~ **Charles Caleb Coulton 1718-1882**

74. *The sign of an intelligent people is their ability to control emotions by the application of reason.* ~ **Marya Manne**

75. *It's hard to convince a fool that his idea is foolish.* ~ **Anonymous**

76. *Everybody is potentially a genius. But if you judge a fish by its ability to climb a tree, it will spend its whole life thinking it's stupid.* ~ **Albert Einstein 1879-1955**

77. *Continuous effort - not strength or intelligence - is the key to unlocking our potential.* ~ **Winston Churchill 1874-1975**

78 *By the way, intelligence to me isn't just being book-smart or having a college degree; it's trusting your gut instincts, being intuitive, thinking outside the box, and sometimes just realizing that things need to change and being smart enough to change it.* ~ **Tabitha Coffey**

79. *Talent hits a target no one else can hit; Genius hits a target no one else can see.* ~ **Arthur Schopenhauer 1788-1860**

80. *A smart man makes a mistake, learns from it, and never makes that mistake again. But a wise man finds a smart man and learns from him how to avoid the mistake altogether.* ~ **Roy H. Williams**

26

SELF CONFIDENCE AND SELF ESTEEM

Self-confidence is the belief in oneself and your abilities and is often used interchangeably with self-esteem, but although there is an over-lap there are also a subtle difference. Self-confidence can refer to how we feel about ourselves and our abilities, whereas self-esteem refers directly to whether or not we acknowledge and value ourselves. A healthy amount of self-liking and self-approval is necessary if we are to have the confidence to meet life's challenges and participate in a social and working environment. In a sense, one could say that having healthy self-esteem leads to being self-confident.
~ Alan Butterly ~

1.   *Trust me when I say that most of the changes I've brought in my life have been sparked by reading some sort of quote. When life seems complicated, sometimes all you need is a different vantage point to look at things differently and a quote lets you do that. A quote lets you look through the eyes of another person, and gives you the opportunity to see their perspective. It allows you to see what they might have learnt in a lifetime, almost instantly. ~ **Alison R.***

2.   *Confidence is at the root of so many attractive human qualities. A sense of humour, a sense of style, a willingness to be who you are regardless what anyone else might say or think.*

~ **Wentworth Miller**

3.   *Confidence is preparation. Everything else is beyond your control.* ~ **Richard Kline**

4.   *If things start happening, don't worry, don't stew, just go right along and you'll start happening too.* ~ **Dr Seuss**

5.   *The more you love the decisions you make the less you need others to love them.* ~ **Anonymous**

6.   *What you think of YOURSELF is far more important than what other people think of you.* ~ **Anonymous**

7.   *We have to learn to be our own best friends because we fall too easily into the trap of being our own worst enemies.* ~ **Roderick Thorp**

8.   *The way to develop self-confidence is to do the thing you fear and get a record of successful experiences behind you.* ~ **William Jennings Bryant 1860-1925**

9.   *If what you see through your eyes do not make you happy, then close your eyes and see through your soul, because your soul can judge your intelligence and feel your beauty and love where the eyes are blinded by the light.* ~ **Anonymous**

10. *It's not what you are that holds you back, it's what you think you are not.* ~ **Anonymous**

11. *Wouldn't it be powerful if you fell in love with yourself so*

deeply that you would do just about anything if you knew it would make you happy? This is precisely how much life loves you and wants you to nurture yourself. The deeper you love yourself, the more the universe will affirm your worth. Then you can enjoy a lifelong love affair that brings you the richest fulfilment from inside out. ~ **Alan Cohen**

12. *Don't wait until everything is just right. It will never be perfect. There will always be challenges, obstacles, and less than perfect conditions. So what? Get started now. With each step you take, you will grow stronger and stronger, more and more skilled, more and more self-confident, and more and more successful.* ~ **Mark Victor Hansen**

13. *Well, we all know that self-esteem comes from what you think of you, not what other people think of you* ~ **Gloria Gaynor**

14. *When you look in the mirror of life, be comfortable and happy knowing that whoever is in your skin can triumph over anything you want. You can take the lows and turn them into highs regardless what life throws at you. That's what having self-esteem and self-confidence really means, nothing more, nothing less.* ~ **Thomas Curtis Clark**

15. *Low self-confidence and low self-esteem isn't a life sentence. With patience and practice you can turn them around so that you become confident and have high self-esteem. Once you master them, everything in your life will change for the better.* ~ **Barrie Davenport**

16. *Once we believe in ourselves, we can risk curiosity, wonder, spontaneous delight, or any experience that reveals the human spirit. ~* **E.E. Cummings 1848-1962**

17. *The more you work at being your real self the more likely you'll feel purposeful and significant in your life. ~* **Wayne W. Dyer**

18. *Self-confidence and self-esteem are the root of so many truly attractive qualities, a sense of humour, a sense of style, a willingness to be who you are no matter what anyone might think or say.... ~* **Wentworth Miller**

19. *When you know who you are, when your mission in life is clear, and you burn with the inner fire of unbreakable will. No cold can touch your heart. No Deluge can dampen your purpose and you know you are alive. ~* **Chief Seattle Duwamish 1789-1866**

20. *It is confidence in our bodies, minds, and spirits that allows us to keep looking for new adventures. ~* **Oprah Winfrey**

21. *Because one believes in oneself, one doesn't try to convince others. Because one is content with oneself, one doesn't need others' approval. Because one accepts oneself, the whole world accepts him or her. ~* **Lao Tzu 604-531 BC**

22. *The moment you doubt whether you can fly you cease forever to be able to do it. ~* **J.M. Barrie 1860-1937**

23. *Trust yourself and put that doubt behind you where it*

belongs. You can step out with a head held high in the air and overcome anything you want. ~ **Dr. Benjamin Spock**

24. A man cannot be comfortable without his own approval. ~ **Mark Twain 1835-1910**

25. Successful people have fear, successful people have doubts, and successful people have worries. They just don't let these feelings stop them. ~ **T. Harvey Eker**

26. You can have anything you want if you are willing to give up the belief that you can't have it. ~ **Dr. Robert Anthony**

27. To love oneself is the beginning of a lifelong romance. ~ **Oscar Wilde 1854-1900**

28. One of the greatest pleasures in life is doing things others said you cannot do. ~ **Anonymous**

29. Real beauty isn't about having a pretty face and an hour glass figure. It's about having a wonderful mind, a caring heart and most importantly, a compassionate soul. ~ **Anonymous**

30. Confidence is a habit that can be developed by acting as if you already had the confidence you desire to have. ~ **Brian Tracy**

31. Inaction breeds doubt and fear. Action breeds confidence and courage. If you want to conquer fear, do not sit home and think about it. Go out and get busy doing the things you always wanted to do. ~ **Dale Carnegie 1888-1956**

32. *You cannot be lonely if you like the person you're alone with. ~ **Wayne Dyer***

33. *Nothing can stop the man with the right mental attitude from achieving his goal; nothing on earth can help the man with the wrong mental attitude. ~ **Thomas Jefferson 1743-1826***

34. *Always remember you are braver than you believe, stronger than you seem, and smarter than you think. ~ **Christopher Robin written by AA Milne 1852-1956***

35. *If you are insecure, guess what? The rest of the world is, too. Do not overestimate the competition and underestimate yourself. You are better than you think. ~ **T. Harvey Eker***

36. *Speak boldly and with intellect. Never hush your voice for someone's comfort. Speak your mind and make other people feel uncomfortable. ~ **Jim Robins***

37. *Build your self-esteem by recalling all the ways you have succeeded, and your brain will be filled with images of you making your achievements happen again and again. Give yourself permission to toot your own horn, and don't wait for anyone to praise you. ~ **Jack Canfield***

38. *Persons of high self-esteem are not driven to make themselves superior to others; they do not seek to prove their value by measuring themselves against a comparative standard. Their joy is being who they are, not being better than someone else. ~ **Nathaniel Brandon***

39. *Aerodynamically the bumblebee shouldn't be able to fly, but the bumblebee doesn't know this so it goes on flying anyway.* ~ **Mary K Ash**

40. *Self-confidence doesn't come when you have all the answers. It comes when you are confident enough to face all the questions.* ~ **Anonymous**

41. *If you're presenting yourself with confidence, you can pull off pretty much anything.* ~ **Katy Perry**

42. *One of the greatest challenges in life is being yourself in a world that is trying to make you like everyone else.* ~ **Anonymous**

43. *When you take risks you learn that there will be times when you succeed and there will be times when you fail, and both are equally important.* ~ **Ellen DeGeneres**

44. *Attract what you expect, reflect what you desire, become what you respect, and mirror what you wish for.* ~ **Anonymous**

45. *Whether you think you can or you think you can't, you're right. Your perception of who you really are counts, don't get it wrong.* ~ **Anonymous**

46. *Don't waste your energy trying to change other people's opinions.....do your thing, and don't care if they like It.* ~ **Tina Fey**

47. *When everything seems to be going against you, remember that the airplane takes off against the wind, not with It.* ~ **Henry Ford 1863-1947**

48. *I don't have an extraordinary degree of self-confidence, but I know the gift I have been given from God and I try to share it with as many people as possible. Having a great voice is not a merit unless you use it properly.* ~ **Andrea Bocelli**

49. *Trust yourself. Create the kind of self that you will be happy to live with all your life. Make the most of yourself by fanning the tiny, inner sparks of possibility into flames of achievement.* ~ **Golda Meir 1898-1978**

50. *You either walk inside your story and own it, or you stand outside your story and hustle for your worthiness.* ~ **Brene Brown**

51. *Being CHALLENGED in life is inevitable, being DEFEATED is optional.* ~ **Anonymous**

52. *If you hear a voice within you say 'you cannot paint,' then by all means paint, and that will voice be silenced.* ~ **Vincent Van Gogh 1853-1890**

53. *Don't wait until everything is just right. It will never be perfect. There will always be challenges, obstacles, and less than perfect conditions. So what? Get started now. With each step you take, you will grow stronger and stronger, more and more skilled, more and more self-confident, and more and more successful.* ~ **Mark Victor Hansen**

54. *When you adopt the viewpoint that there is nothing that exists that is not part of you, that there is no one who exists who is not part of you, that any judgment you make is self-judgment, that any criticism you level is self-criticism, you will wisely extend to yourself an unconditional love that will be the light of the world.* ~ **Harry Palmer**

55. *Every man knows well enough that he is a unique being, only once on this earth; and by no extraordinary chance will such a marvellously picturesque piece of diversity in unity as he is, ever be put together a second time.* ~ **Friedrich Wilhelm Nietzsche 1844-1900**

56. *I've spent most of my life in a prison without bars. I was a prisoner of my fear and my low self-esteem.* ~ **Gerry Coone**

57. *Far away there in the sunshine are my highest aspirations. I may not reach them, but I can look up and see their beauty, believe in them, and try to follow where they lead.* ~ **Louisa May Alcott 1832-1888**

58. *Just think: If I want to be free, I got to be me. Not the me I think you think I should be. Not the me I think my wife thinks I should be. Not the me I think my children think I should be. If I want to be free, I got to be me. If I am not for myself, who will be?* ~ **Pirke Avoth**

59. *Self-pity gets you nowhere. One must have the adventurous daring to accept oneself as a bundle of possibilities and undertake the most interesting game in the world making the*

most of one's best. ~ **Harry Emerson Fosdick 1878-1964**

60. *If only you could sense how important you are to the lives of those you meet; how important you can be to people you may never even dream of. There is something of yourself that you leave at every meeting with another person.* ~ **Fred Rogers**

61. *People are like stained glass windows. They sparkle and shine when the sun is out, but when the darkness sets in their true beauty is revealed only if there is light from within.* ~ **Elisabeth Kubler-Ross**

62. *I think that the power is the principle. The principle of moving forward, as though you have the confidence to move forward, eventually gives you confidence when you look back and see what you've done.* ~ **Robert Downey, Jr.**

63. *You cannot be lonely if you like the person you're alone with.* ~ **Wayne Dyer**

64. *It is not the mountain we conquer, but ourselves.* ~ **Sir Edmund Hillary**

65. *A healthy self-love means we have no compulsion to justify to ourselves or others why we take vacations, why we sleep late, why we buy new shoes, why we spoil ourselves from time to time. We feel comfortable doing things which add quality and beauty to life.* ~ **Andrew Matthews**

66. *Intelligent people tend to have less friends than the average person. The smarter you are the more selective you become.* ~

Nikola Tesla

67. *Grades don't measure intelligence, they measure obedience.* ~ **Anonymous**

68. *Our self-respect tracks our choices. Every time we act in harmony with our authentic self and our heart, we earn our respect. It is that simple. Every choice matters.* ~ **Dan Coppersmith**

69. *Don't rely on someone else for your happiness and self-worth. Only you can be responsible for that. If you can't love and respect yourself – no one else will be able to make that happen. Accept who you are – completely; the good and the bad – and make changes as YOU see fit – not because you think someone else wants you to be different.* ~ **Stacey Charter**

70. *Opinion is the lowest form of human knowledge, while empathy is the highest.* ~ **Anonymous**

71. *It is the mark of an educated mind to be able to entertain a thought without accepting it* ~ **Aristotle 384 BC-322 BC**

72. *Nothing builds self-esteem and self-confidence like accomplishment.* ~ **Thomas Carlyle 1795-1891**

73. *With realization of one's own potential and self-confidence in one's ability, one can build a better world.* ~ **Dalai Lama**

74. *As a father, my first priority is to help my sons set and attain personal goals so they will develop self-confidence and*

individual strength. Engaging in regular fitness activities with my children helps me fulfil those responsibilities. ~ **Alan Thicke**

75. *Lucid dreaming has considerable potential for promoting personal growth and self-development, enhancing self-confidence, improving mental and physical health, facilitating creative problem solving and helping you to progress on the path to self-mastery.* ~ **Stephen LaBerge**

76. *There can be no failure to a man who has not lost his courage, his character, his self-respect, or his self-confidence. He is still a King.* ~ **Orison Swett Marden 1848-1924**

77. *The way to develop self-confidence is to do the thing you fear and get a record of successful experiences behind you.* ~ **William Jennings Bryan 1860-1925**

78. *You are as young as your self-confidence, as old as your fears; as young as your hope, as old as your despair.* ~ **Samuel Ullman 1840-1924**

79. *It is only necessary to have courage, for strength without self-confidence is useless.* ~ **Giacomo Casanova 1725-1798**

80. *Don't ask yourself what the world needs, ask yourself what makes you come alive. And then go and do that. Because what the world needs is people who have come alive.* ~ **Howard Washington Thurman 1899-1981**

27
BEING A SELF STARTER

You grow most in your areas of greatest strength. You will improve the most, be the most creative, be the most inquisitive, and bounce back the fastest in those areas where you have already shown some natural advantage over everyone else - your strengths. This doesn't mean you should ignore your weaknesses. It just means you'll grow most where you're already strong.
~ Marcus Buckingham ~

1.   *The fishing is best where the fewest go, and the collective insecurity of the world makes it easy for people to hit home runs while everyone else is aiming for base hits. There is just less competition for bigger goals. If you are insecure, guess what? The rest of the world is, too. Do not overestimate the competition and underestimate yourself. You are better than you think. ~* **Timothy Ferriss**

2.   *The secret of joy in work is contained in one word - excellence. To know how to do something well is to enjoy it. ~* **Pearl Buck**

3.   *Success is not something you have. It's something you do. It's something you experience when you wake up and act accordingly. Be a self-starter let your first hour set the theme of proactivity and success that is certain to echo throughout the*

*entire day. Today will never happen again so don't waste it with a false start or no real start at all. ~ **Marc Andangel***

4.   *To be successful you must be willing at any moment to sacrifice what you are, for what you will become. ~ **Linchpin***

5.   *You have to wonder at times what you're doing out there. Over the years I have given myself a 1000 reasons to keep running, but it all comes back to when it started. It comes down to self-satisfaction and a sense of achievement. ~ **Al Shape***

6.   *In the real world we don't always live up to our ambitions. But just because we don't always do something, doesn't mean we can't ever do it. ~ **Anonymous***

7.   *Today is a new day. It is a day you have never seen before and a day you will never see again. Stop telling yourself the 'Same crap, different da' That's a lie! How many days has that lie stolen from you? Seize the wonder and uniqueness of today! Recognize that throughout this beautiful day, you have an incredible amount of opportunities to move your life in the direction you really want it to go. ~ **Dr Steve Maraboli***

8.   *The man that moves mountains first began by carrying away a small stone. ~ **Confucius 551-479 BC***

9.   *Either write something worth reading or do something worth writing. ~ **Benjamin Franklin 1706-1790***

10. *People who earn the label 'creative' are really just people who come up with more combinations of ideas, find interesting*

ones faster, and are willing to try them out. The problem is that most schools and organizations train us out of those habits. ~ **Guy Kawasaki**

11. *A master in the art of living draws no sharp distinction between his work and his play; his labour and his leisure; his mind and his body; his education and his recreation. He hardly knows which is which. He simply pursues his vision of excellence through whatever he is doing, and leaves others to determine whether he is working or playing. To himself, he always appears to be doing both. ~* **Lawrence Pearsall Jacks 1860-1955**

12. *Dream big and dare to fail. ~* **Norman Vaughan**

13. *It does not matter how slowly you go as long as you do not stop. ~* **Confucius 551-479 BC**

14. *Build your own dreams, or someone else will hire you to build theirs. ~* **Farrah Gray**

15. *I would rather die full of passion than of boredom. ~* **Vincent van Gogh 1853-1890**

16. *I didn't fail the test. I just found 100 ways to do it wrong. ~* **Benjamin Franklin 1706-1790**

17. *A wise man will make more opportunities than he finds. ~* **Francis Bacon 1561-1626**

18. *Challenges are what make life interesting, and overcoming*

*them is what makes life meaningful. ~ **Joshua J. Marine***

19.   *In everyone's life, at some time, our inner fire goes out. It is then burst into flame by an encounter with another human being. We should all be thankful for those people who rekindle the inner spirit. ~ **Albert Schweitzer 1875-1965***

20.   *Too many of us are not living our dreams because we are living our fears. ~ **Les Brown***

21.   *Tough times never last, but tough people do. ~ **Dr. Robert Schuller***

22.   *Your time is limited, so don't waste it living someone else's life. ~ **Steve Jobs***

23.   *It is never too late to be what you might have been. ~ **George Eliot 1819-1880***

24.   *Just know, when you truly want success, you'll never give up on it. No matter how bad the situation may get. ~ **Anonymous***

25.   *I don't regret the things I've done, I regret the things I didn't do when I had the chance. ~ **Anonymous***

26. *Self-discipline is everything. If you can conquer your physical and mental pain there is nothing you cannot do. ~ **Anonymous***

27. *I am thankful for all of those who said NO to me. It's because of them I'm doing it myself. ~ **Albert Einstein 1879-***

1955

28. *Don't worry about failures, worry about the chances you miss when you don't even try.* ~ **Jack Canfield**

29. *I do not have superior intelligence or faultless looks. I do not captivate a room or run a mile under six minutes. I only succeeded because I was still working after everyone else went to sleep.* ~ **Greg Evans**

30. *Though no one can go back and make a brand new start, anyone can start from now and make a brand new ending.* ~ **Carl Bard**

31. *Be a go getter. Let those first hours of each morning be ones that are full of positive decisions that will set the tone for the rest of the day. Today will be tomorrow so very soon. Don't waste the hours you have as you will never get them back.* ~ **Anonymous**

32. *Not caring what anyone else thinks is the best choice you'll ever make.* ~ **Anonymous**

33. *When you feel like giving up, remember why you held on for so long in the first place.* ~ **Anonymous**

34. *DO NOT claim you want to GROW then run away the moment you feel growing pains.* ~ **Anonymous**

35. *What lies behind us and what lies before us are tiny matters compared to what lies within us.* ~ **Henry S. Haskins 1875-1957**

36. *Challenge yourself with something you know you could never do, and what you'll find is that you can overcome anything* ~ **Anonymous**

37. *All our dreams can come true if we have the courage to pursue them.* ~ **Walt Disney**

38. *If you cannot do great things, do small things in a great way.* ~ **Napoleon Hill 1883-1970**

39. *An obstacle is often a stepping stone.* ~ **William Prescott 1726-1795**

40. *There is only one way to avoid criticism: do nothing, say nothing, and be nothing.* ~ **Aristotle 384-322 BC**

41. *You make a living by what you get; you make a life by what you give.* ~ **Winston Churchill 1874-1965**

42. *Make each day your masterpiece.* ~ **John Wooden**

43. *Don't wait. The time will never be just right.* ~ **Napoleon Hill 1883-1970**

44. *The best dreams happen when you're awake.* ~ **Cherie Gilderbloom**

45. *What you do speaks so loudly that I cannot hear what you say.* ~ **Ralph Waldo Emerson 1803-1883**

46. *You must not only aim right, but draw the bow with all your might.* ~ **Henry David Thoreau 1817-1872**

47. *Even if you fall on your face, remember, you're still moving forward.* ~ **Victor Kiam**

48. *Even if you're on the right track, you'll get run over if you just sit there.* ~ **Will Rogers 1879-1975**

49. *Optimism is one of the most important human traits, because it allows us to evolve our ideas, to improve our situation, and to hope for a better tomorrow.* ~ **Seth Godin**

50. *The more I want to get something done, the less I call it work.* ~ **Richard Bach**

51. *Imagination is your preview of life's coming attractions.* ~ **Albert Einstein 1879-1955**

52. *Obsessed is just a word the lazy use to describe the dedicated.* ~ **Russell Warren**

53. *Whatever course you decide upon, there is always someone to tell you that you are wrong. There are always difficulties arising which tempt you to believe that your critics are right. To map out a course of action and follow it to an end requires courage.* ~ **Ralph Waldo Emerson 1803 -1992**

54. *To be yourself in a world that is constantly trying to make you something else is the greatest accomplishment.* ~ **Ralph Waldo Emerson 1803-1893**

55.   *He who has a built in self-starter is never satisfied where he at. ~* **Anonymous**

56.   *Life has no remote, so get up and change it yourself ~* **Mark A. Cooper**

57,   *Problems are not stop signs, they are guidelines ~* **Robert H. Schuller**

58.   *Be a self-starter. Let your first hour of every day set the theme of success and positive action that will echo throughout the day. Today will never happen again. Don't waste it with a false start or no start at all. You were not born to fail. ~* **Og Mandino**

59.   *How to start is important, very important. But in the end it is how you finish that counts most of all. It is much easier to be a self-starter than a self-finisher. The victor is a race is not the one that dashes of the fastest but the one who leads at the finish. In the race for success speed is less important than stamina. The stickler outlasts the sprinter every time. In today's world we breed many hares but very few tortoises. ~* **B.C. Forbes 1880-1954**

60. *Self-improvement is the real name of the game, and the objective is to strengthen yourself not destroy someone else. ~* **Anonymous.**

61.   *Act as if what you do makes a difference, because it does. ~* **William James 1842-1910**

62. *I do not have superior intelligence or faultless looks. I do not captivate a room or run a mile under six minutes. I only succeeded because I was still working after everyone else went to sleep. ~* **Greg Eva**

63. *The greatest gift you can give someone is your TIME. Because when you give your time you are giving a portion of your life that you will never get back. ~* **Anonymous**

64. *There is only one quality you must possess to win and that is a clearly defined purpose, a goal; the knowledge of what one wants and the all-out desire to go out and get it. ~* **Napoleon Hill 1883-1970**

65. *The will to win, the desire to succeed, the urge to reach your full potential: these are the keys that will unlock the door to personal excellence. ~* **Confucius 551- 479 BC**

66. *Don't wish it were easier. Wish you were better. ~* **Jim Rohn**
67. *Don't put in half of the effort unless you're okay with half of the results. ~* **Anonymous**

68. *The best day of your life is the one on which you decide your life is your own. No apologies or excuses. No one to lean on, rely on, or blame. The gift is yours – it is an amazing journey – and you alone are responsible for the quality of it. This is the day your life really begins. ~* **Bob Moawad**

69. *Never give up on a dream just because of the time it will take to accomplish it. The time will pass anyway. ~* **Earl**

Nightingale

70. *The majority see the obstacles; the few see the objectives; history records the successes of the latter, while oblivion is the reward of the former.* ~ **Alfred Armand Montapert**

71. *The will to win, the desire to succeed, the urge to reach your full potential, these are the keys that unlock the door to ultimate excellence. The spirit and the will to excel are the things that endure. These are so much more important than the events that occur.* ~ **Confucius 551- 479 BC**

72. *Because something doesn't do what you planned it to do doesn't mean it is useless* ~ **Thomas A. Edison 1874 – 1931**

73. *Don't worry about failures; worry about the chances you miss when you don't even try.* ~ **Jack Canfield**

74. *Believe in yourself and all that you are. Know that there is something inside you driving you that is greater than any obstacle.* ~ **Christian D. Larsen 1874-1954**

75. *Destiny is not a matter of chance, it is a matter of choice; it is not a thing to be waited for, it is a thing to be achieved.* ~ **William Jennings Bryant 1860-1925**

76. *Success comes to the person who does today what you were thinking about doing tomorrow.* ~ **Anonymous**

77. *Everyone who's ever taken a shower has an idea. It's the person who gets out of the shower, dries off and does something*

about it who makes a difference. ~ **Nolan Bushnell**

78. *Believe in yourself and all that you believe in. Know that there is something inside you that is greater than any obstacle.* ~ **Christian D. Larsen**

79. *There is a tide in the affairs of men, which taken at the flood, leads on to fortune. Omitted, all the voyage of their life is bound in shallows and in miseries. On such a full sea are we now afloat. And we must take the current when it serves, or lose our ventures.* ~ **William Shakespeare 1564 -1660**

80. *Be a self-starter. Let the first hour of your day set the theme of positive success and action that is certain to echo until tomorrow morning. Today will never happen again. Don't waste it with a false start or no start at all, you were not born to fail.* ~ **Og Mandino**

28

ACCEPTING FAILURE

Keep these concepts in mind: You've failed many times, although you don't remember all of them. You fell down the first time you tried to walk. You almost drowned the first time you tried to swim on your own... You fell off your bike a dozen times before you learn to ride, and the first time you drank a beer or had a whiskey it made you scrunch up your face. Don't worry about failure; it's a part of life. My suggestion to each of you: Worry about the chances you miss when you don't even try.

~ *Sherman Finesilver* ~

1. *Lots of people want to shake your hand during times of success...but what you really want is some who will take your hand and comfort you in moments of failure. ~ **Bertram Hill 1881-1977***

2. *The one who fails and gets back up is so much stronger than the one who never fails. ~ **Anonymous***

3. *If Thomas Edison had believed in failure... we would still be living in darkness. If Henry Ford had given up, we would still be riding on horseback...if Alexander Graham Bell had given in to the clutches of failure, we would be spending less time staring at those small plastic things we call mobile phones that rule our*

*lives ~ **Zoë B***

4.   Nothing in this world can take the place of persistence. Talent will not: nothing is more common than unsuccessful men with talent. Genius will not; unrewarded genius is almost a proverb.   Education will not: the world is full of educated derelicts. Persistence and determination alone are omnipotent. ~ **Calvin Coolidge**

5.   I fail my exams in some subjects but my friend passed. Now he's and engineer in Microsoft and I am the owner. ~ **Bill Gates**

6.   Many of life's failures are people who did not realize how close they were to success when they gave up. ~ **Thomas A. Edison 1847-1931**

7.   Success depends upon previous preparation, and without such preparation there is sure to be failure. ~ **Confucius 551-479 BC**

8.   Think about this. The master has failed more times than the beginner has tried. ~ **Anonymous**

9.   Success consists of going from failure to failure without loss of enthusiasm. ~ **Winston Churchill 1809-1965**

10. I am not discouraged, because every wrong attempt discarded is a step forward. ~ **Thomas A. Edison 1847-1931**

11. Anyone who has never made a mistake has never tried anything new. ~ **Albert Einstein 1879- 1955**

12.   *If we didn't have failure, how would we know what to do next? The process of learning from our mistakes is truly invaluable, and is something we need to run toward, not run from.* ~ **Anonymous**

13.   *I've come to believe that all my past failure and frustrations were actually laying the foundation for the understandings that have created the new level of living I now enjoy.* ~ **Tony Robbins**

14.   *Don't be afraid of missing opportunities. Behind every failure is an opportunity somebody wishes they had missed.* ~ **Lily Tomlin**

15.   *In order to succeed you must fail so that you know what not to do the next time.* ~ **Anthony D'Angelo**

16.   *Success is not built on success. It's built on failure. It's built on disappointment. It's built on frustration. Sometimes it's even built on catastrophe.* ~ **Sumner Redstone**

17.   *What is the point of being alive if you don't try and do something remarkable? You never know you might actually succeed, and you succeeded because you refused to give up.* ~ **John Green**

18.   *I can accept failure, everyone fails at something. But never accept not trying.* ~ **Michael Jordan**

19.   *All people fail at certain times in their lives, the only thing that makes them different is how they manage to stand back up*

or how they choose to fail once again. ~ **Anonymous**

20. *If at first you don't succeed, think how many people you've made happy.* ~ **H. Duane Black**

21. *Win as if you were used to it, lose as if you were enjoying it for a change.* ~ **Ralph Waldo Emerson 1883 – 1882**

22. *Like success, failure is many things to many people. With a Positive Mental Attitude, failure is a learning experience, a rung on the ladder, a plateau at which to get your thoughts in order and prepare to try again.* ~ **W. Clement Stone**

23. *You will always pass failure on your way to success.* ~ **Mickey Rooney**

24. *An expert is a man who has made all the mistakes which can be made in a very narrow field.* ~ **Niels Bohr**

25. *Failure is instructive. The person who really thinks learns as much from his failures as from his successes.* ~ **John Dewey**

26. *You can be discouraged by failure or you can learn from it. So go ahead and make mistakes. Make all you can. Because that's where you'll find success.* ~ **Anonymous**

27. *It's fine to celebrate success but it is more important to heed the lessons of failure.* ~ **Bill Gates**

28. *Failure is the only you chance have to start again only more wisely.* ~ **Henry Ford**

29. *Don't be afraid to fail. Don't waste energy trying to cover up failure. Learn from your failures and go on to the next challenge. It's ok to fail. If you're not failing, you're not growing.* ~ **H. Stanley Judd**

30. *Failure doesn't mean you are a failure.... it just means you haven't succeeded yet.* ~ **Robert Schuller**

31. *Failure cannot cope with persistence.* ~ **Napoleon Hill 1883-1970**

32. *Creativity is allowing yourself to make mistakes. Art is knowing which ones to keep.* ~ **Scott Adams**

33. *I never make stupid mistakes, only very, very clever ones.* ~ **John Peel**

34. *Why do I talk about the benefits of failure? Simply because failure meant a stripping away of the inessential. I stopped pretending to myself that I was anything other than what I was and began to direct all my energy into finishing the only work that mattered to me.* ~ **J.K. Rowling**

35. *Failure doesn't mean the game is over it means try again only this time with experience.* ~ **Len Shlesinger**

36. *There is no such thing as a bed of roses all your life. But failure will never stand in the way of success if you learn from it.* ~ **Hank Aaron**

37. *The better a man is, the more mistakes he will make, for the more new things he will try.* ~ **Peter F Drucker**

38. *When defeat comes, accept it as a signal that your plans are not sound, rebuild those plans, and set sail once more toward your coveted goal.* ~ **Napoleon Hill 1883-1970**

39. *It's not how we make mistakes that defines us, but how we correct them.* ~ **Bo Bennet**

40. *When one door closes another door opens, but we so often look so long and so regretfully upon the closed door, that we do not see the ones which open for us.* ~ **Alexander Graham Bell 1847- 1922**

41. *If you have never seen failure then you have never seen success.* ~ **Anonymous**

42. *Failure should be our teacher, not our undertaker. Failure is a delay, not a defeat. It is a temporary detour, not a dead end. Failure is something we can avoid only by saying nothing, doing nothing, and being nothing.* ~ **Denis Waitley**

43. *You'll never be brave if you don't get hurt. You'll never learn if you don't make mistakes. You'll never be successful if you don't encounter failure.* ~ **Anonymous**

44. *There are two kinds of people in this world: those who want to get things done, and those who don't want to make mistakes.* ~ **John Maxwell**

45. *A failure is not always a mistake, it may simply be the best one can do under the circumstances. The real mistake is to stop trying.* ~ **B.F. Skinner**

46. *An inventor fails 999 times, and if he succeeds once, he's in. He treats his failures simply as practice shots.* ~ **Charles F. Kettering**

47. *The greatest mistake you can make in life is to be continually fearing you will make one.* ~ **Elbert Hubbard 1856-1915**

48. *Success represents the 1% of your work which results from the 99% that is called failure.* ~ **Soichiro Honda**

49. *Negative results are just what I want. They're just as valuable to me as positive results. I can never find the thing that does the job best until I find the ones that don't.* ~ **Thomas A. Edison 1847-1931**

50. *If you look at great human civilizations, from the Roman Empire to the Soviet Union, you will see that most do not fail simply due to external threats but because of internal weakness, corruption, or a failure to manifest the values and ideals they espouse.* ~ **Cory Booker**

51. *If you're not prepared to fail then you will never come up with anything original.* ~ **Ken Robinson**

52. *You build on failure. You use it as a stepping stone. Close the door on the past. You don't try to forget the mistakes, but*

you don't dwell on it. You don't let it have any of your energy, or any of your time, or any of your space. ~ **Johnny Cash**

53. *Forget about the consequences of failure. Failure is only a temporary change in direction to set you straight for your next success.* ~ **Denis Waitley**

54. *I really don't think life is about the I-could-have-been. Life is only about the I-tried-to-do. I don't mind the failure but I can't imagine that I'd forgive myself if I didn't try.* ~ **Nikki Giovanni**

55. *No man ever achieved worthwhile success who did not, at one time or other, find himself with at least one foot hanging well over the brink of failure.* ~ **Napoleon Hill 1883-1970**

56. *A person who doubts himself is like a man who would enlist in the ranks of his enemies and bear arms against himself. He makes his failure certain by himself being the first person to be convinced of it.* ~ **Ambrose Bierce**

57. *A man may fail many times but he isn't a failure until he begins to blame somebody else.* ~ **John Burroughs**

58. *Successful people do not fear failure they understand it is necessary to grow and learn from.* ~ **Robert Kiyosaki**

59. *It's fine to celebrate success but it far more important to heed the lessons of failure* ~ **Bill Gates**

60. *In the real world very smart people fail and mediocre people*

rise. Part of what makes people fail or succeed are skills that have absolutely nothing to do with IQ. Also the idea the IQ can be tested using a test is erroneous. ~ **Camille Paglia**

61.   *I have news for you, failure is unimportant. It takes courage and hard work to make a complete fool of yourself* ~ **Charlie Chaplin 1899-1977**

62. *Good people are good because they've come to wisdom through failure. You get very little wisdom from success you know.* ~ **William Saroyan**

63.   *You don't learn to walk by following rules, you learn to walk by falling over* ~ **Richard Branson**

64. *Success or failure is caused more by metal attitude than by mental capacity* ~ **Anonymous**

65. *Everyone fails sometimes in their lives, the one thing that makes them different is......how they managed to stand up, or how they managed to carry on again.* ~ **Lifehack.org**

66. *Every time you fail, if you're really smart you learn not to do it a second time.* ~ **Roger Payne**

67. *You are not a failure as failure is an event. Today ends tonight. You begin again tomorrow and try again until you get it right.* ~ **Anonymous**

68. *The only man who never makes a mistake is the man who never does anything.* ~ **Theodore Roosevelt 1858 – 1919**

69. *Success is not final, failure is not fatal. It is the courage to continue that counts. Failure will never overtake me if my determination to succeed is strong enough. Success is the result of perfection, hard work, learning from my mistakes, loyalty and persistence.* ~ **Winston Churchill 1874-1975**

70. *Part of being a man is learning to take responsibility for your successes and for your failures. You can't go blaming others or being jealous. Seeing somebody else's success as your failure is a cancerous way to live.* ~ **Kevin Bacon**

71. *Success is most often achieved by those who don't know that failure is inevitable.* ~ **Coco Chanel**

72. *When we give ourselves permission to fail, we, at the same time, give ourselves permission to excel.* ~ **Eloise Ristad**

73. *If you're not prepared to be wrong, you'll never come up with anything original.* ~ **Ken Robinson**

74. *If you don't try at anything, you can't fail... it takes back bone to lead the life you want* ~ **Richard Yates**

75. *When you take risks you learn that there will be times when you succeed and there will be times when you fail, and both are equally important.* ~ **Ellen DeGeneres**

76. *Fear regret more than failure* ~ **Anonymous**

77. *There is only one thing that makes a dream impossible to*

achieve: the fear of failure. ~ **Paulo Coelho**

78. *Pain is temporary. Quitting lasts forever.* ~ **Lance Armstrong**

79. *It's failure that gives you the proper perspective on success.* ~ **Ellen DeGeneres**

80. *What do you first do when you learn to swim? You make mistakes, do you not? And what happens? You make other mistakes, and when you have made all the mistakes you possibly can without drowning – and some of them many times over – what do you find? That you can swim? Well – life is just the same as learning to swim! Do not be afraid of making mistakes, for there is no other way of learning how to live!* ~ **Alfred Adler 1870-1937**

29
ETHICAL BEHAVIOUR

Ethics in the workplace refers to the standard of conduct that members of a team or business should apply in their work relationships. Ethics are derived from human values such as respect, responsibility, integrity, and the personal behaviour each team member person holds. Upholding ethics in the workplace allows team leaders, managers and team members to maintain proper boundaries by respecting the personal space and work space of others as well as obeying specified rules when communicating with one another.
~ Fiona Miller ~

1. Your children's work ethic at school and when they play is down to you. They listen, watch what you do, and then copy it. If you continually set a bad example it is unlikely they will develop a good example. So think about that every time you swear, every time you complain about work, and every very time you promise to play with them then find an excuse not to. ~ **David Popenoe**

2. The harder thing to do, and the right thing to do, are usually one and the same. ~ **Anonymous**

3. Ethics has no need of rules, it's a stand-alone commitment. ~ **Albert Camus**

4. *Ethical behaviour tends to be good for business and involves demonstrating respect for key moral principles that include honesty, fairness, equality, dignity, diversity and individual rights. It should not only apply to your staff but to your customers too.* ~ **Anonymous**

5. *Honesty is the cornerstone of all success, without which confidence and ability to perform shall cease to exist.* ~ **Mary Kay Ash**

6. *Don't worry about being a genius. Don't worry about being clever. Trust to hard work, perseverance, determination and honesty. The best motto on a long march: Don't grumble, plug on.* ~ **Sir Fredrick Treves 1853-1923**

7. *Aspire to decency. Practice civility toward one another. Admire and emulate ethical behaviour wherever you find it. Apply a rigid standard of morality to your lives; and if, periodically, you fail as you surely will, adjust your lives, not the standards.* ~ **Ted Koppel**

8. *Moral authority comes from following universal and timeless principles like honesty, integrity, treating people with respect.* ~ **Stephen Covey**

9. *The greatest homage we can pay to truth is to use it.* ~ **Ralph Waldo Emerson**

10. *If networks are to be consistently efficient and effective...it will only come about on the basis of a high level of trust and the*

existence of shared ethical behaviour between network members. ~ **Francis Fukuyama**

11.   People should not be afraid of exposing their government corruption. Governments should be afraid of the people exposing their corruption. ~ **V for Vendetta**

12.   When you live for a strong purpose, then hard work isn't an option. It's a necessity. ~ **Steve Pavlina**

13.   Do what you have to today so you can do what you want to tomorrow. ~ **Anonymous**

14.   There are no easy methods of learning difficult things; the method is to close your door, give out that you are not at home, and work to high standards. ~ **Joseph de Maistre**

15.   If you have an idea of what you want to do in your future, you must go at it with almost monastic obsession, be it music, the ballet or just a basic degree. You have to go at it single-mindedly and let nothing get in your way. ~ **Henry Rollins**

16. The strongest thing that any human being has going is their own integrity and their own heart. As soon as you start veering away from that, the solidity that you need in order to be able to stand up for what you believe in and deliver what's really inside, it's just not going to be there. ~ **Herbie Hancock**

17.   The winds and waves are always on the side of the ablest navigators. ~ **Edward Gibbon**

18.   Hard work spotlights the character of people: some turn up their sleeves, some turn up their noses, and some don't turn up at all. ~ **Sam Ewing**

19.   Ethical behaviour is doing the right thing when no one else is watching- even when doing the wrong thing is acceptable. ~ **Aldo Leopold**

20.   Relativity applies to Physics not Ethics. ~ **Albert Einstein 1879-1955**

21.   Be impeccable with your word and sincere in your actions. ~ **Robert Palmer**

22.   Speak with integrity. Say only what you mean. Avoid using the word to speak against yourself or to gossip about others. Use the power of your word in the direction of truth and love. ~ **Don Miguel Ruiz**

23.   A life lived with integrity - even if it lacks the trappings of fame and fortune is a shining star in whose light others may follow in the years to come. ~ **Denis Waitley**

24.   Wisdom is knowing the right path to take. Integrity is taking it. ~ **M.H. McKee 1859-1950**

25.   I don't think of myself as a role model for others, but I like to live my life by my own integrity. So, in that sense, I might be a positive influence. I do believe you should get over your insecurities and just try to be the best you can. ~**Lily Cole**

26. *Never do anything against conscience even if the state demands it.* ~ **Albert Einstein 1879-1955**

27. *Character is what emerges from all the little things you were too busy to do yesterday, but did anyway.* ~ **Mignon McLaughlin**

28. *The highest compact we can make with our fellow is, - Let there be truth between us two forever more.* ~ **Ralph Waldo Emerson**

29. *Honesty is the first chapter in the book of wisdom.* ~ **Thomas Jefferson**

30. *To restore and keep the public's confidence in the integrity of their government and its officials - it must be open, honest and transparent.* ~ **John Lynch**

31. *In failing circumstances sometimes no one can be relied on to keep their integrity. But when it goes everyone knows and you can't go back and pick it up again.* ~ **Ralph Waldo Emerson 1803-1882**

32. *The world will not be destroyed by those who do evil, but by those who watch them without doing anything.* ~ **Albert Einstein 1878-1955**

33. *In the end you should always do the right thing even if it's hard.* ~ **Nicholas Sparks**

34. *The question is, when so many others cut corners, shave the*

truth, self-deal, believe in the fast buck, and follow the crowd along the low road of least resistance, can we even afford to travel the high road of ethical behaviour? Frankly, we can't afford anything else. Any other competitive angle is a pure crapshoot in today's business world. Companies with shaky ethics and shabby standards will be crippled as they try to compete in our changing world. ~ **Price Pritchett**

35. Honesty, integrity and accountability, the values which should be the hallmark of this government, have instead been thrown under the bus by an arrogant majority, casualties in a misguided campaign to shield from accountability those who abuse this house. ~ **Louise Slaughter**

36. The glue that holds all relationships together - including the relationship between the leader and the led - is trust, and trust is based on integrity. ~ **Brian Tracy**

37. Integrity is the first step to true greatness. Men love to praise, but are slow to practice it. To maintain it in high places costs self-denial; in all places it is liable to opposition, but its end is glorious, and the universe will yet do it homage. ~ **Charles Simmons**

38. Whoever is careless with the truth in small matters cannot be trusted with important matters. ~ **Albert Einstein 1979 - 1955**

39. Leadership requires five ingredients-brains, energy, determination, trust, and ethics. The key challenges today are in terms of the last two - trust and ethics. ~ **Fred Hilmer**

40. *Don't make misrepresentations to anyone you deal with. If you believe the other person may have misunderstood you, correct any misunderstanding you find exists. Honesty is integral to ethical behaviour, and trustworthiness is essential for good, lasting relationships.* ~ **Buck Rogers**

41. *A man without ethics is a wild beast let loose on this world to do as much damage as he can.* ~ **Anonymous**

42. *Integrity is not a conditional word. It doesn't blow in the wind or change with the weather. It is your inner image of yourself, and if you look in there and see a man who won't cheat, then you know he never will.* ~ **John D. MacDonald**

43. *The view is much better when it is earned through honestly and hard work.* ~ **Dean Drummond**

44. *Success is no accident. It is hard work, perseverance, leaning, studying, sacrifice, honesty, and most of all, love of what you are doing or learning to do.* ~ **Pele**

45. *Achievement of your happiness is the only moral purpose of your life, and that happiness, not pain or mindless self-indulgence, is the proof of your moral integrity, since it is the proof and the result of your loyalty to the achievement of your values.* ~ **Ayn Rand**

46. *There are truths on this side of the Pyrenees which are falsehoods on the other.* ~ **Michel de Montaigne 1533-1592**

47. *It is easy to dodge our responsibilities, but we cannot dodge the consequences of dodging our responsibilities. ~ **Josiah Charles Stamp 1880-1941***

48. *Don't assume, ask. Be kind. Tell the truth. Don't say anything you can't stand behind fully. Have integrity. Tell people how you feel. ~ **Warsan Shire***

49. *We all have a path to take; sometimes it's hidden under the weeds, so you might have to work a little, but a little hard work never hurt an honest man. ~ **Mike Dolan***

50. *Try to find the path of least resistance and use it without harming others. Live with integrity and morality, not only with people but with all beings. ~ **Steven Segal***

51. *Ethos is not just an abstract intellectual discipline. It is about the conflicts that arise in trying to meet real human needs and values. ~ **John Ziman***

52. *Integrity is the first step to true greatness. Men love to praise, but are slow to practice it. To maintain it in high places costs self-denial; in all places it is liable to opposition, but its end is glorious, and the universe will yet do it homage. ~ **Charles Simmons***

53. *Never rob your character to enrich your pocket ~ **James Lendall Basfor***

54. *Doors don't slam open, and honest is something you are or you are not. ~ **John M. Shanahan***

55.   *Trust men and they will be true to you; treat them greatly and they will show themselves great.* ~ **Ralph Waldo Emerson**

56. *Just trust yourself, then you will know how to live.* ~ **Johann Wolfgang von Goethe 1749-1842**

57.   *Better to trust the man who is frequently in error than the one who is never in doubt.* ~ **Eric Sevareid**

58. *The greatness of a man is not in how much wealth he acquires, but in his integrity and his ability to affect those around him positively.* ~ **Bob Marley**

59. *For it is mutual trust, even more than mutual interest that holds human associations together. Our friends seldom profit us but they make us feel safe... Marriage is a scheme to accomplish exactly that same end.* ~ **H. L. Mencken 1880-1896**

60. *The world is becoming more complicated every day, my fellow citizens. No man ought to be foolish enough to think that he understands it all. And, therefore, I am glad that there are some simple things in the world. One of the simple things is principle. Honesty is a perfectly simple thing.* ~ **Woodrow Wilson 1856-1924**

61.   *The leaders who work most effectively, it seems to me, never say 'I.' And that's not because they have trained themselves not to say 'I.' They don't think 'I.' They think 'we'; they think 'team.' They understand their job to be to make the team function. They accept responsibility and don't sidestep it, but 'we' gets the*

credit.... *This is what creates trust, what enables you to get the task done.* ~ **Peter F Drucker**

62. *Achievement of your happiness is the only moral purpose of your life, and that happiness, not pain or mindless self-indulgence, is the proof of your moral integrity, since it is the proof and the result of your loyalty to the achievement of your values.* ~ **Ayn Rand**

63. *Ethics is not definable, is not implementable, because it is not conscious; it involves not only our thinking, but also our feeling.* ~ **Valdemar W. Setzer**

64. *No matter what the situation never let your emotions overpower your intelligence and your honour.* ~ **Turcois Ominek**

65. *We need people in our lives with whom we can be as open as possible.* ~ **Anonymous**

66. *In a thieves market place it is difficult not to be marked as a thief.* ~ *'Ali Baba and the Forty Thieves'*

67. *When people honour each other, there is a trust established that leads to synergy, interdependence, and deep respect. Both parties make decisions and choices based on what is right, what is best, what is valued most highly.* ~ **Blaine Lee**

68. *Honest men who are resolved to find a way for themselves will always find opportunities enough; and if they do not find them, they will eventually make them.* ~ **Samuel Smiles 1812-**

1904

69. Do not waste a minute, not a second, in trying to demonstrate to others the merit of your own performance. If your work does not vindicate itself, you cannot vindicate it, but you can labour steadily on to something that needs no advocate but it. ~ **Thomas Wentworth Higginson 1823-1911**

70. If ethics are poor at the top, that behaviour is copied down through the organization, ~ **Robert Noyce**

71. Trust each other again and again. When the trust level gets high enough, people transcend apparent limits, discovering new and awesome abilities for which they were previously unaware. ~ **David Armistead**

72. God gives every bird its food, but he does not throw it into its nest. ~ **J.G. Holland 1819-1891**

73. We're never so vulnerable than when we trust someone - but paradoxically, if we cannot trust, neither can we find love or joy. ~ **Walter Anderson**

74. The chief lesson I have learned in a long life is that the only way to make a man trustworthy is to trust him; and the surest way to make him untrustworthy is to distrust him and show your distrust. ~ **Henry L. Stimson 1867-1950**

75. The best way to find out if you can trust somebody is to trust them. ~ **Ernest Hemingway**

76. *Let me define a leader. He must have vision and passion and not be afraid of any problem. Instead, he should know how to defeat it. Most importantly, he must work with integrity.* ~ **A. P. J. Abdul Kalam**

77. *In the 17th and 18th Century politicians often needed to know how the public felt about the work they were doing in Parliament. Since there were no forms of electronic communication they used to send their assistants to local taverns and other such establishments. They were told to 'go sip' some ale and listen to people's conversations and political concerns. The assistants were told to 'go sip' here, and 'go sip' there. The two words 'go sip' were eventually combined when referring to the local opinion and, thus we now have the have the term 'gossip.'* ~ **Roger Payne**

78. *Being honest will not necessarily get you a lot of friends, but it will always get you the right ones.* ~ **Anonymous**

79. *Your conscience is the measure of the honesty of your selfishness. Listen to it carefully and never cheat it.* ~ **Richard Bach**

80. *Integrity choosing your thoughts and actions based on values rather than personal gain* ~ **Anonymous**

30
TAKING RISKS

Don't listen to those who say 'you taking too big a chance.' If Michelangelo had he would have painted the floor of the Sistine Chapel not the ceiling, and it would surely be rubbed out by today. Most important, don't listen when the little voice of fear inside you rears its ugly head and says, 'they're all smarter than you out there. They're more talented, they're taller, blonder, prettier, luckier, and they have connections.' I firmly believe that if you follow a path that interests you, not to the exclusion of love, sensitivity, and cooperation with others, but with the strength of conviction that you can move others by your own efforts and do not make success or failure the criteria by which you live the chances are you'll be a person worthy of your own respects.

~ *Neil Simon* ~

1.   The biggest risk is not taking any risk. In a world that is changing really quickly, the only strategy that is guaranteed to fail is not taking any risks. ~ **Mark Zuckerberg**

2.   Remembering that I'll be dead soon is the most important tool I've ever encountered to help me make the big choices in life. Because almost everything - all external expectations, all pride, all fear of embarrassment or failure - these things just fall away in the face of death, leaving only what is truly important.

~ Steve Jobs

3.   The biggest risk is not taking any risk... In a world that changing really quickly, the only strategy that is guaranteed to fail is not taking risks. ~ **Mark Zuckerman**

4.   Once we believe in ourselves we can risk curiosity, wonder, spontaneous delight, or any experience that reveals the human spirit. ~ **E. E. Cummings 1894-1962**

5.   Abject fear is the main source of superstition, and one of the main sources of cruelty. To conquer fear is the beginning of wisdom. ~ **Bertrand Russell**

6.   Life is all about taking risks. If you never take a risk you will NEVER achieve your dreams. ~ **Anonymous**

7.   Never be afraid to try something new. Remember, amateurs built the ark; professionals built the Titanic. ~ **Anonymous**

8.   The fishermen know that the sea is dangerous and the storm terrible, but they have never found these dangers sufficient reason for remaining ashore. ~ **Vincent van Gogh 1853-1890**

9.   If you don't take any risks you might as well fall flat on your face as you lean over too far backward. ~ **James Thurber 1894-1961**

10.   The young do not know enough to be prudent, and therefore they attempt the impossible and achieve it, generation after

*generation. ~ **Pearl S. Buck***

11.   *Taking a new step, uttering a new word, is what people fear most. ~ **Fyodor Dostoevsky***

12.   *My record was so bad that I was first rejected by the Peace Corps as a poor risk and possible troublemaker and was accepted as a volunteer only after a great deal of explaining and arguing ~ **Paul Theroux***

13.   *Never allow waiting to become a habit forming. Live your dreams and take risks. Life is happening to you right now. ~ **Anonymous***

14.   *The first step toward success is taken when you refuse to be a captive of the environment in which you first find yourself. ~ **Mark Cain***

15.   *Experience teaches slowly, and at the cost of mistakes. ~ **James A. Froude***

16.   *To dare is to lose one's footing momentarily. To not dare is to lose oneself. ~ **Soren Kierkegaard***

17.   *There are 30,000 days in your life. When I was 24, I realized I'm almost 9,000 days down. There are no warm-ups, no practice rounds, no reset buttons. Your biggest risk isn't failing, it's getting too comfortable. Every day, we're writing a few more words of a story. I wanted my story to be an adventure and that's made all the difference. ~ **Drew Houston***

18. *I really don't think life is about the I-could-have-beens. Life is only about the I-tried-to-do. I don't mind the failure but I can't imagine that I'd forgive myself if I didn't try.* ~ **Nikki Giovanni**

19. *What's the biggest risk: Taking the risk, or not taking the risk? What will you accomplish by not taking the risk? What will you accomplish by taking the risk, even if you fail?* ~ **Kya Aliana**

20. *It seems to be a law of nature, inflexible and inexorable, that those who will not risk cannot win.* ~ **John Paul Jones 1747-1792**

21. *I must not fear. Fear is the mind-killer. Fear is the little-death that brings total obliteration. I will face my fear. I will permit it to pass over me and through me. And when it has gone past I will turn the inner eye to see its path. Where the fear has gone there will be nothing. Only I will remain.* ~ **Frank Herbert**

22. *The dangers of life are infinite, including safety.* ~ **Goethe**

23. *You must accept that you might fail; then, if you do your best and still don't win, at least you can be satisfied that you've tried. If you don't accept failure as a possibility, you don't set high goals, you don't branch out, you don't try, and you don't take the risk.* ~ **Rosalynn Carter**

24. *In the end we only regret the chances we didn't take, relationships we were afraid to have, and the decisions we waited too long to make.* ~ **Anonymous**

25. *The risk of a wrong decision is preferable to the terror of indecision.* ~ **Moshe ben Maimon (Maimonides) 1135-1204**

26. *It is better by noble boldness to run the risk of being subject to half the evils we anticipate than to remain in cowardly listlessness for fear of what might happen.* ~ **Herodotus 484-425 BC**

27. *There's something liberating about not pretending. Dare to embarrass yourself, take risks.* ~ **Drew Barrymore**

28. *Nobody can go back and start a new beginning, but anyone can start today and make a new ending.* ~ **Anonymous**

29. *Creative people who can't help but explore other mental territories are at greater risk, just as someone who climbs a mountain is more at risk than someone who just walks along a village lane.* ~ **R. D. Laing**

30. *One who fears failure limits his activities. Failure is only the opportunity to more intelligently begin again.* ~ **Henry Ford**

31. *Untrinque Paratus (Be ready for anything) Motto of the British Parachute Regiment.* ~ **R.P.**

32. *When in doubt, make a fool of yourself. There is a microscopically thin line between being brilliantly creative and acting like the most gigantic idiot on earth. So what the hell, leap.* ~ **Cynthia Heimel**

*33. Anyone who takes himself too seriously always runs the risk of looking ridiculous; anyone who can consistently laugh at himself does not. ~ **Vaclav Havel***

*34. Often the difference between a successful man and a failure is not one's better abilities or ideas, but the courage that one has to bet on his idea, to take a calculated risk, and to act. ~ **1889-1975***

*35. If it's on your mind it's not going to go away so it's worth taking the risk. ~ **Paulo Coelho***

*36. We must risk going too far to find out how far we can go. ~ **Anonymous***

*37. Our lives improve only when we take chances, and the first and most difficult risk we can take is to be honest with ourselves. ~ **Walter Anderson***

*38. Security is mostly a superstition. It does not exist in nature, nor do the children of men as a whole experience it. Avoiding danger is no safer in the long run than outright exposure. Life is either a daring adventure, or NOTHING. ~ **Helen Keller 1889-1968***

*39. Accept that all of us can be hurt, that all of us can and surely will at times fail. Other vulnerabilities, like being embarrassed or risking love, can be terrifying, too. I think we should follow a simple rule: if we can take the worst, take the risk. ~ **Joyce Brothers***

40. *Everyone wants to be a diamond but very few are willing to get cut.* ~ **Anonymous**

41. *You have to leave the city of your comfort and go into the wilderness of your intuition. You can't get there by bus, only by hard work and risk and by not quite knowing what you're doing. What you'll discover will be wonderful. What you'll discover will be yourself.* ~ **Alan Alda**

42. *A man would do nothing, if he waited until he could do it so well that no one would find fault with what he has done.* ~ **Cardinal Newman**

43. *Creative risk taking is essential to success in any goal where the stakes are high. Thoughtless risks are destructive, of course, but perhaps even more wasteful is thoughtless caution, which prompts inaction and promotes failure to seize opportunity.* ~ **Gary Ryan Blair**

44. *Yes, risk taking is inherently failure prone, otherwise, it would be called sure thing taking.* ~ **Anonymous**

45. *Don't wait for the perfect moment, take the moment and make it perfect.* ~ **Zoey Sayward**

46. *And the day came when the risk it took to remain tight inside the flowers bud was more painful than the risk it took to blossom.* ~ **Anais Nin**

47. *Test fast, fail fast, adjust fast.* ~ **Tom Peters**

48. *What you have to do and the way you have to do it is incredibly simple. Whether you are willing to do it is another matter.* ~ **Peter F. Drucker**

49. *Don't be afraid to take a big step. You can't cross a chasm in two small jumps.* ~ **David Lloyd George 1863-1945**

50. *The way to develop self-confidence is to do the thing you fear and get a record of successful experiences behind you. Destiny is not a matter of chance, it is a matter of choice; it is not a thing to be waited for, it is a thing to be achieved.* ~ **William Jennings Bryan 1860-1925**

51. *The fear of death is the most unjustified of all fears, for there's no risk of accident for someone who's dead.* ~ **Albert Einstein 1879-1955**

52. *Life is inherently risky. There is only one big risk you should avoid at all costs, and that is the risk of doing nothing.* ~ **Denis Waitley**

53. *The time to take counsel of your fears is before you make an important battle decision. That's the time to listen to every fear you can imagine! When you have collected all the facts and fears and made your decision, turn off all your fears and go ahead!* ~ **General George S. Patton**

54. *Security is mostly a superstition. It does not exist in nature, nor do the children of men as a whole experience it. Avoiding danger is no safer in the long run than outright exposure. Life is either a daring adventure or nothing.* ~ **Helen Keller 1889-**

1968

55. *Whatever you can do, or dream you can, begin it. Boldness has genius, power and magic in it. ~ **Johann Wolfgang von Goethe 1749-1832***

56. *It is only by risking our persons from one hour to another that we live at all. ~ **William James 1842-1910***

57. *The dangers of life are infinite, and among them is safety. ~ **Johann Wolfgang von Goethe 1749 1832***

58. *In the future you will be angry because of the things you failed to do than those you did do. So throw off the bowlines, sail away from the safe harbour, catch the trade winds in your sails. ~ **Mark Twain 1935 – 1910***

59. *EXPLORE!   DREAM!   DISCOVER!   CONQUER!   ~ **Anonymous***

60. *Everything you've done so far in life has a certain amount of risk attached to it, so why be afraid to take a calculated risk and leap into the unknown and try something entirely new that could be life changing. If you don't take the risk you will never know ~ **Hal Rogers***

61. *When you want something you've never had you have to do something you've never done. ~ **Anonymous***

62. *Simply thinking 'Here goes nothing' could be the start of EVERTHING. ~ **Drew Wagner***

63. *If you are taking a risk, what you really saying is 'I believe in tomorrow and I want to be a part of it!'* ~ **Linda Ellerbee**

64. *Life is full of risk from driving the car to crossing the road. Team Leading is no different.* ~ **R.P.**

65. *Success seems to be connected with action. Successful people keep moving. They make mistakes, but they don't quit.* ~ **Conrad Hilton 1887-1979**

66. *If you're offered a seat on a rocket ship, don't ask what seat! Just get on.* ~ **Sheryl Sandberg**

67. *I always did something I was a little not ready to do. I think that's how you grow. When there's that moment of 'Wow, I'm not really sure I can do this,' and you push through those moments, that's when you have a breakthrough.* ~ **Marissa Mayer**

68. *Pearls don't lie on the seashore. If you want one, you must dive for it.* ~ **Chinese proverb**

69. *You can't outwit fate by standing on the sidelines placing little side bets about the outcome of life. Either you wade in and risk everything you have to play the game or you don't play at all. And if you don't play you can't win.* ~ **Judith McNaught**

70. *The universe has no restrictions. You place restrictions on the universe with your expectations.* ~ **Deepak Chopra**

71. *You get what you settle for.* ~ **TV show Thelma and Louise**

72. *I refuse to accept other people's ideas of happiness for me. As if there's a 'one size fits all' standard for happiness.* ~ **Kanye West**

73. *Do not accept what others assume is your rightful place in the world. If everyone did that nobody would ever better themselves.* ~ **Mel Stone**

74. *Always go with your passions. Never ask yourself if it's realistic or not.* ~ **Deepak Chopra**

75. *I don't think you're human if you don't get nervous.* ~ **Sidney Crosby**

76. *Think big and don't listen to people who tell you it can't be done. Life's too short to think small.* ~ **Tim Ferriss**

77. *I've missed more than 9000 shots in my career. I've lost almost 300 games. 26 times I've been trusted to take the game winning shot and missed. I've failed over and over and over again in my life. And that is why I succeed.* ~ **Michael Jordan**

78. *Your dreams are ballbusters; they're not the yellow brick road stuff.* ~ **Kelly Cutrone**

79. *If we listened to our intellect, we'd never have a love affair. We'd never have a friendship. We'd never go into business because we'd be too cynical. Well, that's nonsense. You've got to jump off cliffs all the time and build your wings on the way*

down. ~ **Annie Dillard**

80. *When I let go of what I am, I become what I might be.* ~ **Lao Tzu 604-501 BC**

81. *Often the difference between a successful person and a failure is not one has better abilities or ideas, but the courage that one has to bet on one's ideas, to take a calculated risk – and to act.* ~ **Andre Malraux**

31
SETTING STANDARDS

Setting employee performance standards, and then monitoring their progress is extremely important in the development of your team. A team leader should work closely with the team members to develop a set of standards that both they can understand and can commit to. When team members take part in creating their own performance standards, they have an increased feeling of responsibility for reaching, and often exceeding, those standards.

~ *Roger Payne* ~

1. *Just remember, accepting the prevailing standards often means that you don't have any standards of your own to live up to.* ~ **Jean Toomer**

2. *You will always get what you expect in people. If you set a reasonable standard and say no more or no less, you'll get it. The key is setting the right standards.* ~ **Liz Betrey**

3. *Let's not be afraid to speak the common sense and the truth: you can't have high standards without good discipline.* ~ **William Hague**

4. *You can become an even better leader by constantly setting high standards for yourself and then by doing everything*

possible to live up to those standards. ~ **Brian Tracy**

5. Don't blame people for disappointing you, blame yourself for expecting too much from them. ~ **Anonymous**

6. We are motivated by goals that have deep meaning, by dreams that need completion, by pure love that needs expressing, then we truly live life. ~ **Greg Anderson**

7. Don't lower your expectations to meet your performance. Raise your level of performance to meet your expectations. ~ **Kalari aka Lyrikal**

8. We do it because we can, 'cause we know how. We do it whether people remember us or not, in spite of the fact that there's no shiny reward at the end of the day...other than the work itself ~ **Anonymous**

9. Never let anyone tell you that your standards are too high. There is nothing wrong with wanting the best for yourself and if they cannot match them then they clearly aren't up to your standards. ~ **Anonymous**

10. Focus on the journey, not the destination. Joy is found in finishing an activity but in doing it. ~ **Greg Anderson**

11. You can become a far better person by consistently setting higher and higher standards for yourself and then by doing everything possible to live up to those standards. ~ **Brian Tracy**

12. But we must remember that while social morals are indeed

subjective, there is an objective spiritual core within us that, via its capacity for empathy and longing for freedom and happiness, knows universal rights from universal wrongs. The virtues of compassion, humility, service, wisdom, strength, discretion, and courage are not limited to the human domain, for they are truly universal. ~ **Montalk**

13.   Sometimes the issue is simply their ceiling is your floor. ~ **A.J. Zone**

14.   A man needs to look, not down, but up to standards set so much above his ordinary self as to make him feel that he is himself spiritually the underdog. ~ **Irving Babbitt 1865-1933**

15.   When you set standards and stick to them, there will be people in your life who will fall away; let them. ~ **Anonymous**

16.   Leadership is lifting a person's vision to high sights, the raising of a person's performance to a higher standard, the building of a personality beyond its normal limitations. ~ **Peter F Drucker**

17.   Soldiers, when committed to a task, can't compromise. It's unrelenting devotion to the standards of duty and courage, absolute loyalty to others, not letting the task go until it's been done. ~ **John Keegan**

18.   You can't please everyone. When you're too focused on living up to other people's standards, you aren't spending enough time raising your own. Some people may whisper, complain and judge. But for the most part, it's all in your head.

The Team Leadership Bucket List

*People care less about your actions than you think. Why? They have their own problems! ~ **Kris Carr***

19. *I have my own high standards for what I want in a partner and how I want to be treated. I bring a lot to the table. I'm not talking about material things but what I have to offer as a person love and loyalty and all the things that make a good relationship. ~ **Jennifer Lopez***

20. *I do have high standards. I look at everything I have done and think, 'Why wasn't that better?' Part of my motivation is from crippling self-doubt I have got to prove myself wrong. ~ **Michael Palin***

21. *Not everyone is qualified to join this team. To enlist you have to both meet our high standards and be motivated to serve this country...motivation or qualification are not enough. ~ **Bryan Hilferty***

22. *You've always got to work with the best if you can, and of course, the best are the best because they're different. They expect certain standards, and they're usually very difficult people to work with. ~ **Malcolm McDowell***

23. *You will always get what you expect in people. If you set a reasonable standard in people no more or no less. You'll get it. The key is to set the right standards. ~ **Liz Betry***

24. *Sometimes you want things so bad you will kind of lower your standards, and I've learned that once you do that, it's really hard to go back, to get people to respect you and respect your*

craft. ~ **Tamar Braxton**

25. *Standards means doing it right when no one is looking.* ~ **Henry Ford 1863 1947**

26. *You have been condition to be who you are. This also means YOU can condition yourself to be who you want.* ~ **Blair Singer**

27. *Fraud in government is no different from infidelity in marriage or plagiarism in scholarly work.   Even people committed to high moral standards succumb.* ~ **Miroslav Volf**

28. *Aim above morality. Be not simply good, be good for something.* ~ **Henry David Thoreau 1817-1862**

29. *Stay strong and make everyone wonder why you're still smiling.* ~ **Anonymous**

30. *I spend some of my time brooding about people who seem addicted to double standards those who take an allegedly principled stand on a Monday, then switch firmly to the opposite principle on Tuesday if it is to their advantage.* ~ **John Leo**

31. *In order to say 'YES' to your priorities you must be prepared to say 'NO' to something else.* ~ **Anonymous**

32. *Success is liking yourself, liking what you do, and liking how you do it.* ~ **Maya Angelou**

33. *Don't do anything you wouldn't be willing to explain on*

television. ~ Arjay Miller

34, *A 'No' uttered from deepest conviction is better and greater than a 'Yes' merely uttered to please, or what is worse, to avoid trouble. ~ Mahatma Gandhi 1869-1968*

35. *Never for the sake of peace and quiet deny your convictions. ~ Dag Hammarskjold*

36. *If we don't fight for what we 'stand for' with our passionate words and honest actions, do we really 'stand' for anything? ~ Tiffany Madison*

37. *Creative risk taking is essential to success in any goal where the stakes are high. Thoughtless risks are destructive, of course, but perhaps even more wasteful is thoughtless caution which prompts inaction and promotes failure to seize opportunity. ~ Gary Ryan Blair*

38. *When you have to start compromising yourself or your morals for the people around you, it's probably time to change the people around you. ~ Anonymous*

39. *The nicest thing about standards is that there are so many of them to choose from. ~ Ken Olsen*

40. *Don't judge the past by the standards of today. It won't work. They're incompatible. ~ Richelle Mead*

41. *Raise your standards as high as you can live with, avoid wasting your time on routine problems, and always try to work*

as closely as possible at the boundary of your abilities. ~ **Edsger W. Dijkstra**

42. *When you do what you fear most, then you can do ANYTHING.* ~ **Stephen Richards**

43. *Do this, because it is the only way of discovering how that boundary should be moved forward.* ~ **Edward Dolan**

44. *Standards only move in one direction. At the beginning of the world, standards were established and they've been slipping ever since.* ~ **Edward Stevenson 1820-1897**

45. *We do it because we can, 'cause we know how. We do it whether people remember us or not, in spite of the fact that there's no shiny reward at the end of the day...other than the work itself.* ~ **Anonymous**

46. *Whatever is worth doing at all, is worth doing well.* ~ **John Chesterfield**

47. *Living at risk is jumping off the cliff and building your wings on the way down.* ~ **Ray Bradbury**

48. *Hold yourself responsible for a higher standard than anybody else expects of you.* ~ **Henry Ward Beecher 1813-1887**

49. *It is important that people know what you stand for. It's equally important that they know what you won't stand for.* ~ **Mary Waldrip**

50. When we breathe it in, soot can interfere with our lungs and increase the risk of asthma attacks, lung cancer and even premature death. The smallest particles can pass into the blood stream and cause heart disease, stroke and reproductive complications. ~ **Sheldon Whitehouse**

51. The way you treat yourself sets the standard for others on how you want to be treated yourself. Don't settle for anything other than RESPECT. ~ **Anonymous**

52. The measure of a man's real character is what he would do if he knew he never would be found out. ~ **Thomas B. Macaulay 1800-1859**

53. Raise your standards for the one thing over which you have complete control, YOURSELF. It means you've committed to being intelligent, flexible, and creative enough to consistently find a way to look at your life in a fashion that makes any experience enriching. ~ **Anthony Robbins**

54. I will never apologise for being me and anyone else who asks me to be any different should apologise to me. ~ **Raymond Terrance**

55. One has to set high standards. I can never accept mediocrity. ~ **Patrece Motsepe**

56. Never lower YOUR standards for anyone or anything. Self-respect cannot be bought. ~ **Vicky Eveline**

57. Cinderella is proof that a pair of shoes lift you out of the

*doldrums and can change your life. ~ **Billy Osborne***

58.   *The price of excellent is discipline. The cost of mediocrity is disappointment. ~ **William Arthur Ward***

59.   *The greatest danger for all of us is not that we aim high and miss but that we aim low and achieve it. ~ **Michelangelo 1475-1574***

60.   *The secret of change is not to fight it for all your worth but to adapt to it for all your worth. ~ **Socrates 471-399 BC***

61.   *The quality of a leader is defined by the standards they set for themselves and their team. ~ **Barry Clover***

62.   *A 'No' uttered from deepest conviction is better and greater than a 'Yes' merely uttered to please, or what is worse, to avoid trouble. ~ **Mahatma Gandhi 1869-1948***

63.   *When you hold out for high standards, people are impressed - but they don't always like you for it. Not everybody will be on your side in your struggle to do what's right and ethical. In fact, sometimes even you won't be on your side. You'll wrestle with inner conflict, torn between what you should do and what you want to do. You'll also aggravate other people. Seems when you walk the straight and narrow you always step on someone's toes. Don't count on the ethics of excellence to make you popular. ~ **Price Pritchett***

64.   *Sometimes the issue is their ethics isn't as high as yours. If that is so then they can dramatically improve their ethics or*

move on. ~ **Anonymous.**

65. *High standards means I expect people to behave properly, not like children.* ~ **Anonymous**

66. *It is better to risk starving to death then surrender. If you give up on your dreams, what's left?* ~ **Jim Carry**

67. *Let every man judge according to his own standards, by what he has himself read, not by what others tell him.* ~ **Albert Einstein 1879-1955**

68. *Any time you sincerely want to make a change, the first thing you must do is to raise your standards. When people ask me what really changed my life eight years ago, I tell them that absolutely the most important thing was changing what I demanded of myself. I wrote down all the things I would no longer accept in my life, all the things I would no longer tolerate, and all the things that I aspired to becoming.* ~ **Anthony Robbins**

69. *The nicest thing about standards is that there are so many of them to choose from.* ~ **Andres S. Tannenbaum**

70. *You can become an even better person by constantly setting higher and higher standards for yourself and then by doing everything possible to live up to those standards.* ~ **Brian Tracy**

71. *There are many hypotheses in science which are wrong. That's perfectly all right; they're the aperture to finding out what's right. Science is a self-correcting process. To be accepted,*

new ideas must survive the most rigorous standards of evidence and scrutiny. ~ **Dr Carl Sagen**

72. I've also seen that great men are often lonely. This is understandable, because they have built such high standards for themselves that they often feel alone. But that same loneliness is part of their ability to create. ~ **Yousuf Karsh**

73. Successful people are always looking for opportunities to help others. Unsuccessful people are always asking, 'What's in it for me? ~ **Brian Tracy**

74. I will deal with them according to their conduct, and by their own standards I will judge them. ~ **Ezekiel 12:10-22**

75. Apparently I am too picky.....why shouldn't I be? It's my time, my life, my energy so why shouldn't I value it? Why shouldn't I set high standards? If I'm confident with what I have to offer why shouldn't I choose carefully who I offer it to? ~ **Anonymous**

76. It is those who have this imperative demand for the best in their natures, and who will accept nothing short of it, that hold the banners of progress, that set the standards, the ideals, for others ~ **Orison Swett Marden 1828-1924**

77. We may be surprised at the people we find in heaven. God has a soft spot for sinners. His standards are quite low. ~ **Bishop Desmond Tutu**

78. Undermine their pompous authority, reject their low moral

*standards, make anarchy and disorder your trademarks. Cause as much chaos and disruption as possible but don't let them take you ALIVE. ~ '**Sid Vicious**'*

79. *Let us be about setting high standards for life, love, creativity, and wisdom. If our expectations in these areas are low, we are not likely to experience wellness. Setting high standards makes every day and every decade worth looking forward to. ~ **Greg Anderson***

80. *The idea for which this nation stands will not survive if the highest goal free man can set themselves is an amiable mediocrity. Excellence implies striving for the highest standards in every phase of life. ~ **William Arthur Ward***

32
BEING TRUTHFUL

Almost two thousand years ago, Truth was put on trial and judged by people who were devoted to lies. In fact, truth faced six trials in less than one full day, three of which were religious, and three that were legal. In the end, few people involved in those events could answer the question, 'What is truth.' Truth as we know it today it is derived from the Old English 'trèowe'. In fact the exact meaning of truth is still difficult to pin down because there are so many different interpretations of it. But we generally accept that it means to be honest, loyal, sincere, reliable, trustworthy, and genuine. Whichever way you look at it, if someone in the team is found wanting in any of those qualities then the team is going to have major problems until it is sorted out one way or another.

~ *Roger Payne* ~

1. If you are honest with people they will most likely be honest with you. And if they are not it is still better for you to always tell the truth. ~ **Catherine Pulsifer**

2. To be persuasive we must be believable. To be believable we must be credible, and to be credible we must be truthful. ~ **Edward R. Murrow**

3. Supporting the truth, even when it is unpopular, shows the capacity for honesty and integrity. ~ **Steve Brunkhorst**

4.   *We must make the world honest before we can honestly say to our children that honesty is the best policy.* ~ **George Bernard Shaw 1856-1950**

5.   *All truth passes through three stages. FIRST, it is ridiculed, SECOND it is violently opposed, and THIRD, it is accepted as self-evident.* ~ **Arthur Schopenhauer 1788-1860**

6.   *Speak your truth quietly and clearly; and listen to others, even the dull and ignorant; they too have their story.* ~ **Max Ehrman 1872-1945**

7.   *There are only three mistakes one can make along the road to truth; not going all the way, being on the wrong side of the road and most important of all, not starting.* ~ **Robert Page-Simpson**

8.   *Telling a truth is not only a matter of character, but is also a matter of appreciating factual situations and representing them without bias.* ~ **M. K. Soni**

9.   *A lie travels round the world while truth is putting her boots on.* ~ **French Proverb**

10.   *Honesty is fearing a negative response and telling the truth anyway.* ~ **Michelle C. Ustaszeski**

11.   *All parents want their child to be honest but often forget to place emphasis on being trustworthy even though this is also a*

form of honesty. ~ **James R. Morrison,**

12.   Those who corrupt the public mind are just as evil as those who steal from the public purse. ~ **Adlai Stevenson**

13.   Honesty is just as important a factor in one's communication skills as trust. ~ **Ross Elkins.**

14.   A lie has speed, but truth has endurance. ~ **Edgar J. Mohn**

15.   The speed of communications is wondrous to behold. It is also true that speed can multiply the distribution of information that we know to be untrue. ~ **Edward R. Murrow**

16.   Everything we hear is an opinion, not a fact. Everything we see is a perspective, not the truth. ~ **Marcus Aurelius (Marcus Aurelius Antoninus Augustus) 121-180 AD**

17.   Few men have a good enough memory to make a successful liar. ~ **Abraham Lincoln 1809-1865**

18.   If you want to be truly happy, set a goal that commands your thoughts, liberates your soul, and inspires your hopes. ~ **Andrew Carnegie 1837-1919**

19.   The greatest advantage of speaking the truth is that you don't have to remember what you said. ~ **Anonymous**

20. We tell lies when we are afraid....afraid of what we don't know, afraid of what others will think, afraid of what will be found out about us. But every time we tell a lie the thing we fear

*most grows stronger. ~ **Tad Williams***

21.   *Truth fears no questions. ~ **Anonymous***

22.   *Men occasionally stumble over the truth, but most of them pick themselves up and hurry off as if nothing had happened. ~ **Winston Churchill 1874-1975***

23.   *The truth is more important than the facts. ~ **Frank Lloyd Wright***

24.   *It is not without good reason, that he who has not a good memory should never take upon him the trade of lying. ~ **Michel de Montaigne 1533 1592***

25.   *People who are brutally honest get more satisfaction out of the brutality than out of the honesty. ~ **Richard J. Neil***

26.   *Man is least himself when he talks in his own person. Give him a mask, and he will tell you the truth. ~ **Oscar Wilde 1854-1900***

27.   *Today I bent the truth to be kind, and I have no regret, for I am far surer of what is kind than I am of what is true. ~ **Robert Brault***

28.   *Some people will not tolerate emotional honesty in communication. They would rather defend their dishonesty on the grounds that it might hurt others. Therefore, having rationalized their phoniness into nobility, they settle for superficial relationships. ~ **Anonymous***

29. *Beware of the half-truth. You may have gotten hold of the wrong half.* ~ **Anonymous**

30. *A lie will easily get you out of a scrape, and yet, strangely and beautifully, rapture possesses you when you have taken the scrape and left out the lie.* ~ **Charles Edward Montague 1867-1928**

31. *Some people create their own storms, then get unhappy when it rains.* ~ **Anonymous**

32. *Those who think it is permissible to tell white lies soon grow colour-blind.* ~ **Austin O'Malley 1859-1932**

33. *The least initial deviation from the truth is multiplied later a thousand fold.* ~ **Aristotle 384-382 BC**

34. *With lies you may get ahead in the world but you can never go back.* ~ **Russian Proverb**

35. *The hardest tumble a man can take is to fall off his own bluff.* ~ **Ambrose Bierce 1842-1914**

36. *Truth is the most valuable thing we have, so I try to conserve it.* ~ **Mark Twain 1835-1910**

37. *Honesty is never seen sitting astride the fence.* ~ **Lemuel K. Washburn 1876-1928**

38. *A lie may take care of the present, but it has no future.* ~

Anonymous

39. I never lie because I don't fear anyone. You only lie when you're afraid. ~ **John Gotti**

40. Worse than telling a lie is spending the rest of your life staying true to a lie. ~ **Robert Brault**

41. We tell lies when we are afraid, afraid of what we don't know, afraid of what others will think, afraid of what will be found out about us. But every time we tell a lie, the thing that we fear grows stronger. ~ **Tad Williams**

42. A truth that's told with bad intent beats all the lies you can invent. ~ **William Blake 1727-1857**

43. Honesty is the first chapter of the book of wisdom. ~ **Thomas Jefferson 1743-1826**

44. There are only two ways of telling the complete truth anonymously and posthumously. ~ **Thomas Sowell**

45. Keep away from people who try to belittle your ambitions, small people always do that, but the really great people make you feel that you, too, can become great just like them. ~ **Mark Twain 1835-1910**

46. When you tell a lie, you steal someone's right to the truth. ~ **Khaled Hosseini**

47. There is no well-defined boundary between honesty and

dishonesty. The frontiers of one blend with the outside limits of the other, and he who attempts to tread this dangerous ground may be sometimes in one domain and sometimes in the other. **~ O. Henry (William Sidney Porter) 1862-1910**

48. Pretty much all the honest truth telling in the world is done by children. **~ Oliver Wendell Holmes 1809-1894**

49. Never be afraid to raise your voice for honesty and truth and compassion against injustice and lying and greed. If people all over the world...would do this, it would change the earth. **~ William Faulkner 1897-1962**

50. We need more people speaking out. Our world is not overrun with rebels and free thinkers. It's overrun with sheep and conformists. **~ Bill Maher**

51. Every lie is two lies, the lie we tell others and the lie we tell ourselves to justify it. **~ Robert Brault**

52. It takes years to build up a good reputation. It only takes one lie and in one second you can ruin it forever. **~ Anonymous**

53. Before speaking, resist the temptation to tell people only what they want to hear. **~ W. Dyer**

54. All truth passes through three stages: First it is ridiculed, second it is violently opposed and third it is accepted as being self-evident. **~ Anonymous**

55. Better to slip with your foot than your tongue. **~ Benjamin**

Franklin 1706-1790

56. *Just because everybody's doing something, doesn't mean its right.* ~ **Anonymous**

57. *To announce that there must be no criticism of the President, or that we are to stand by the President, right or wrong, is not only unpatriotic and servile, but is morally treasonable to the American public.* ~ **Theodore Roosevelt 1858-1919**

58. *If we are not ashamed to think it, we should not be ashamed to say it.* ~ **Marcus Tullius Cicero 106-43 BC**

59. *If an offence come out of the truth, better is it that the offence come than that the truth be concealed.* ~ **Thomas Hardy 1840-1928**

60. *It has always been the prerogative of children and halfwits to point out that the emperor has no clothes. But a halfwit remains a halfwit, and the emperor remains an emperor.* ~ **Neil Gaiman**

61. *It is hard to believe that a man is telling the truth when you know that you would lie if you were in his place.* ~ **Henry Louis Mencken 1880-1956**

62. *Honesty is the first chapter of the book of wisdom.* ~ **Thomas Jefferson 1743-1826**

63. *I don't mind lying, but I hate inaccuracy.* ~ **Samuel Butler**

1835-1902

64. *If you shut up truth and bury it under the ground, it will but grow, and gather to itself such explosive power that the day it bursts through it will blow up everything in its way.* ~ **Emile Zola 1840-1902**

65. *Truth has power. And if we all gravitate toward similar ideas, maybe we do so because those ideas are true ... written deep within us. And when we hear the truth, even if we don't understand it, we feel that truth resonate within us ... vibrating with our unconscious wisdom. Perhaps the truth is not learned by us, but rather, the truth is recalled ... remembered ... recognized ... as that which is already inside us.* ~ **Dan Brown**

66. *Truth is like the town whore. Everybody knows her, but nonetheless, it's embarrassing to meet her on the street.* ~ **Wolfgang Borchert**

67. *Truth never lost ground by enquiry.* ~ **William Penn 1644-1718**

68. *Truth can hardly be expected to adapt herself to the crooked policy and wily sinuosities of worldly affairs; for truth, like light, travels only in straight lines.* ~ **Charles Caleb Colton 1780-1832**

69. *When others asked the truth of me, I was convinced it was not the truth they wanted, but an illusion they could bear to live with.* ~ **Anaïs Nin**

70. *When you have eliminated the impossible, whatever remains, however improbable, must be the truth.* ~ **Sir Arthur Conan Doyle 1859-1930**

71. *When you cannot control what is happening to you, challenge yourself to control the way you respond to what is happening. That's where your real power lies.* ~ **Anonymous**

72. *Truth, after all, wears a different face to everybody, and it would be too tedious to wait till all were agreed. She is said to lie at the bottom of a well, for the very reason, perhaps, that whoever looks down in search of her sees his own image at the bottom, and is persuaded not only that he has seen the goddess, but that she is far better looking than he had imagined.* ~ **James Russell Lowell 1819-1891**

73. *Talent will get you in the door, but character will keep you in the room.* ~ **Anonymous**

74. *There is nothing which rots morale more quickly and more completely than the feeling that those in authority do not know their own minds.* ~ **Lionel Urwick 1891-1983**

75. *How wrong people always were when they said: 'It's better to know the worst than go on not knowing either way.' No; they had it exactly the wrong way round. Tell me the truth, doctor, I'd sooner know. But only if the truth is what I want to hear.* ~ **Kingsley Amis**

76. *Political language is designed to make lies sound truthful and murder respectable, and to give an appearance of solidity*

to pure wind. ~ **George Orwell**

77. *Torture will make even the truthful tell lies.* ~ **Publilius Syrus 85-93 BC**

78. *A man is never more truthful than when he acknowledges himself as a liar.* ~ **Mark Twain 1835-1910**

79. *The Five Levels of Truth-Telling: First, you tell the truth to yourself about yourself. Then you tell the truth to yourself about another. At the third level, you tell the truth about yourself to another. Then you tell your truth about another to that other. And finally, you tell the truth to everyone about everything.* ~ **Neale Donald Walsch**

80. **The Poem 'The Six Men of Indostan':**
It was six men of Indostan to learning much inclined, who went to see the Elephant (Though all of them were blind), that each by observation might satisfy his mind.
The First approached the Elephant, and happening to fall against his broad and sturdy side, At once began to bawl: "God bless me! but the Elephant Is very like a WALL!"
The Second, feeling of the tusk, cried, "Ho, what have we here, so very round and smooth and sharp? To me 'tis mighty clear, this wonder of an Elephant Is very like a SPEAR!"
The third approached the animal and happening to take the squirming trunk within his hands, thus boldly up and spake: "I see," quoth he, "the Elephant Is very like a SNAKE!"
The Fourth reached out an eager hand, and felt about the knee "What most this wondrous beast is like," quoth he:

"Tis clear enough the Elephant Is very like a TREE!"
The fifth, who chanced to touch the ear, said: "E'en the blindest man can tell what this resembles most; Deny the fact who can, this marvel of an Elephant is very like a FAN!"
The Sixth no sooner had begun about the beast to grope, than seizing on the swinging tail that fell within his scope, "I see," quoth he, "the Elephant Is very like a ROPE!"
*And so these men of Indostan disputed loud and long, each in his own opinion exceeding stiff and strong, though each was partly in the right, and all were in the wrong! ~ **John Godfrey Saxe 1816-1887***

33
INSPIRING YOUR TEAM MEMBERS

Life is like the old 'Brownie Instamatic Camera'. You must focus on what's important and capture the good times. Once you have pressed the shutter and taken all your shots, you develop the result from the negatives. If things are slightly blurred and don't look perfect; take another shot from a slightly different angle. Eventually you'll get it right and the portrait can sit on your wall.

*~ **Anonymous** ~*

1. *Be the team leader who makes everyone around them feel like somebody. ~ **Anonymous***

2. *As I look back on my life, I realise that every time I thought I was being REJECTED from something good, I realised I was being RE-DIRECTED to something better ~ **Anonymous***

3. *WORRYING does not empty tomorrow of its troubles, it simply empties TODAY of its strength. ~ **Corrie T. Boone***

4. *Perfection is not attainable, but if we chase perfection we can catch excellence. ~ **Vince Lombardi***

5. *You fall, you rise, you make mistakes, you live, you learn. You're human, not perfect. You've been hurt, but you're alive.*

Think of what a precious privilege it is to be alive to breathe, to think, to enjoy, and to chase after something you love. Sometimes there is sadness in your journey, but there is also lots of beauty. We must keep putting one foot in front of the other even when we're hurt, for we never know what is waiting just around the bend for us. ~ **Anonymous**

6.   *Life is 10% what happens to you and 90% of how you react to it.* ~ **Charles Swindoll**

7.   *Believe you can and you're halfway there.* ~ **Theodore Roosevelt 1858-1919**

8.   *Remember no one can make you feel inferior without your consent.* ~ **Eleanor Roosevelt 1884- 1962**

9.   *Don't call it a dream, call it a plan.* ~ **Anonymous**

10. *I can't change the direction of the wind, but I can adjust my sails to always reach my destination.* ~ **Jimmy Dean**

11. *Sometimes you have to forget what has gone and simply appreciate what you have and look forward to what's coming next.* ~ **Anonymous**

12. *Stop hating yourself for everything you aren't and start liking yourself for everything you already are.* ~ **Recoveryexperts.com**

13. *I am thankful for all the difficult people who have come into my life for they have shown me what I never want to be.* ~

Carrol Spinks

14.   Strive not to be a success, but rather to be of value. ~ **Albert Einstein 1879-1955**

15.   Sometimes the smallest step in the right direction can end up being the biggest step of your life. Tip toe if you must, but take the step. ~ **Anonymous**

16.   I CAN AND I WILL....watch me! ~ **Ann Brown**

17.   Sometimes you find yourself in the middle of nowhere. And sometimes in the middle of nowhere you find yourself. ~ **Anonymous**

18.   The most common way people give up their power is by thinking they don't have any. ~ **Alice Walker**

19.   It is during our darkest moments that we must focus to see the light. ~ **Aristotle Onassis**

20.   Don't judge each day by the harvest you reap but by the seeds that you plant. ~ **Robert Louis Stevenson 1850 1894**

21.   Change your thoughts and you change your world. ~ **Norman Vincent Peale 1898-1983**

22.   The question isn't who is going to let me; it's who is going to stop me. ~ **Ayn Rand**

23.   Life is NOT about waiting for the storm to pass but about

learning to dance in the rain. ~ **Maddy Caldwell**

24. *Doubt kills more dreams that failure ever has.* ~ **Anonymous**

25. *Look for something positive in each day even if on some days you have to look a little harder.* ~ **Recoveryexperts.com**

26. *I have learned over the years that when one's mind is made up, this diminishes any fear I had.* ~ **Rosa Parks**

27. *I would rather die of passion than of boredom.* ~ **Vincent van Gogh 1853-1890**

28. *A truly rich man is one whose children run into his arms when his hands are empty.* ~ **Anonymous**

29. *I have been impressed with the urgency of doing. Knowing is not enough; we must apply. Being willing is not enough; we must do.* ~ **Leonardo da Vinci 1452-1590**

30. *If you want to lift yourself up, lift up someone else up along with you.* ~ **Booker T. Washington 1856-1915**

31. *Limitations live only in our minds. But if we use our imaginations, our possibilities become limitless.* ~ **Jamie Paolinetti**

32. *As I look back on my life, I realize that every time I was being rejected from something good, I was actually being redirected to something better.* ~ **Anonymous**

33. *You have complete control over only one thing in the universe — you're thinking! You can decide what you are going to think in any given situation. Your thoughts and feelings determine your actions and determine the results you get. It all starts with your thoughts. ~* **Brian Tracy**

34. *Everything has beauty, but not everyone can see it. ~* **Confucius 551-479 BC**

35. *Action is the foundational key to all success. ~* **Pablo Picasso 1881-1973**

36. *Strength doesn't come from what you can do. It comes from doing the things you thought you couldn't do. ~* **Anonymous**

37. *Take wrong turns. Talk to strangers. Open unmarked doors. And if you see a group of people in a field, go find out what they are doing. Do things without always knowing how they'll turn out. ~* **Randall Munroe**

38. *Life can only be understood backwards; but it must be lived forwards. ~* **Søren Kierkegaard**

39. *Your life will never change until you change something you do every day. The secret of your personal success can be found in your daily routine. ~* **John C. Maxwell**

40. *There is no elevator to success, everyone you has to take the stairs, and sometimes they come back down only to turn around and go up a second time having learned from the first time. ~*

Anonymous

41. *The only person you are destined to become is the person you decide to be.* ~ **Ralph Waldo Emerson 1803-1882**

42. *We can't help everyone, but everyone can help someone.* ~ **Ronald Reagan**

43. *Everything you've ever wanted is on the other side of fear.* ~ **George Addair 1823-1899**

44. *We can easily forgive a child who is afraid of the dark; the real tragedy of life is when men are afraid of the light.* ~ **Plato 428-348 BC**

45. *Don't wait for the perfect moment, take the moment and make it perfect.* ~ **Zoey Sayward**

46. *A little spark of KINDNESS can put a COLLOSAL BURST of sunshine into someone's day* ~ **Anonymous**

47. *Keep your face always toward the sunshine and shadows will fall behind you.* ~ **Walt Whitman 1818-1892**

48. *Your work is going to fill a large part of your life, and the only way to be truly satisfied is to do what you believe is great work. And the only way to do great work is to love what you do. If you haven't found it yet, keep looking. Don't settle. As with all matters of the heart, you'll know when you find it.* ~ **Steve Jobs**

49. *A pessimist, they say, sees a glass as being half empty; an*

optimist sees the same glass as half full. But a giving person sees a glass of water and starts looking for someone who might be thirsty. ~ **G. Donald Gale**

50. If you take care of your people, your people will take care of your customers and your business will take care of itself. ~ **J.W. Marriot**

51. If you are willing to do more than you are paid to do, eventually you will be paid to do more than you do. ~ **Anonymous**

52. The distance between insanity and genius is measured only by success. ~ **Bruce Feirstein**

53. Every day might not be good, but in every day there is some good – go find it, then tomorrow find some more. Soon there is more good than bad and all because you never gave up looking for it ~ **Roger Payne**

54. Focus on the journey, not the destination. Joy is found not in finishing an activity but in doing it. ~ **Greg Anderson**

55. Average leaders raise the bar on themselves; good leaders raise the bar for others; great leaders inspire others to raise their own bar. ~ **Orrin Woodward**

56. I survived because the fire within me was stronger than the fire around me. ~ **Anonymous**

57. The two most important days in your life are the day you

are born and the day you find out why. ~ **Mark Twain 1835-1910**

58. *Life shrinks or expands in proportion to one's courage. ~* **Anais Nin**

59. *Work and self-worth are the two factors in pride that interact with each other and that tend to increase the strong sense of pride found in superior work teams. When people do something of obvious worth, they feel a strong sense of personal worth. ~* **Dennis Kinlaw**

60. *Teamwork means that you are willing to compromise when it is best for the team in its efforts at reaching a goal. ~* **Byron Pulsifer**

61. *The past is your lesson. The present is your gift. The future is your motivation. ~* **Anonymous**

62. *If it scares you then it might be a good thing to try. ~* **Seth Getting**

63. *Someday everything will make perfect sense. So for now, laugh at the confusion, smile though the tears, and keep reminding yourself that everything happens for a reason. ~* **Anonymous**

64. *There is no royal road to anything. One thing at a time, all things in succession. That which grows fast, withers as rapidly. That which grows slowly, endures. ~* **Josiah Gilbert Holland 1819- 1891**

65. *The quickest way to double your money is to fold it over and put it back in your pocket.* ~ **Will Rogers 1874-1937**

66. *When I hear somebody sigh, 'Life is hard,' I am always tempted to ask, 'Compared to what?'* ~ **Sydney Harris**

67. *Choose to be optimistic. It feels much better.* ~ **Dhali Lama**

68. *When I was 5 years old, my mother always told me that happiness was the key to life. When I went to school, they asked me what I wanted to be when I grew up. I wrote down 'happy'. They told me I didn't understand the assignment, and I told them they didn't understand life.* ~ **John Lennon**

69. *A river cuts through rock not because of its power but because of its persistence.* ~ **Anonymous**

70. *A creative person is motivated by the desire to achieve not by the desire to win.* ~ **Ann Rand**

71. *Creativity is discontent translated into arts and craft.* ~ **Eric Hoffer**

72. *Learn the rules like a professional, so you can break them like an artist.* ~ **Pablo Picasso 1881-1973**

73. *There are painters who transform the sun to a yellow spot, but there are others who, with the help of their art and their intelligence, transform a yellow spot into sun.* ~ **Pablo Picasso 1881-1973**

74. *Go and make interesting mistakes, make amazing mistakes, make glorious and fantastic mistakes. Break rules. Leave the world more interesting for your being here.* ~ **Neil Gaiman**

75. *We dance for laughter, we dance for tears, we dance for madness, we dance for fears, we dance for hopes, we dance for screams, we are the dancers, we create the dreams.* ~ **Albert Einstein 1879-1955**

76. *The object isn't to make art, it's to be in that wonderful state which makes art inevitable.* ~ **Robert Henri 1865-1929**

77. *If the doors of perception were cleansed everything would appear to man as it is, infinite.* ~ **William Blake**

78. *Where is the wisdom that we have lost in knowledge? Where is the knowledge we have lost in information?* ~ **T.S. Elliot 1888-1965**

79. *Imagination grows by exercise, and contrary to common belief, is more powerful in the mature than in the young.* ~ **W. Somerset Maugham 1874-1075**

80. *Don't spend your life with someone you can live with. Spend your life with someone you cannot live without.* ~ **Anonymous**

34
TEAM ACCOUNTABILITY

To ensure a job was well done the ancient Romans had a tradition. Whenever one of their engineers constructed an arch, as the capstone was hoisted into place, the engineer assumed accountability for it in the most profound way possible, he stood underneath the arch for 30 minutes after the capstone was put in place. It's a pity we don't have a similar rule in our businesses today.

*~ **Michael Armstrong** ~*

1.   *It's not only what We do, but what We do not do for which We are accountable.* *~ **Jean Baptiste Poquelin***

2.   *It is not only what we do, but also what we do not do for which we are accountable.* *~ **Molière (Jean Baptiste Poquelin) 1622-1673***

3.   *The majority of your problems can be solved in three words 'take personal responsibility'.* *~ **Anonymous***

4.   *Quit making excuses, putting it off. Complaining about it, crying over it, believing you can't do it, worrying you can, waiting until you're older, skinnier, richer, braver, or all round better at it. Suck it up, hold on tight, say a prayer, make a plan and JUST DO IT!* *~ **Nike Shoe Advertisement***

5. *When it comes to privacy and accountability, people always demand the former for themselves and the latter for everyone else.* ~ **David Brin**

6. *Everything you do is based on the choices you make. It's not your parents, your past relationships, your job, the economy, the weather, an argument or your age that is to blame. You and only you are responsible for every decision and choice you make. Period.* ~ **Anonymous**

7. *You will never become who you want to be if you keep blaming everyone else for who you are. Be yourself, live at your own pace, accept your mistakes and learn from them.* ~ **Anonymous**

8. *My belief is that personal freedom cannot grow beyond personal responsibility. The more people that learn to be fully accountable for their lives, the more freedom each of us can enjoy and the more fulfilling all of our lives will be.* ~ **Reed Konsler**

9. *We are accountable for our decisions in our personal life so why shouldn't we be just as accountable in our work life.* ~ **Catherine Pulsifer**

10. *Creating a culture of integrity and accountability not only improves effectiveness, it also generates a respectful, enjoyable and life-giving setting in which to work.* ~ **Tom Hanson**

11. *When you can truly understand how others experience*

your behaviour, without defending or judging, you then have the ability to produce a breakthrough in your leadership role. Everything starts with your self-awareness. You cannot take charge without taking accountability, and you cannot take accountability without understanding how you avoid it. ~ **Loretta Malandro**

12. *Life is not accountable to us. We are accountable to life.* ~ **Denis Waitley**

13. *My grandfather once told me that there were two kinds of people: those who do the work and those who take the credit. He told me to try very hard to be in the first group; there was much less competition.* ~ **Indira Gandhi**

14. *If we want unity, we must all be unifiers. If we want accountability, each of us must be accountable for all we do.* ~ **Christine Gregoire**

15. *The happiest people in the world are those who feel absolutely terrific about themselves, and this is the natural outgrowth of accepting total responsibility for every part of their life.* ~ **Brian Tracy**

16. *If I am going to trash others for their dumb predictions or actions, I must at least hold myself to the same sort of accountability.* ~ **Barry Ritholz**

17. *Leaders must develop a lower threshold for alibis and become better communicators and enforcers of what they want done. Holding people accountable to high standards and results*

is nothing to apologize for. Failing to stretch them to their potential is. ~ **Dave Anderson**

18.   There is only one real failure in life that is possible, and that is, not to be accountable and true to the best one knows. ~ **Anonymous**

19.   One thing I detest most about the financial press is the lack of accountability. All sorts of nonsense is said without penalty. ~ **Barry Ritholz**

20.   I can't explain why I made so many mistakes, why I repeated them knowing I was digging a hole too deep to climb out of, only I know I did. I can't explain it, but I own it. No one forced me to do it. I could have been influenced, or manipulated, but at the end, I said YES, nobody forced me. Therefore rather than make excuses, I chose to be accountable. Why is this so IMPORTANT? Accountability takes me from a victim mentality to a victor mentality. It puts me in the driver's seat and in control of my next move. I can't explain the past; I don't have too. I just have to learn from it and make sure it doesn't happen again. ~ **Anonymous**

21.   When bad things happen, resist the urge to blame others. Instead, find something you can do to fix the problem. ~ **Anonymous**

22.   The victim mindset dilutes the human potential. By not accepting personal responsibility for our circumstances, we greatly reduce our power to change them. ~ **Steve Maraboli**

23. *It is easier to fight for one's principles than to live up to them.* ~ **Alfred Adler 1870-1937**

24. *It is easy to dodge our responsibilities, but we cannot dodge the consequences of dodging our responsibilities.* ~ **Sir Josiah Stamp 1880-1941**

25. *Never promise more than you can perform.* ~ **Publilius Syrus 85-9 BC**

26. *Whether you accept it or not, every single day you are accountable for what you do; therefore you are leading by example. It can be positive or negative, you are still influencing those around you.* ~ **Rob Liano**

27. *No one is responsible for achieving YOUR goals, but YOU. At some in your life a decision has to be made and YOU have to take ownership of your future.* ~ **Wendy Nicole Anderson**

28. *You cannot talk about leadership without talking about responsibility and accountability. You cannot separate the two. A leader must delegate responsibility and provide freedom to make decisions, and then be held accountable for the results.* ~ **Buck Rogers**

29. *For most people, blaming others is a subconscious mechanism for avoiding accountability. In reality, the only thing in your way is YOU.* ~ **Steve Maraboli**

30. *No snowflake in an avalanche ever feels responsible.* ~ **George Burns**

31. Accountability on a strong team occurs directly among its members. For it to thrive, a leader must demonstrate a willingness to confront difficult issues. The best opportunity for holding one another accountable occurs during meetings, and the regular review of a team scoreboard provides a clear context for doing so. ~ **Patrick M. Lencioni**

32. Accountability separates the wishers in life from the action takers that care enough about their future to account for their daily actions. ~ **John Di Lemme**

33. There are two primary choices in life: to accept conditions as they exist, or accept the responsibility for changing them. ~ **Denis Waitley**

34. When a man points a finger at someone else, he should remember that four of his fingers are pointing at himself. ~ **Louis Nizer**

35. A person may cause evil to others not only by his actions but by his inaction, and in either case he is justly accountable to them for injury. ~ **John Stuart Mill**

36. He that is good for making excuses is seldom good for anything else. ~ **Benjamin Franklin 1706-1790**

37. We are solely responsible for our choices, and we have to accept the consequences of every deed, word, and thought throughout our lives. ~ **Elizabeth Kubler-Ross**

38. The four steps to accountability: SEE IT (Acknowledge it). OWN IT (Take Responsibility for it). SOLVE IT (Determine what you can do). DO IT (Take Action). ~ **Anonymous**

39. It has always been my belief that a man should do his best, regardless of how much he receives for his services, or the number of people he may be serving or the class of people served. ~ **Napoleon Hill 1833-1970**

40. Accountability is an expensive gift, don't expect it from cheap people. ~ **J.M.C.**

41. Accept responsibility for your actions. Be accountable for your results. Take ownership of your mistakes. When you can do this then there is nothing that you cannot achieve. ~ **Audrey Marlene**

42. Chess helps you to concentrate, improves your logic. It teaches you to play by the rules and take responsibility for your actions, how to problem solve in an uncertain environment. ~ **Garry Kasparov**

43. More people would learn from their mistakes if they weren't so busy denying them. ~ **Harold J. Smith**

44. When it comes to privacy and accountability, people always demand the former for themselves and the latter for everyone else ~ **David Brin**

45. Accountability separates the wishers in life from the action takers that care enough about their future to account for their

daily actions. ~ **John Di Lemme**

46. *It is easier to fight for one's principles than to live up to them.* ~ **Alfred Adler 1870-1937**

47. *Our Government is a body of men holding themselves accountable to nobody and they ought not to be trusted by anybody.* ~ **Thomas Paine 1737-1809**

48. *The four Pillars of accountability (Webster's Dictionary): RESPONSIBILITY: A duty that binds you to a course of action. ANSWERABILITY: Being called to account. TRUSTWORTHINESS: A trait of being worthy of trust and confidence. LIABILITY: Being legally bound to a debt or obligation.* ~ **Anonymous**

49. *Everything you do is based upon the choices you make. It's not your parents, your past relationships, your job, the weather, an argument or your age to blame, You and only you are responsible for every decision and choice you make, YOU are accountable, nobody else.* ~ **Anonymous**

50. *My philosophy is that not only are you responsible for your life, but doing the best at this moment puts you I the best place for the next moment.* ~ **Oprah Winfrey**

51. *Accountability separates the wishers in life from the action takers that care enough about their future to account for their daily actions.* ~ **John Di Lemme**

52. *The most important thing to understand is you're not*

setting out to 'create' your values, you're setting out to 'uncover' them. ~ **Anonymous**

53. If you hang out with chickens, you're going to cluck. If you hang out with eagles, you're going to fly ~ **Steve Maraboli**

54. In life there's only two options: Make progress or make excuses. ~ **Anonymous**

55. It is not only what we do, but for what we don't do for which we are accountable. ~ **John Baptiste Molière**

56. Courage is the first of human qualities because it is the quality which guarantees all others. ~ **Winston Churchill 1874-1975**

57. The great thing in this world is not so much where you stand, as in what direction you are facing. ~ **Oliver Wendell Holmes**

58. Vulnerability is the birthplace of love, belonging, joy, courage, empathy, and creativity. It is the source of our hope, empathy, accountability, and authenticity. ~ **Brenė Brown**

59. When we are really honest with ourselves we must admit our lives are all that really belong to us. So it is how we use our lives that determines the kind of men we are. ~ **Caesar Chave**

60. A duty dodged is like a debt unpaid; it is only deferred, and we must come back and settle the account at last. ~ **Joseph Fort Newton 1876-1950**

61. *Accountability separates the wishers in life from the action-takers that care enough about their future to account for their daily actions.* ~ **John Di Lemme**

62. *A memorandum is written not to inform the reader but to protect the writer.* ~ **Dean Acheson 1843-1971**

63. *If you let other people do it for you, they will often do it to you.* ~ **Robert Anthony**

64. *God judges men according to the use they make of the light which he gives them.* ~ **Joseph Smith 1806-1844**

65. *It is not only what we do, but also what we do not do, for which we are accountable.* ~ **Jean Baptiste Poquelin 1622-1673**

66. *Every person's work, whether it be literature or music or pictures or architecture or anything else, is always a portrait of that person.* ~ **Samuel Butler**

67. *Think of these things, whence you came, where you are going, and to whom you must account.* ~ **Benjamin Franklin 1706-1790**

68. *Duties are not performed for duty's sake, but because their neglect would make the man uncomfortable. A man performs but one duty - the duty of contenting his spirit, the duty of making himself agreeable to himself.* ~ **Mark Twain 1835-1910**

69. *If a picture speaks a thousand words, your actions forever*

record what you believe in. ~ **Jerry Fernandez**

70. *And no creature is hidden from his sight, but all are naked and exposed to the eyes of him to whom we must give account.* ~ **Hebrews 4:13**

71. *Our tradition calls for a commitment to accountability. This is not an assumption - this is a promise that I will be there for you; and I can count on you being there for me.* ~ **Bob Ladouceur**

72. *Responsibility equals accountability equals ownership. And a sense of ownership is the most powerful weapon a team or organization can have.* ~ **Pat Summitt**

73. *We have a problem when the same people who make the law get to decide whether or not they themselves have broken the law.* ~ **Michel Templet**

74. *Good team coaches hold players' accountable, only great team players hold players accountable.* ~ **Joe Dumars**

75. *It's not what happens to you, but how you react to it that matters.* ~ **Epictetus 55-135 AD**

76. *The greatest discovery of our generation is that human beings can alter their lives by altering their attitudes of mind. As you think, so shall you be.* ~ **William James 1842-1910**

77. *When it comes to privacy and accountability, people always demand the former for themselves and the latter for everyone*

else. ~ **David Brin**

78. When we fail to set boundaries and hold people accountable, we feel used and mistreated. This is why we sometimes attack who they are, which is far more hurtful than addressing a behaviour or a choice. ~ **Brené Brown**

79. It is not only what we do, but also what we do not do, for which we are accountable. ~ **Moliere 1522-1573**

80. A body of men holding themselves accountable to nobody ought not to be trusted by anybody. ~ **Thomas Paine 1737-1809**

35
TEAM SUCCESS

We are the team with the biggest heart, the best possible preparation, the deepest passion, the strongest togetherness, and the unquenchable fire in our bellies to win. Nothing can stop us. Let's get together and capture greatness and never let it go.

~ *Ty Howard* ~

1. *Success isn't just about what you achieve in life, success is what you also inspire others to achieve.* ~ **Anonymous**

2. *Success isn't a result of spontaneous combustion. You must set yourself and your team on fire.* ~ **Arnold H. Glasow**

3. *Success occurs when opportunity meets preparation.* ~ **Zig Ziglar**

4. *The road to success and the road to failure are almost exactly the same except for a strong dose of enthusiasm.* ~ **Colin R. Davis**

5. *Success usually comes to those who are too busy to be looking for it.* ~ **Henry David Thoreau 1817 1862**

6. *Success is the child of drudgery and perseverance. It cannot*

be coaxed or bribed; pay the price and it is yours. ~ **Orison Swett Marden 1848-1924**

7. *SUCCESS is: See your goal - Understand the obstacles - Clear your mind of self-doubt - Create a positive mental picture - Embrace the challenge - Stay on track - Show everyone you can achieve it.* ~ **Anonymous**

8. *There are two types of people who will tell you that you cannot make a difference in this world: those who are afraid to try and those who are afraid you will succeed.* ~ **Ray Goforth**

9. *Successful people do what unsuccessful people are not willing to do. Don't wish it were easier; wish they were better.* ~ **Jim Rohn**

10. *Success isn't measured by money or power or social rank. Success is measured by your discipline and inner peace.* ~ **Mike Ditka**

11. *At first they will ask WHY are you doing it. And then they will ask HOW you did it.* ~ **Anonymous**

12. *Think twice before you speak, because your words and influence will plant the seeds of success or failure in the mind of another.* ~ **Napoleon Hill 1883-1970**

13. *I owe my success to having listened respectfully to the very best advice, and then going away and doing the exact opposite.* ~ **G. K. Chesterton 1874-1936**

14, *Would you like me to give you a formula for success? It's quite simple, really: Double your rate of failure. You are thinking of failure as the enemy of success. But it isn't at all. You can be discouraged by failure or you can learn from it, so go ahead and make mistakes. Make all you can because remember that's where you will find success.* ~ **Thomas J. Watson 1874-1956**

15. *If you are willing to do more than you are paid to do, eventually you will be paid to do more than you do.* ~ **Anonymous**

16. *If you are not willing to risk the usual, you will have to settle for the ordinary.* ~ **Jim Rohn**

17. *The ones who are crazy enough to think they can change the world, are the ones that do.* ~ **Anonymous**

18. *Do one thing every day that scares you.* ~ **Anonymous**

19. *When you think about it all your success's take place outside your comfort zone.* ~ **Anonymous**

20. *People who succeed have momentum. The more they succeed, the more they want to succeed, and the more they find a way to succeed. Similarly, when someone is failing, the tendency is to get on a downward spiral that can even become a self-fulfilling prophecy.* ~ **Tony Robbins**

21. *Don't let the fear of losing be greater than the excitement of winning.* ~ **Robert Kiyosaki**

22. *If you really look closely, most overnight successes took a long time.* ~ **Steve Jobs**

23. *The real test is not whether you avoid this failure, because you won't. It's whether you let it harden or shame you into inaction, or whether you learn from it; whether you choose to persevere.* ~ **Barack Obama**

24. *All you need in this life is ignorance and confidence, and then success is sure.* ~ **Mark Twain 1835-1910**

25. *Do something you really like, and hopefully it pays the rent. As far as I'm concerned, that's success.* ~ **Tom Petty**

26. *It had long since come to my attention that people of accomplishment rarely sat back and let things happen to them. They went out and happened to things.* ~ **Leonardo da Vinci 1452-1519**

27. *Unity is strength. Where there is teamwork and collaboration, wonderful things can be achieved.* ~ **Mattie J.T. Stephenek**

28. *Success seems to be connected with action. Successful people keep moving. They make mistakes, but they don't quit.* ~ **Conrad Hilton 1887-1979**

29. *If you really want to do something, you'll find a way. If you don't, you'll find an excuse.* ~ **Jim Rohn**

30. *Success is how high you bounce when you hit bottom.* ~
General George S. Patton

31. *Success is not the key to happiness. Happiness is the key to
success. If you love what you are doing, you will be successful.*
~ **Albert Schweitzer 1875-1965**

32. *To know even one life has breathed easier because you have
lived. This is to have succeeded.* ~ **Bessie Anderson Stanley
1879-1952**

33. *Success is not measured by what you accomplish, but by
the opposition you have encountered, and the courage with
which you have maintained the struggle against overwhelming
odds.* ~ **Orison Swett Marden 1848-1924**

34. *Some people dream of success while others wake up and
work at it.* ~ **Winston Churchill 1874- 1965**

35. *Always be yourself, express yourself, have faith in yourself,
do not go out and look for a successful personality and
duplicate it.* ~ **Bruce Lee**

36. *The difference between who you are and who you want to
be is what you do.* ~ **Anonymous**

37. *A successful man is one who can lay a firm foundation with
the bricks that others throw at him.* ~ **David Brinkley**

38. *Success seems to be largely a matter of hanging on after
others have let go.* ~ **William Feather 1898-1931**

39. *In order to succeed, we must first believe that we can.* ~ **Nikos Kazantzakis 1883-1957**

40. *There's always failure. And there's always disappointment. And there's always loss. But the secret is learning from the loss, and realizing that none of those holes are vacuums.* ~ **Michael J. Fox**

41. *Don't be distracted by criticism as the only taste of success some people get is to take a bite out of you.* ~ **Zig Ziglar**

42. *The secret of success is to do the common thing uncommonly well.* ~ **John D. Rockefeller Jr. 1874 1960**

43. *If you want something you've never had, you must be willing to do something you've never done.* ~ **Thomas Jefferson 1743-1826**

44. *There is a powerful driving force inside every human being that, once unleashed, can make any vision, dream, or desire a reality.* ~ **Anthony Robbins**

45. *The secret to success is to know something nobody else knows.* ~ **Aristotle Onassis**

46. *To be successful you have to be lucky, or a little mad, or very talented, or find yourself in a rapid growth field.* ~ **Edward de Bono**

47. *I never did anything worth doing by accident, nor did any of*

my inventions come indirectly through accident, except the phonograph. No, when I have fully decided that a result is worth getting, I go about it, and make trial after trial, until it comes. ~ **Thomas Edison 1874-1931**

48. *Success is neither magical nor mysterious. Success is the natural consequence of consistently applying the basic fundamentals.* ~ **Jim Rohn**

49. *Would you like me to give you a formula for success? It's quite simple, really: Double your rate of failure. You are thinking of failure as the enemy of success. But it isn't at all. You can be discouraged by failure or you can learn from it, so go ahead and make mistakes. Make all you can. Because remember that's where you will find success.* ~ **Thomas J. Watson 1874-1956**

50. *Success is simple. Do what's right, the right way, at the right time.* ~ **Arnold H. Glasow**

51. *You can teach a student a lesson for a day; but if you can teach him to learn by creating curiosity, he will continue the learning process as long as he lives.* ~ **Clay P. Bedford**

52. *The best teamwork comes from men who are working independently toward one goal in unison.* ~ **James Cash Penney**

53. *When two people meet, there are really six people present. There is each man as he sees himself, each man as he wants to be seen, and each man as he really is.* ~ **Michael De Saintamo**

54. *A group becomes a team when all members are sure enough of themselves and their contributions to praise the skill of others.* ~ **Anonymous**

55. *Remember: upon the conduct of each depends the fate of all.* ~ **Alexander the Great 356-323 BC**

56. *It is a fact that in the right formation, the lifting power of many wings can achieve twice the distance of any bird flying alone.* ~ **Anonymous**

57. *The basic building block of good team building is for a leader to promote the feeling that every human being is unique and adds value.* ~ **Anonymous**

58. *Respect your fellow human being, treat them fairly, disagree with them honestly, enjoy their friendship, explore your thoughts about one another candidly, work together for a common goal and help one another achieve it.* ~ **Bill Bradley**

59. *It is hard work, perseverance, learning, studying, sacrifice and most of all, love of what you are doing or learning to do. Success is the result of perfection, hard work, learning from failure, loyalty, and persistence. Success is not final, failure is not fatal: it is the courage to continue that counts.* ~ **Winston Churchill 1874-1973**

60. *Many ideas grow better when transplanted into another mind than the one where they sprang up.* ~ **Oliver Wendell Holmes 1841-1935**

61.   Find a group of people who challenge and inspire you, spend a lot of time with them, and it will change your life. ~ **Amy Poehler**

62. You need to be aware of what others are doing, applaud their efforts, acknowledge their successes, and encourage them in their pursuits. When we all help one another, everybody wins. ~ **Jim Stovall**

63. There is no such thing as a self-made man. You will reach your goals only with the help of others. ~ **George Shinn**

64. Cooperation is the thorough conviction that nobody can get there unless everybody gets there. ~ **Virginia Burden**

65. None of us, including me, ever do great things. But we can all do small things, with great love, and together we can do something wonderful. ~ **Mother Teresa**

66. With an enthusiastic team you can achieve almost anything. ~ **Tahir Shah**

67. Recipe for success: heat up and idea, take action, mix it with passion and belief, then add a dash of persistence. ~ **Anonymous**

68. A single leaf working alone provides no shade. ~ **Chuck Page**

69. Cooperation is the thorough conviction that nobody can get there unless everybody gets there. ~ **Virginia Burden**

70. *One piece of log creates a small fire, adequate to warm you up, add just a few more pieces to blast an immense bonfire, large enough to warm up your entire circle of friends; needless to say that individuality counts but teamwork dynamites.* ~ **Jin Kwon**

71. *Every adversity, every failure, every heartache carries with it the seed of an equal or greater benefit.* ~ **Napoleon Hill 1883-1970**

72. *So powerful is the light of unity that it can illuminate the whole earth.* ~ **Bahá'u'lláh**

73. *If we were all determined to play the first violin we should never have an ensemble. Therefore, respect every musician in his proper place.* ~ **Robert Schumann 1810-1856**

74. *Teamwork is neither 'good' nor 'desirable.' It is a fact. Wherever people work together or play together they do so as a team. Which team to use for what purpose is a crucial, difficult and a risky decision that is even harder to unmake. Managements have yet to learn how to make it.* ~ **Peter F. Drucker**

75. *In order to become a leading home run hitter, a batter must be surrounded by good hitters, otherwise, the pitchers will 'pitch around' him. Likewise, many successful people became that way from being on a good team.* ~ **Laing Burns Jr**

76. *When he took time to help the man up the mountain, lo, he*

scaled it himself. ~ **Tibetan proverb**

77. *People have been known to achieve more as a result of working with others than against them.* ~ **Dr. Allan Fromme**

78. *A failure will not appear until a unit has passed final inspection.* ~ **Arthur Bloc**

79. *When your team is winning, be ready to be tough, because winning can make you soft. On the other hand, when you team is losing, stick by them. Keep believing.* ~ **Bo Schembechle**

80. *People keep asking me why I don't want to grow, get bigger. There's nothing wrong with staying small. You can do big things with a small team of good people who you trust.* ~ **Jason Fried**

*Cooking the leadership cake. First look up the recipe, read it and understand it. Get the ingredients and mix them with passion in a bowl of enthusiasm. Sprinkle in small amounts of loyalty, respect, truthfulness, integrity and fairness. When thoroughly mixed turn on the oven with the teambuilding switch and turn the communication timer to the correct time. Wait until it is coked. Remove it from the oven and cut it into equal slices, one for each team member and one for yourself - enjoy - Cook frequently ~ **Roger Payne***

36
QUALITY CONTROL

Quality is about using the right things to produce a perfect commodity so that the consumer or end user will not have any complains or queries about the product.
~ Stephen Nicholas ~

1.   *Quality is never an accident; it is always the result of high intention, sincere effort, intelligent direction and skilful execution; it represents the wise choice of many alternatives. ~* **William A. L Foster 1819-1900**

2.   *Checklists turn out to be the basic tools of the quality and productivity revolution in aviation, engineering and construction field that combines high risk and complexity. Checklists seem lowly and simplistic but they help fill in the gaps in our brains and between our brains. ~ Atul Gawande*

3.   *Knowledge comes by taking things apart: analysis. But wisdom comes by putting things together so they always fit perfectly. ~* **John A. Morrison 1814-1904**

4.   *You can say the right thing about a quality control and nobody will listen. You've got to say it in such a way that people will feel it in their gut. Because if they don't feel it, nothing will happen. ~ William Bernbach*

5.   *Quality is more important than quantity. One home run is much better than two doubles. ~ **Steve Jobs***

6.   *Quality is never an accident. It is always a result of good and intelligent efforts. ~ **Anonymous***

7.   *Marketing is what you do when your product is no good. ~ **Edwin Land***

8.   *Where you find quality you will find a craftsman, not a quality control expert. ~ **Robert Brault***

9.   *Quality control is implemented to detect and correct things when they occur. Quality assurance is implemented to prevent things before they happen. ~ **W. Edwards Demming***

10.   *It is common sense to take a method and try it. If it fails, admit it frankly and try another. But above all, try something. ~ **Franklin D. Roosevelt 1882-1945***

11.   *Quality in a service or product is not what you put into it. It is what the client or customer gets out of it. ~ **Peter F Drucker***

12.   *Your friends should motivate and inspire you. Your work circle should be well rounded and supportive. Keep it tight. Always aim for quality instead of quantity, ALWAYS. ~ **Kristy M. Lopez***

13.   *Quality is never an accident. It's always the result of*

intelligent effort. -- **Anonymous**

14.   *To say we've always done it that way opens the door for YOUR competitors to do it better.* ~ **Mark Arnson**

15.   *Quality in a product or service is not what the supplier puts in. It is what the customer gets out and is willing to pay for. A product is not quality because it is hard to make and cost a lot of money, as manufacturers believe. This is incompetence. Customers pay only for what is of use to them and gives them value. Nothing else constitutes quality.* ~ **Peter F. Drucker**

16.   *If you don't have time to do it right first time you better have time to do it over.* ~ **Anonymous**

17.   *Give them quality. That's the best kind of advertising.* ~ **Milton Hersey**

18.   *Quality is not act. It is a habit.* ~ **Aristotle 384-322 AD**

19.   *Do or do not... there is no try.* ~ **Yoda. (From 'Star Wars', 1977**

20.   *Quality is simple. It's people that are complicated.* ~ **Harry Forsha**

21.   *Quality is the best business plan.* ~ **John Lasseter**

22.   *Every action is an opportunity to improve.* ~ **Mark Graban**

23.   *Quality means doing it right when no one is looking.* ~

Henry Ford 1863-1947

24. *Be a yardstick of quality. Some people aren't used to an environment where excellence is expected. ~ **Steve Jobs***

25. *We simply cannot rely on mass inspection to improve quality, though there are times when 100% inspection is necessary. As Harold S. Didge said many years ago. 'You cannot inspect quality into a product. The quality is there or it isn't by the time it's inspected.' ~ **W. Edwards Deming***

26, *Quality begins on the inside...then works its way out. ~ **Bob Moawad***

27. *Quality is not what happens when what you do matches your intentions. It is what happens when what you do matches your customers' expectations. ~ **Guaspari***

28. *Total quality management is a journey, not a destination. ~ **Brian Berry***

29. *Nothing great was ever achieved without enthusiasm. ~ **Ralph Waldo Emerson 1803-1882***

30. *It is our choices that show who we really are, far more than our abilities. ~ **J.K. Rowling***

31. *By a yardstick of quality. Some people aren't used to an environment where excellence is expected. ~ **Steve Jobs***

32. *Be passionate about solving the problem, not proving your*

solution. ~ **Nathan Furr**

33. *Productivity and efficiency can be achieved only step by step with sustained hard work, relentless attention to details, and insistence on the highest standards of quality and performance.* ~ **J.R.D. Tata**

34. *If you look at a building by Mies van de Rohe, it might look very simple, but close up the sheer quality of construction, materials and thought, an inspirational.* ~ **David Chipperfield**

35. *Can you say, 'We are so confident in our quality that we can guarantee it in writing? If not then why not?'* ~ **Anonymous**

36. *All excellence involves discipline and tenacity of purpose.* ~ **John W. Gardner**

37. *Without changing our patterns of thought, we will not be able to solve the problems that we created with our current patterns of thought.* ~ **Albert Einstein 1879-1955**

38. *The most dangerous kind of waste is the waste we do not recognize.* ~ **Shigeo Shingo**

39. *Every action is an opportunity to improve.* ~ **Mark Graban**

40. *Problems breed problems, and the lack of a disciplined method of openly attacking them breeds more problems.* ~ **Philip Crosby**

41. *If a thing's worth doing, it's worth doing well.* ~ **Chinese**

Proverb

42. More business is lost every year through neglect than through any other cause. ~ **Rose Fitzgerald Kennedy 1890-1995**

43. It's actually very surprising how little we think about the quality of our decision making and how we could improve it. ~ **Noreena Hertz**

44. If you can't explain it simply, you don't understand it well enough. ~ **Albert Einstein 1879-1955**

45. A real decision is measured by the fact that you've taken a new action. If there's no action, you haven't truly decided. ~ **Tony Robbins**

46. Success is the sum of small efforts, repeated day in and day out. ~ **Robert Collier**

47. Regardless what you do always be the yardstick of quality. Some people aren't used to an environment where excellence is expected. ~ **Anonymous**

48. Customers are the most important assets any company has, even though they don't show up on the balance sheet. ~ **John Berry**

49. Quality is the result of high intention, sincere effort, and intelligent direction: which represents the wise choice of many alternatives. ~ **Anonymous**

50. *European nations began World War I with a glamorous vision of war, only to be psychologically shattered by the realities of the trenches. The experience changed the way people referred to the glamour of battle; they treated it no longer as a positive quality but as a dangerous illusion* ~ **Virginia Postrel**

51. *Quality control should be vitally important to you. By handling everything but the manufacturing process, you should be able to keep the cost reasonable and maintain your relationship with your customers thereby ensuring their satisfaction.* ~ **Tim Johnson**

52. *Quality is like buying oats. If you want nice, clean, fresh oats you must be prepared to pay a fair price. However. If you can be satisfied with oats that have already been through the horse that comes a little cheaper.* ~ **Anonymous**

53. *Innovate. Innovation distinguishes a leader from a follower. Delegate. Let other top executives do 50% of your routine work to be able to spend 50% your time on the new stuff. Say no to 1,000 things to make sure you don't get on the wrong track or try to do too much. Concentrate on really important creations and radical innovation. Hire people who want to make the best things in the world. You need a very product oriented culture, even in a technology company. Lots of companies have tons of great engineers and smart people. But ultimately, there needs to be some gravitational force that pulls it all together.* ~ **Steve Jobs**

54. *When you find quality you will find a craftsman not a*

quality control expert. ~ **Robert Bault**

55. *Quality begins on the inside.....then works its way out.* ~ **Bob Moawad**

56. *Quality is never an accident, it is always the result of high intention, sincere effort, intelligent direction and skilful execution; it represents the wise choice of many alternatives.* ~ **William A Foster**

57. *Quality control is implemented to correct problems when they occur: whereas quality assurance is implemented to prevent problems happening.* ~ **Anonymous**

58. *Quality is FREE, it's inequality things that cost money.* ~ **Phillip B Crosby**

59. *The ideas of control and improvement are often confused with one another. That is because quality control and quality improvement are inseparable.* ~ **Shinobo Ishihara 1879-1963**

60. *Learn continually. There's always 'one more thing' to learn. Cross-pollinate ideas with others both within and outside your company. Learn from customers, competitors and partners. If you partner with someone whom you don't like, learn to like them – praise them and benefit from them. Learn to criticize your enemies openly, but honestly. It all makes for a quality product.* ~ **Steve Jobs**

61. *Ask for feedback from people with diverse backgrounds. Each one will tell you one useful thing. If you're at the top of the*

chain, sometimes people won't give you honest feedback because they're afraid. In this case, disguise yourself, or get feedback from other sources. Focus on those who will use your product – always listen to your customers first. ~ **Steve Jobs**

62, Quality does not only begin with a letter Q, It must be followed by U. ~ **Anonymous**

63. Once upon a time the web was full of quality sites now it is full of spam, shady operators, and blatant falsehoods. Outside of a relatively small percentage of high quality sites, most of the web is chock full of popup ads and other interruptive come-ons. It's nearly impossible to find signal in that noise, and the web is in danger of being overrun by all that crap. ~ **John Battelle**

64. Quality is simple. People are complicated. ~ **Harry Forsha**

65. Quality is not what happens when what you do matches your intentions. It is what happens when what you do matches your customers' expectations. ~ **Guaspari**

66. Customers are the most important assets any company has, even though they don't show up on the balance sheet. ~ **J.M. Berry 1860-1937**

67. Build it like you would for your family. ~ **Lenny Taylor**

68. It is easier to do a job right than to explain why you didn't. ~ **Anonymous**

69 Most electrical products are now designed to last only 5

years, that's the new quality control, called planned obsolescence. ~ **Bill Henshore**

70. *Give the work force a chance to work with pride, and the 3 per cent that apparently don't care will erode itself by peer pressure* ~ **W. Edwards Deming**

71. *Quality means building the customer's point of view into every aspect of a product from design to final recycling.* ~ **Anonymous**

72. *Profits are the result, the by-product of great service.* ~ **Anonymous**

73. *Quality is brought about by attention to detail and pride in your workmanship, nothing else.* ~ **Miles Osborne**

74. *If you don't have time to do it right you must have time to do it over.* ~ **Unknown**

75. *A foolish consistency is the hobgoblin of little minds.* ~ **Ralph Waldo Emerson 1803-1882**

76. *The society which scorns excellence in plumbing because plumbing is a humble activity and tolerates shoddiness in philosophy because it is an exalted activity will have neither good plumbing nor good philosophy. Neither its piped nor its theories will hold water.* ~ **John Gardner 1897-1935**

77. *You can't fake quality any more than you can fake a good meal.* ~ **William S. Burroughs**

78. *If you want a quality, act as if you already had it.* ~ **William James 1842-1910**

79. *The quality of a person's life is in direct proportion to their commitment to excellence, regardless of their chosen field of endeavour.* ~ **Vince Lombardi**

80. *People forget how fast you did a job – but they remember how well you did it.* ~ **Anonymous**

*Reflect upon you present blessings, of which
every man has many-not on your past
misfortunes, of which all men have some.*
~ Charles Dickens 1812-1870

37
HAVING MEETINGS

A meeting is a formal or informal gathering of team members called to debate certain issues and problems, and to make decisions. Formal meetings are held at specific times, at a definite place, and usually for a laid down time limit, using an agreed upon agenda.

~ Roger Payne ~

1.   *If you want to make meetings more efficient and productive, you should think about having deliberate conversations so it becomes a quality experience for everyone not simply a gathering for no apparent reason. ~ (1 to 14)* **Paul Axtell**

2.   *Meetings should make everyone leaving feeling more connected, valued and fulfilled, even though your main aim was to achieve the meeting outcomes.*

3.   *Beforehand make sure everyone knows what the meeting is about and where it is.*

4.   *Before the meeting think about what you are going to say about the meeting objectives.*

5.   *Watch everyone as they arrive and notice what their body language is telling you. 'Read the room' before you start, gauging the overall feeling.*

6.   *Ask people to turn off all electronic devices as interruptions from them going off will stop the flow of the meeting.*

7.   *Throughout the meeting 'actively listen' to team members as they should feel they have an important input.*

8.   *Demonstrate empathy. People associate attention with caring — your attention matters. Observe, listen, ask thoughtful questions, and avoid distractions and multitasking.*

9.   *Set up and manage the conversation. It's important to establish some guidelines about distraction. Tell everyone that you will monitor conversations to keep the flow of the meeting going. Ask people to allow other team members to speak and to wait until they have finished before asking questions.*

10.   *Include enough time so that every topic gets thoroughly discuss. This means having fewer agenda items and more time allocated to each topic. As a target, put 20% fewer items on your agenda and allow 20% more time for each item.*

11.   *Slow down the conversation to include everyone, but don't allow the conversation to be dominated by one person.*

12,   *Ask yourself: Who would be great at starting the conversation? Who is affected by the outcome and therefore needs to be asked for their view? Who is most likely to have a different view? Who are the old hands who might sense whether we are making a mistake or missing something?*

13. Begin each meeting with a question: 'Does anyone have anything to say or ask before we begin?' Ask it deliberately and with a tone that signals that this conversation matters to you. And then wait. Pausing tells everyone that you're interested in what they might say — that this conversation matters. Don't spoil your pauses by making remarks about the lack of response or slowness of a response. People often need a few moments to reflect.

*14. Crafting a quality experience in your meetings takes time, but it's worth it. ~ **Paul Axtell***

*15. You will never see eye to eye if you never meet face to face. ~ **Warren Buffet***

*16. When leaders know how to control great meetings, there's less time wasted and less frustration, and you have more energy to do the work that matters, realize your full potential, and do great things. ~ **Justin Rosenstein***

*17. Nothing beats personal interaction that occurs at a well-run meeting. It's still the best way to build a rapport, and that can only enhance business performance. ~ **Anonymous***

18. Fortunately or unfortunately, the one predictable thing in any team is the crisis. When it comes you depend on the leader: In this instance their job is to ensure the team is battle-ready and organised by using short sharp meetings. This boosts morale and gives the team a feeling of trust and control so it knows where it's going and what it is doing. ~ **Peter F. Drucker**

19. *The critical factor in any meeting is CONTROL. If you control it properly it will run well. If you let it get out of hand then it will soon become a talkfest and a waste of time.* ~ **Catherine Wright**

20. *When I run a meeting, I start by subtracting those that don't need to be there, reducing it down to its most essential people who will get everything done.* ~ **Richard Saul Wurman**

21. *A Meeting is a deliberate assembly of individuals called to debate specific issues and problems, and then to take decisions. For small teams a 15 minute meeting over a cup of coffee at the beginning of the working day when everyone is alert is worth far more than a 40 minute one at the end of the day when everyone is tired.* ~ **Andrew Revis**

22. *We are visual creatures. When you doodle an image that captures the essence of an idea, you not only remember it, but you also help other people understand and act on it which is generally the point of meetings in the first place.* ~ **Tom Wujec**

23. *Until one is committed to a meeting there is hesitancy, the chance to draw back. There is one elementary truth the ignorance of which can kill countless ideas and splendid plans. The moment one definitely commits oneself a whole stream of events issues from the decision, raising in one's mind all manner of things which no man could have dreamt would have come his way.* ~ **William J. Murry 1894-1987**

24. *Management's job is to convey leadership's message in a compelling and inspiring way. Not just in meetings, but also by example.* ~ **Jeffrey Gitomer**

25. *Avoid any specific discussion of public policy at public meetings.* ~ **Quintus Tullius Cicero 106-43 BC**

26. *Great things in teams are never done by one person; they are done by everyone, and that means getting together at meetings to sort the major problems out and delegating the minor ones to individuals to sort out (Delegation).* ~ **Anonymous**

27. *If a video meeting is not possible, then a phone link up could be the answer. If that won't work for you, you may have to go back to the old e-mail...poor you.* ~ **Tim Scannell**

28. *People in most organizations are always attached to the obsolete, like regular weekly meetings and things that should have worked but did not, the things that once were productive and no longer are.* ~ **Peter F. Drucker**

29. *The amount of meetings I've been in – people would be shocked. But that's how you gain experience, how you can gain knowledge, being in meetings and participating. You learn and grow.* ~ **Tiger Woods**

30. *With many of our staff working remotely, wireless connectivity is crucial and has streamlined our scheduling processes by enabling our administrators to view the*

*availability of our remote staff before scheduling new meetings with them. These remote users are then notified directly on their devices of these new meetings, eliminating the need for endless phone calls, voicemails and emails. ~ **David Barnett***

31. *Those who have dispersed workplaces, it would appear, are trying to get back together and regroup so that they can ascertain, do they have clear leadership, do they have a mission, can they do operations? It appears that the old fashioned meeting is making a comeback. ~ **John Stufflebeem***

32. *Most of our meetings are held to discuss problems which would never arise if we had fewer meetings. ~ **Anonymous***

33. *Each friend represents a world in us, a world possibly not born until they arrived, and it is only by this meeting that a new world is born. ~ **Anäis Nin***

34. *It is a matter of principle that we always carry out by committee anything in which any one would be able to do alone. ~ **Frank Moore Colby***

35. *Meetings have a bad rap because most people who run them like to listen to their own voices while stopping other people speak. ~ **Anonymous***

36. *A committee is a group of people who individually can do nothing, but who, as a group, can meet and decide that nothing can be done. ~ **Anonymous***

37. *You know, when I sit in meetings and things are very tense and people take things extremely seriously and they invest a lot of their ego, I sometimes think to myself, 'Come on, there's life and there's death and there is love.' And all of that ego business is nonsense compared to that.* ~ **Christine Lagarde**

38. *A camel looks like a horse that was planned by a committee.* ~ **Anonymous**

39. *Nothing replaces being in the same room, face to face, breathing the same air and reading and feeling each other's micro expressions.* ~ **Peter Guber**

40. *To get something done a committee should consist of no more than three people, two of whom are absent.* ~ **Robert Copeland**

41. *Constant meetings are a symptom of bad organization. The fewer meetings the better.* ~ **Peter F. Drucker**

42. *Effective meetings don't happen by accident, the happen by design.* ~ **Anonymous**

43. *No institution can possibly survive if it needs geniuses or supermen to manage it. It must be organized in such a way as to be able to get along under a leadership composed of average human beings who periodically get together and discuss how to move forward.* ~ **Peter F. Drucker**

44. *The reason meetings don't work is they aren't controlled properly, and they aren't controlled properly because team*

leaders don't know how to control them. A small amount of research into how to run a meeting goes a long way. ~ **Roger Payne**

45. *Law of Triviality. Briefly stated, means that the time spent on any item of the meeting agenda will be in inverse proportion to the sum involved.* ~ **Anonymous**

46. *Meetings without an agenda are like a restaurant without a menu.* ~ **Susan B. Wilson**

47. *What is the point of having a meeting agenda if you don't stick to it?* ~ **Anonymous**

48. *Videoconferences still need a reason for everyone being there. They still need an agenda, they still need to be controlled, and they still need you to sit across the table and look people in the eye.* ~ **James Bishop**

49. *When a meeting is cancelled for no apparent reason who loses besides our team members? I'll tell you who. The workers who depend on our business. The hospitality industry. Hotel housekeepers. Restaurant servers. The airlines.* ~ **John Stumpf**

50. *My team has a meeting for 10 minutes each morning around the coffee machine while having a cup of coffee. We don't waste time, we talk about the problems we're having and how to solve them. If it's something big then we arrange for a longer meeting later on in the morning and sort it out.* ~ **David Meadows**

51. *This meeting was like many of the meetings that I would go to over the course of two years.* ~ **Paul O'Neill**

The only way I can describe it is that, well, the president is like a blind man in a roomful of deaf people. There is no discernible connection. ~ **Paul O'Neill**

52. *Always go into meetings or negotiations with a positive attitude. Tell yourself you're going to make this the best deal for all parties.* ~ **Natalie Massenet**

53. *The least productive people are usually the ones who are most in favour of holding regular meetings.* ~ **Thomas Sowell**

54. *Whether meetings are by remote means, in a meeting room, or first thing in the morning in the coffee room, they have A PURPOSE, and that purpose is to PASS essential information within the team. They ARE NOT for have a 'washer woman chin wag' between team members.* ~ **Roger Payne**

55. *The Corporate World is drowning in meetings. To make one thing clear, I am not against communication. Quick one-on-ones can be extremely effective. I am talking about those hour long recurring meetings, devoid of a clear agenda, and attended by many who drone on and on about nothing. I dread them.* ~ **Sebastian Thrun**

56. *A typical day for me involves a lot of meetings. I only wish more than half of them were worth the effort.* ~ **Sophia Amoruso**

57. *Our meetings are held to discuss the many problems which would never arise if we held fewer meetings.* ~ **Ashleigh Brilliant**

58. *Meetings are indispensable to people who do not want to do anything.* ~ **John K Galbraith**

59. *A Committee is a group of men who individually can do nothing but as a group decide that nothing can be done.* ~ **Anonymous**

60. *A meeting is where people speak up, say nothing, then everyone agrees!* ~ **Anonymous**

61. *Whoever invented the meeting must have had Hollywood in mind. I think they should consider giving Oscars for meetings: Best Meeting of the Year, Best Supporting Meeting, Best Meeting Based on Material from Another Meeting.* ~ **William Goldman**

62. *Business is a combination of war and sport and you find it all at a company take over meeting.* ~ **Conrad Hemmings**

63. *One look at an email can rob you of fifteen minutes of focus. One call on your cell phone, one tweet, one instant message can destroy your schedule, forcing you to move meetings, or blow off really important things, like love, and friendship.* ~ **Jacqueline Leo**

64. *But for me to have the opportunity to stand in front of a bunch of executives and present myself, I had to hustle in my*

own way. I can't tell you how frustrating it was that they didn't get that. No joke I'd leave meetings crying all the time. ~ **Kanye West**

65. These days there are two types of people in the business community: those who produce results and those who sit at meetings and give you reasons why they didn't. ~ **Peter F. Drucker**

66. A committee is a 'cul-de-sac' down which ideas are lured and then quietly strangled. ~ **Sir Barnett Cocks**

67. A conference is a gathering of important people who singly can do nothing but together can decide nothing can be done. ~ **Fred Allen**

68. If computers get too powerful, we can organize them into committees. That'll do them in. ~ **Anonymous**

69. If Columbus had an advisory committee he would probably still be at the dock. ~ **Arthur Goldberg**

70. Our meetings are held to discuss many problems which would never arise if we held fewer meetings. ~ **Ashleigh Brilliant**

71. A meeting is a group of unwilling people chosen by the team leader to discuss absolutely nothing. It will take a minimum of one hour including a coffee break. ~ **Anonymous**

72.   *Would you believe it? I was once called to a meeting where our team leader spent forty-five minutes telling us why meetings were important for good communication.* ~ **Harold Watts**

73. *I am ready to meet my Maker. Whether my Maker is prepared for the ordeal of meeting me is another matter.* ~ **Winston Churchill 1874-1975**

74. *A 'Normal' person is the sort of person that might be designed by a committee. You know, 'Each person puts in a pretty colour and it comes out grey'* ~ **Alan Sherman**

75. *If we can't solve it via email, IM, texting, faxing or phone call we'll resort to a face to face meeting, that'll fool them.* ~ **Anonymous**

76.   *I don't believe a committee can write a book. It can, oh, govern a country, perhaps, but I don't believe it can write a book.* ~ **Arnold Toynbee**

77. *Meetings are by definition a concession to a deficient organization. For one either meets or one works. One cannot do both at the same time.* ~ **Peter F Drucker**

78. *More business decisions occur over lunch and dinner than at any other time, including meetings, yet no MBA courses are given on the subject.* ~ **Peter F. Drucker**

79. *People who enjoy meetings shouldn't be in charge of anything.* ~ **Thomas Sowell**

80. *Civilisation began during a union stop work meeting outside the factory cave when a caveman threw the first verbal insult at a none-union member instead of a rock. The very next day the Human Resource Department got involved because the caveman should have been out hunting Mammals at the time.*
~ **Anonymous**

"Six mistakes mankind keeps making century after century: Believing that personal gain can be made by crushing others; Worrying about things that cannot be changed or corrected; Insisting that a thing is impossible because we cannot accomplish it now; Refusing to set aside trivial preferences; Neglecting the development and refinement of the mind; Attempting to compel others to believe and live as we do." ~
Marcus Tulius Cicero 106-43 BCE

38
MY FAVOURITE QUOTES

All my favourite quotes come from an author far better than I, Terry Pratchett, who was once described as the master of laugh out loud fiction. He has created a world (Discworld) that is as round and flat as a geological pizza, but without the anchovies and garlic; a world full of trolls, dwarfs, wizards, witches, undead, human characters, and Death, who as you'd expect, is a 7 foot hooded skeleton with piercing green eyes, a scythe, who SPEAKS IN A VOICE LIKE THE SLAMMING OF COFFIN LIDS. However, he also likes a good curry, kittens, and finds the lives of mortals endlessly fascinating. Pratchett uses this world to reflect on his own culture with entertaining and gloriously funny results. It's an accomplishment nothing short on verbal magic.

~ *The Chicago Tribune* ~

1.   *Never trust any complicated cocktail that remains perfectly clear until the last ingredient goes in, and then immediately clouds.*

2.   *Charles Dickens, as you know, never got round to starting his home page.*

3.   *The thought that someone could voluntarily give up the*

prospect of being bored for fifty years made him feel quite weak. With fifty years ahead of him, he thought, he could elevate tedium to the status of an art form. There would be no end to the things he wouldn't do.

4. *She'd tried being alone with her thoughts once, but had never tried it again. It had been too dull.*

5. *I once had a book that had two authors, and they were both the same person.*

6. *It's not worth doing something unless you were doing something that someone, somewhere, would much rather you weren't doing.*

7. *Although the scythe isn't pre-eminent among the weapons of war, anyone who has been on the wrong end of, say, a peasants' revolt, will know that in skilled hands it is fearsome weapon as peasants have a nasty habit of cutting your legs from underneath you so you end up looking into their belly buttons.*

8. *Stories of imagination tend to upset those without one.*

9. *Coming back to where you started from is not the same as not leaving!*

10. *It's still magic even if you know how it's done!*

11. *There are times in life when people must know when not to let go. Balloons are designed to teach small children this.*

12.   Geography is just physics slowed down, with a couple of trees stuck in it.

13.   Sometimes it is better to light a flamethrower than curse the darkness.

14.   An education was a bit like a communicable sexual disease. It made you unsuitable for a lot of jobs and then you had the urge to pass it on.

15.   They say a little knowledge is a dangerous thing, but it's not one half so bad as a lot of ignorance.

16.   Opera happens because a large number of things amazingly fail to go wrong.

17.   Light thinks it travels faster than anything but it is wrong. No matter how fast light travels, it finds the darkness has always got there first, and is waiting for it.

18.   There is a rumour going around that I have found God. I think this is unlikely because I have enough difficulty finding my keys, and there is empirical evidence that they exist.

19.   Taxation is just a sophisticated way of demanding money with menaces.

20.   Real stupidity beats artificial intelligence every time.

21.   History was full of the bones of good men who'd followed bad orders in the hope that they could soften the blow. Oh, yes,

there were worse things they could do, but most of them began right where they started to follow the bad orders.

22. Constable Nobby Nobbs had any amount of ways of passing the time, since guard duty in Lancre involved such an awful lot of it. There was Getting the Nostrils Really Clean, that was a good one. Or Farting Tunes, aromatic but interesting, especially in the long drawn out bits. Or standing on one leg. Or holding his breath, and counting was something he often fell back on when he couldn't think of anything else and his meals hadn't been too rich in carbohydrates.

23. It is a mistake trying to cheer up camels. You may as well drop meringues into a black hole.

24. It's not for nothing that advanced mathematics tended to be invented in hot countries. It's because of the morphic resonance of all the camels, who have that disdainful expression and famous curled lip as a natural result of an ability to do quadratic equations.

25. Sergeant Fred Colon thought that someone could voluntarily give up the prospect of being bored for fifty years made him feel quite weak. With fifty years ahead of him, he thought, he could elevate tedium to the status of an art form. There would be no end to the things he wouldn't do. He could become quite famous doing it too.

26. Human beings make life so interesting. Do you know, that in a universe so full of wonders, they have managed to invent utter boredom?

27. *Police Corporal Detritus the huge living rock Troll in human shape, with basic intelligence and personality was learning about weapons safety. Sergeant Fred Colon held out the enormous crossbow and said very deliberately, 'When Mister Safety Catch Is Not On, Don't Point Mister Crossbow At Yourself As He Is Definitely Not Your Friend.' Corporal Detritus took the huge thing and slowly turn it toward himself and as he did so 20 police constables cleared the Police Station in less then point one of a second. No sooner was the last one outside the station precincts than there was a loud thwang followed by a 'Whoops!'*

28. *People who would not believe a High Priest if he said the sky was blue, and was able to produce signed affidavits to this effect from a white haired old mother and three Vestal virgins, would trust just about anything whispered in their ear by a complete drunken stranger in a pub. Although Tronk wasn't religious, when he hit his thumb with an eight pound hammer it was nice to be able to blaspheme.*

29. *Hoc envied his fellow students who believed in Gods that were intangible and lived a long way away on top of a mountain. A fellow could really believe in gods like that. But it was extremely hard to believe in a God when you saw him at breakfast every day.*

30. *They all stared at the branch. There wasn't just one flower out there, there were dozens, although the pink frogs weren't able to think like this because frogs can't count beyond one, so they saw lots and lots of one's.*

31. *He stood there looking at the figure and thought, 'Some things are fairly obvious when it's a seven foot skeleton wearing a hooded black cloak and two bright blue dots staring at you where the eyes should have been, especially as its carrying a scythe in one skeletal hand and beckoning me with the other. But the clincher was the white horse he was sitting on that was floating two feet above the ground.'*

32. *No! Please! I'll tell you whatever you want to know!' the man yelled. 'Really?' said Commander Vimes leaning across the table in the interview room. 'What's the orbital velocity of the moon?' 'WHAT?' 'Oh, you'd like something simpler?'*

33. *In the beginning there was nothing, which exploded.*

34. *'Do you do fried rat?' said Glod. 'Best damn fried rat in the city,' said Cut Me Own Throat Dibbler the proprietor of the stall. 'Okay. Give me four fried rats and some dwarf bread,' said Imp. 'And some coke,' said Lias, patiently. 'You mean rat heads or rat legs?' said Dibbler. 'No. Just four fried rats and some dwarf bread.' said imp. 'And some coke.' added Lias. 'You want ketchup on those rats?' 'No.' 'You sure?' 'No ketchup.' 'And some coke.' said Lias.*

35. *God does not play dice with the universe; He plays an ineffable game of His own devising, which might be compared, from the perspective of any of the other players [i.e. everybody], to being involved in an obscure and complex variant of poker in a pitch dark room, with blank cards, for infinite stakes, with a Dealer who won't tell you the rules, and who smiles all the time.*

36. *The vermine is a small checkered black and white relative of the lemming, found in the cold Hublandish regions. Its skin is extremely rare and highly valued, especially by the vermine itself; unfortunately the selfish little bastard will do anything rather than let go of it.*

37. *Many people, meeting Aziraphale for the first time, formed three impressions: that he was English, that he was intelligent, and that he was gayer than a tree full of monkeys on nitrous oxide.*

38. *Studies have shown that an ant can carry one hundred times its own weight, but there is no limit to the lifting power of the average tiny eighty year old Spanish peasant grandmother.*

39. *'DON'T THINK OF IT AS DYING,' said Death. 'JUST THINK OF IT AS LEAVING EARLY TO AVOID THE RUSH.' 'I meant,' said Ipslore bitterly, 'what is there in this world that truly makes living worthwhile?' Death thought about it. 'CATS.' He said eventually. 'CATS ARE NICE.*

40. *I get it,' said the prisoner. 'Good Cop, Bad Cop, eh?' 'If you like.' said Vimes. But we're a bit short staffed here at the moment, so if I give you a cigarette would you mind lighting it and then kicking yourself in the teeth?'*

41. *People are a curious species. They actually wonder how the snow-plough driver gets to work, or how the makers of dictionaries look up the spelling of words.*

42. *Most Gods throw dice, but Fate plays chess, and you don't find out till too late that he's been playing with two queens all along.*

43. *The Four Horsemen of the Apocralypse are anthropomorphic personifications of the events that people have most feared since the beginning of history, namely Death, War, Famine and Pestilence. Normally each would be working on the phenomenon that he personifies. On the special occasion that the end of the world is expected, the Four will gather to Ride forward. Like all people who work together they are moderately friends with each other. Their work fields are often overlapping, but each is often too busy to socialize with the others. There was once a fifth horseman, Kaos, but he left them before they were famous because of artistic disagreements. He is now known as Ronnie Soak, a very successful dairy products merchant.*

44. *Mind you, the Elizabethans had so many words for the female genitals that it is quite hard to speak a sentence of modern English without inadvertently mentioning at least three of them.*

45. *Let's see, now... in HOGFATHER there are a number of stabbings, someone's killed by a man made of knives, someone's killed by the dark, and someone just been killed by a wardrobe. It's a book about the magic of childhood. You can tell.*

46. *Greebo had spent an irritating two minutes in that box. Technically, a cat locked in a box may be alive or it may be dead. You never know until you look. In fact, the mere act of opening the box will determine the state of the cat, although in this case*

there were three determinate states the cat could be in: these
being Alive, Dead, and Bloody Furious.

47. *It's very hard to talk quantum mechanics using a language
originally designed to tell other monkeys where the ripe fruit is.*

48. *Few religions are definite about the size of Heaven, but on
the planet Earth the Book of Revelation (ch. XXI, v.16) gives it
as a cube 12,000 furlongs on a side. This is somewhat less than
500,000,000,000,000,000,000 cubic feet. Even allowing that
the Heavenly Host and other essential services take up at least
two thirds of this space, this leaves about one million cubic feet
of space for each human occupant – assuming that every
creature that could be called 'human' is allowed in, and that the
human race eventually totals a thousand times the number of
humans alive up until now. This is such a generous amount of
space that it suggests that room has also been provided for
some alien races or- a happy thought – that pets are allowed.*

49. *The presence of beer always greases the rungs of the
evolutionary ladder.*

50. *"If complete and utter chaos was lightning, then Sam Vines
would be the sort to stand on a hilltop in a thunderstorm
wearing wet copper armour and shouting 'All gods are
bastards!"*

51. *Fantasy is an exercise bicycle for the mind. It might not take
you anywhere, but it tones up the muscles that can. Of course,
I could be wrong.*

52. *Any philosophical remark that begins with 'I reckon' was probably unlikely to come up with a world-shattering insight or even a new un-shattered one.*

53. *The Fool was vaguely aware that you could tell which direction the Hub valley lay by seeing which side of the trees the moss grew on. A quick inspection of the nearby trunks indicated that, in defiance of all normal geography, the Hub lay everywhere.*

54. *This is a bit of the continent, sticking out into the warmer sea to the south-east. Most of its inhabitants call it Florida. Actually, they don't. Most of its inhabitants don't call it anything. They don't even know it exists. Most of them have six legs, and buzz. A lot of them have eight legs and spend a lot of time in webs waiting for six-legged inhabitants to arrive for lunch. Many of the rest have four legs, and bark or moo or even lie in swamps pretending to be logs. In fact, only a tiny proportion of the inhabitants of Florida have two legs, and even most of them don't call it Florida. They just go tweet, and fly around a lot.*

55. *People look down on stuff like geography and meteorology, and not only because they're standing on one and being soaked by the other. They don't look quite like real science. But geography is only physics slowed down and with a few trees stuck on it, and meteorology is full of excitingly fashionable chaos and complexity.*

56. *Map-making had never been a precise art on the Discworld. People tended to start off with good intentions and then get so*

carried away with the spouting whales, monsters, waves, and other twiddley bits of cartographic furniture that they often forgot to put the boring mountains and rivers in at all.

57. Lu-Tze, when they found him, was looking calmly up at an enormous mammoth. Under its huge hairy brow its eyes were squinting with the effort both of seeing him and of getting all three of its brain cells lines up so that it could decide whether to trample on him or gouge him out of the frost-bound landscape. One brain cell was saying 'gouge', one was going for 'trample' but the third had wandered off and was thinking about as much sex as possible.

58. Mrs Ogg, who'd had six husbands and eighteen children, had a very vague attitude to sex except in humorously anatomical areas including her armpits.

59. An hour ago Cutwell had thumbed through the index of The Monster Fun Grimoire and had cautiously assembled a number of common household ingredients and put a match to them. Funny thing about eyebrows, he mused. You never really noticed them until they'd gone.

60. There is no such thing as a whisper in Ankh-Morpork when the sum involved had the word 'thousand' in it somewhere; people could hear you think kind of money in Ankh Morpork

61. He moved very much like a man who'd got his ideas about stealth from watching adventure films.

62. You didn't want to be a warrior Glod?' 'Never. It takes a

woman nine months to make a new human. Why waste her effort?

63. Most human food with the possible exception of the custard pie has never been designed for offensive purposes.

64. Dwarfs were said to be the keenest of financial negotiators, second only in acumen and effrontery to little old ladies.

65. It was said that everything in Ankh-Morpork was for sale except for the beer and the women, both of which one merely hired.

66. Nanny Ogg could see the future in the froth on a beer mug. It invariably showed that she was going to enjoy a refreshing drink which she almost certainly was not going to pay for.

67. Ponder Stibbons, wizard, had once got one hundred percent in a prescience exam by getting there the previous day.

68. Granny Weatherwax had nothing against fortune-telling provided it was done badly by people with no talent for it. It was a different matter if people who ought to know better did it, though. She considered that the future was a frail enough thing at best, and if people looked at it hard they changed it. Granny had some quite complex theories about space and time and why they shouldn't be tinkered with, but fortunately good fortune-tellers were rare and anyway people preferred bad fortune-tellers, who could be relied upon for the correct dose of uplift and optimism. Granny knew all about bad fortune-telling. It was harder than the real thing. You needed a good imagination.

69. There was no such thing as absolute control, not in a fully functioning universe. There was just a variable amount of lack of control.

70. There might have been more efficient ways to build a world. You might start with a ball of molten iron and then coat it with successive layers of rock, like an old-fashioned gobstopper. And you'd have a very efficient planet, but it wouldn't look so nice. Besides, things would drop off the bottom.

71. 'Look,' said Magrat desperately, 'why don't I go by myself?' 'Cos you ain't experienced at fairy godmothering,' said Granny Weatherwax. This was too much even for Magrat's generous soul. Well, nor are you,' she said. 'That's true,' Granny conceded. 'But the point is...the point is...the point is we've not been experienced for a lot longer than you.'

72. Stopping a battle is much harder than starting it. Starting it only requires you to shout 'Attack!' but when you want to stop it, everyone is busy.

73. Fate always wins. Most of the Gods throw dice but Fate plays chess, and you don't find out until it's too late that he's been using two queens all along.

74. Other theories about the ultimate start involve Gods creating the universe out of the ribs, entrails and testicles of their father. There are quite a lot of these. They are interesting, not for what they tell you about cosmology, but for what they say about people. Gods like a joke as much as anyone else.

75. *The problem with Destiny, of course, is that she is often not careful where she puts her finger.*

76. *Destiny was funny stuff, he knew that. You couldn't trust it. Often you couldn't even see it. Just when you knew you had it cornered it turned out to be something else – coincidence, maybe, or providence. You barred the door against it, and it was standing behind you. Then just when you thought you had it nailed down it walked away with the hammer.*

77. *Battle elephants were the fashion lately. They weren't much good for anything except trampling on their own troops when they inevitably panicked, so the military minds on both sides had responded by breeding bigger elephants.*

78. *The idea that winter could actually be enjoyable would never have occurred to Ramtop people, who had eighteen different words for snow. All of them, unfortunately, unprintable*

79. *Death - He really liked black. It went with anything, except his horse Binky, who was pure white.*

80. *Loyalty was a great thing, but no army lieutenant should be forced to choose between their General and a circus with elephants.*

Always be wary of any helpful item that weighs less than its operating manual.
~ Terry Pratchett ~

About the Author

Roger Payne was born in South Wales at the end of the Second World War. He began his working life as a fifteen year old in the Junior Leaders Regiment Royal Artillery and when he was seventeen and a half he attempted the fearsome selection course for the Army's elite Parachute Regiment and finally entered into its ranks after completing a parachute course.

Nine years later he accepted a position in the Australian Army to train men for Vietnam. He eventually rose to the position of Chief Instructor of fitness training to the Corps of Infantry.

In that time he gained diplomas in Human Movement and Human Resource Management. He also received the highest award a serving member of the Defence Forces could receive, The Chief of the Defence Force Commendation, then one year later an unprecedented Order of Australia, one of the highest awards an Australian citizen can achieve.

He is still the only Australian serviceman to receive both. He left the military in 1993 and became an adviser on leadership and team building to the Australian Mines Rescue Service and coordinator of team leadership skills in the

National Mines Rescue Competition attended by teams from all over the world.

Roger is now retired and has written a number of published books about the World War II, one of which *'Paras - Voices of the British Airborne Forces in the Second World War'* is still selling on Amazon and other sites. He is in the process of writing two other military books.

The Team Building Bucket List is his first attempt at a book on team building and leadership.